Scott Sedita's *Ultimate* Guide To Making It In Hollywood

…and New York, Atlanta, Vancouver, Chicago, and Any Other Industry City!

"In an industry that is notoriously overwhelming and in-consistent, Scott Sedita's greatest talent is his ability to remind you that you still have some control. He inspires confidence, hard work, and dedication by providing a formulaic, yet organic, approach to acting."

-HOLLY TAYLOR, *Actor*

"I believe the main reason I continue to work is because I strive to be confident and real. I would have had no chance of achieving either of those if it wasn't for Scott Sedita. His ability to prepare the actor for both the craft of acting and the accompanying business is unparalleled in my experience."

-GEOFF STULTS, *Actor*

"Scott Sedita is an inspiration in person and on the page. His new book is a recipe for success for anyone who really wants it!"
-MARY LOU BELLI, *Emmy Award-Winning Director*

"Scott's acting classes were life changing for me. He gave me invaluable tools to navigating not only the audition process but the business as a whole. I am forever grateful for his guidance."
-MARISA RAMIREZ, *Actor*

"Scott Sedita has a fresh, unique approach to 'making it' as an actor. This is a book for actors that want to be in it for the long haul and are focused on achieving success."
-MARK TESCHNER, *Emmy Award-Winning Casting Director*

"Not only is Scott Sedita incredibly skilled at coaching, but his advice and words of wisdom have been indispensable to me. And now he shares it with all of you."
-JENNIFER FINNIGAN, *Actor*

"Scott writes in a very specific and detailed format, providing a fantastic roadmap for any person wanting to become an actor. Everything you need to be successful...it's in there."
-STEW STRUNK AND TRACY STEINSAPIR, *Talent Managers*

"I always recommend Scott's books and classes to actors who have talent but need no-nonsense, practicable direction to make the most of it. No guru, no flatterer, no flim-flam name-dropper, Scott combines a shrewd business sense with absolute truth-telling."
-DAVID RAMBO, *Writer/Producer*

"Scott helped transform the way I audition, which undoubtedly led to much more success than I would've had without his insight. He has such a unique approach to the process, and he knows what works! His knowledge of the craft and the business is invaluable."
-JT NEAL, *Actor*

"Scott Sedita's simple and practical concepts will assist the actor to have both the confidence and the tools to start on that very difficult path to becoming a working actor."
— VICTORIA MORRIS, *Talent Agent*

"There are very few teachers who are not only able to educate their students but impact them so profoundly that it changes their very lives. For me, Scott Sedita was one of those teachers. I can honestly say that Scott has been one of the biggest influences on my life and there's no way I would be where I am today without him!"
— JOSEPH DAVID-JONES, *Actor*

"This book is like having a personal life coach guiding you through your acting career. A MUST READ!"
— TERRY BERLAND, *Casting Director*

"Scott's classes and books are so informative and have given me the acting chops that I confidently use today on projects. I'm thankful for what he has added to my Hollywood journey."
— MEAGAN TANDY, *Actor*

"As an actor, it's crucial to have the right coach as a part of your team. I love connecting the right clients to Scott. He's direct and fiercely passionate about actors being their best, as artists and professionals."
— KANICA SUY, *Talent Manager*

"I owe the invaluable lessons I learned from Scott Sedita to every job I've booked since working at the studio. Studying with Scott gave me expansive industry knowledge, earned audition confidence, and proper guidance to pursue Hollywood in the capacity I've desired. Working with him is a great honor."
— NICO GREETHAM, *Actor*

"Scott knows the business from many angles—as an agent, casting director, and acting coach. This book is full of invaluable advice and insight into the world of acting."

-SUSAN VASH, *Casting Director*

"An insightful and inspirational blueprint for achieving success in the world of Hollywood. It will unlock treasures that an actor needs to attain and sustain a thriving career in the entertainment industry."

-MARA SANTINO, *Talent Manager*

"Scott Sedita gave me the guidance I needed to not only sharpen my craft but actually launch my career. It's pretty simple: listen to Scott to become a better actor and book better jobs."

-CHRIS COY, *Actor*

"Scott Sedita's new book offers a step-by-step approach to becoming a successful working actor. He is an actor's coach."

-TJ STEIN, *Talent Manager*

"Scott's book is so smart, so complete, so full of real, practical advice that I'm actually tempted to step from behind the camera to in front of the camera!"

-ROB LOTTERSTEIN, *Writer/Producer*

"Scott highlights the real obstacles that face the professional actor, and gives the advice and counsel so desperately needed. He demystifies and debunks years of silly thinking that has plagued millions of actors as they embark on a career in acting."

-PETER KLUGE, *Talent Manager*

"Finally, a great self-help book for actors! Thank you, Scott!"
-CONCHATA FERRELL, *Emmy Award-Winning Actor*

"Sedita helped me evolve from a retired NFL football player to a skilled and fearless actor. His insight on being specific in every aspect of auditioning was a game changer for me. Honored to be an alum!"
-THOMAS Q. JONES, *Actor*

"Imagine you have a really good friend who knows EVERYTHING about the acting game and you'll have some idea what it's like to read this engaging and informative book."
-JED SEIDEL, *Writer/Producer*

"Scott Sedita's Ultimate Guide To Making It In Hollywood will inspire and empower you to become a successful actor. Get ready for some changes with this book!"
-JAY KENNETH JOHNSON, *Actor*

"Scott has always had a great grasp on this industry. Talent, Confidence, and Perseverance is what he preaches, and truer words have never been spoken. Thanks Scott!"
-ERIC LADIN, *Actor*

"I had a great time working with Scott Sedita. He challenges you to always do your very best. His classes are set in a fun and supportive atmosphere, where the actor feels safe to make mistakes. Scott's class is where it's at!"
-KEVIN ALEJANDRO, *Actor*

Scott Sedita's *Ultimate* Guide To Making It In Hollywood

…and New York, Atlanta, Vancouver, Chicago, and Any Other Industry City!

Scott Sedita

Atides Publishing, Los Angeles, California

Scott Sedita's *Ultimate* Guide To Making It In Hollywood

...and New York, Atlanta, Vancouver, Chicago, and Any Other Industry City!

Published by:
Atides Publishing
526 N. Larchmont Blvd.
Los Angeles, CA 90004, USA

2nd Edition completely revised

ISBN: 978-0-9770641-6-8

Library of Congress Control Number: 2008923937

Cover photo: satoriportrait.com
Cover and interior design: zenrage
Editor: Jim Martyka

First printing: 2008
Second printing: 2022
Printed in the United States of America

To all my students who inspire me and challenge me to become a better teacher and a more creative human being. You all make me proud and help me remember why I'm doing this in the first place.

CONTENTS

SECTION TWO

<u>SECTION THREE</u>

MY STORY

The choices you make

On your journey as an artist, you will be faced with opportunities, obstacles and, most of all, choices. Who you are and who you become are dictated by the choices you make in your life and in your career. And those choices become your story.

This is my story.

I grew up in Glen Cove, New York, a suburb of New York City. My parents were divorced, so I was raised by a single mom who worked twelve hours a day to support her family. Five days a week my mom boarded the train to Manhattan where she worked as a legal secretary at a prominent law firm. My mother was a working woman at a time when most of her peers were homemakers.

I was what was called a "latchkey kid," meaning I was a child who returned home from school to an empty house. Except my house wasn't empty; it had a brand-new RCA color television (my mom got it in the divorce settlement), and it was filled with great comedy, drama, variety, talk, and game shows that kept me engaged, enlightened, and entertained. And it kept me company. Television was my babysitter.

I was born with the innate ability to act, write, and direct, so if I wasn't watching TV (or "the boobtube," as my mom called it), I was usually putting on mini extravaganzas with the neighborhood kids in my rickety garage. Or I was acting in elementary school plays. While I considered myself a leading man, I was always placed in the chorus. I guess it wasn't likely that a fat, funny, four-eyed kid would play Tom Sawyer or Prince Charming. But I made the most of it, much to the chagrin of my school director who would shout out to me, "You're just a member of the chorus, Scott! Not *the* chorus!"

By high school, that fat, funny, four-eyed kid grew into a fit, funny, contact lens-wearing teen who was now getting lead roles in high school plays and community theatre shows. I also started making comedic short films using a Super 8mm camera and my friends as the actors. I loved being behind the camera and had a knack for working with those in front of the camera. I also liked playing with different camera tricks. I became the prince of stop motion technology—I could make anyone, or anything (including my dog) disappear and then reappear. It was my homage to my favorite show, *Bewitched*.

My last two years of high school were busy with writing and directing short films as well as producing and acting in big elaborate stage productions in the high school auditorium and community centers. When it was time for college, I had a choice to make: should I study filmmaking or acting? I chose acting.

I was accepted into the acting program at Boston University's School of Fine Arts (SFA). Once there, I started taking notice of my fellow actors; some were brimming with talent while others had a harder time accessing it. I noticed the different degrees of confidence each actor possessed; some entered the program with a strong sense of self-worth already instilled in them, while others seemed uncertain, hesitant, and self-conscious. There was also a clear distinction between the actors who had more drive, passion, and perseverance about the prospects of an acting career than those who didn't.

By the end of my first year of acting school, I'd been cast in a few plays, and I had written and directed my own shows. I had made a name for myself and was invited back for a second year.

But my sophomore year proved more challenging. My acting classes were more difficult and the criticism from my teachers became harsher. My confidence started to wane. I'd leave my acting classes feeling deflated, disheartened, and like a failure. This opened the door for fear to set in. Fear of not being good enough, fear of humiliation, fear of being a disappointment to my family and to myself. I knew I had to face my fear, but I had no psychological tools to combat it. I developed a fear of acting.

That fear was overriding my desire to be an actor. When I returned from Christmas vacation, I sat down with the dean of SFA and told her that this upcoming semester would be my last in the acting program. I talked like a young man who knew exactly what he wanted. But in reality, it was my fear doing the talking.

I did feel a great sense of relief. And, surprisingly, in that last semester, I did my best acting work ever! Apparently, knowing that I was leaving acting took the pressure off and got me out of my head, and freed me to explore and be present without the fear. It's deceptive how quickly fear can vanish by simply walking away from what's causing it, even if the cause is that thing that you love. Fear can fool you like that.

I left acting school, but I didn't go far. I went across the street to Boston University's Film School to pursue my other passions: writing and directing for TV and film. For the next two years, I worked diligently at making as many films as possible. In film school, we were only taught about the technical aspects of filmmaking. They weren't particular about having actors in our films; they said just to use our roommates as "talent." But I only wanted to work with trained actors.

Naturally, I enlisted my theatre school friends to appear in all my student productions. And, since I knew the dean of SFA, I successfully campaigned to get theatre students school credit for acting in B.U. Film School projects, something that was previously not an option. There was one friend in particular that I put in many of my films who grew up to—wait for it—win an Academy Award for Best Actress! I guess you could say, I was her first film director (more on this famous actress later).

During the summers, I also worked hard to make industry contacts in Los Angeles. My plan was to have a job in L.A. by the time I graduated college. And I did! On graduation day, I had a job in Hollywood waiting for me as a production assistant (PA) for a TV series. But the day *after* graduation, I got a phone call informing me that there was a writers strike, and my PA position was gone.

With no other options, no money, and student loans looming, I moved in with my mother who now lived in New York City…in a one-bedroom apartment. I slept in the living room on an ottoman, which (amazingly) converted into a single bed. I loved my mom, but I needed my own place. I took the first job I was offered, which changed the course of my career.

I started work as an agent's assistant for a prestigious boutique talent agency called Writers & Artists. I soon realized that I had another talent, and that was *spotting* talent. I quickly became very adept at my job.

I worked for Writers & Artists for less than a year when I accepted a position as a SAG-franchised agent at the Mary Ellen White Agency. I was twenty-two years old and the youngest agent in New York City. Every night, I went out to various plays and showcases to discover new actors. I signed them, nurtured them, and groomed them for success. And it worked! Or should I say, *they* worked.

After a two-year stint at the Mary Ellen White Agency, I moved to a new agency called Frontier Booking International (FBI). There I became a young, Armani suit-wearing, hot shot agent who seemed to have the golden touch.

During my time at FBI, I was instrumental in discovering and building the careers of several top stars, including Courteney Cox, Matt LeBlanc, Christopher Meloni, Teri Polo, Robin Givens, Jerry O'Connell, Debbie Gibson, Dylan Walsh, and Vincent D'Onofrio, to name a few. As an agent, I worked very closely with my clients, guiding them in their careers and seeing them grow as artists.

Considering my acting training, I often coached my clients before their auditions to help them with their sides. I also did it to have a clearer idea of what they were going to do in the audition room, so when I spoke to the casting director about their audition, I could buffer any negative feedback by turning it into something positive: "Totally with you, she's gotta study, *but* what a great look and personality, right?!" I was always able to get my clients back into the room.

Being an agent was exciting, but there was something nagging at me. I still had the need and desire to explore my creativity. I wanted to write. I started taking screenwriting classes after work. Then, one day, I had an epiphany. I was sitting at my desk, leaned down to open a drawer, and I was suddenly hit with the thought, "Does being an agent *still* make me happy?" The answer was "No."

After eight years of representing actors, I decided to call it quits. At the top of my game and making a fantastic salary (especially for being under thirty), I made the choice to give up being a talent agent. I left my family, friends, and my Armani suits behind and drove cross country to Los Angeles (in an old '81 Chevy) to pursue a whole new career as a TV writer.

I had a great beginning. I got a literary agent, took meetings with network execs and showrunners, and booked some TV writing gigs for Howie Mandel and Bobcat Goldthwait. As I was waiting for my big break to get a writing gig on a TV show, I found a great survival job in casting that would soon present a whole new career opportunity.

I worked with the late casting director Danny Goldman, where I got a unique perspective on the casting process. Danny cast commercials, so I got to audition hundreds of actors a week. I very quickly recognized the differences between the talented versus the not-so-talented and the experienced actor versus the "green" actor. I saw, once again, how an actor's confidence and belief in oneself plays a major role in auditioning as well as booking the job.

In casting sessions, I witnessed how important it was for actors to understand who they were and what types they played best. The actors who knew themselves were the ones that consistently worked. I also witnessed how actors—through various forms of fear—sabotaged themselves in an audition or worse, in the callback.

During this time, my writing career wasn't happening quickly enough for me. I had the talent and confidence, but I lacked the perseverance (and patience) to keep doing what a TV writer must do: write as many spec scripts as possible until one gets you a steady job.

I was now in my mid-thirties and at another crossroads, and I was taking stock in what I wanted to do with my life. Then I ran into an actress I had represented at FBI.

She asked me to coach her for a sitcom audition, just like I did when I was her theatrical agent. I did, and she booked the job. This led me to start offering acting classes at Danny Goldman's as well as private coaching sessions, which helped many actors to book jobs on films and TV shows.

I quickly discovered that I loved coaching actors. There was a thrill in watching an actor seek, find, and speak the truth. I took what I learned from acting school and applied it to my coaching. And actors responded well to my style, my techniques and my straightforward approach to giving feedback. With my experience as an agent and casting director, I also educated actors about the "business of the business." I not only wanted actors to learn the craft of acting, but I also wanted them to learn what it takes to have an acting career.

I found a whole new kind of satisfaction in teaching and coaching that I had never experienced before. The choice became clear: I wanted to redirect all my creative energy into a career as an acting coach.

One evening after work, I drove to Larchmont, a quaint, hip section of Hollywood, to meet a friend for coffee. On the way, I spotted a "Space for Rent" sign on a building on Larchmont Boulevard. I thought, "When I open my acting studio, *this* will be a great location: upscale, quiet, and safe for my young actors." So, I stopped and checked out the space. It was perfect! Naively, I told the leasing agent I wanted it, but not for three months, (when I'd be ready to tackle such an undertaking). He dryly replied, "It'll be rented by then, kid." Without a beat, I said, "I'll take it!"

I invested in the one person I believed in the most... me. I opened Scott Sedita Acting Studios (SSAS) in January of 1998 with high hopes and only ten students—which didn't even cover my rent. I worked 24/7 for the toughest boss I ever had...also me. During the day, I ran the business and coached actors. At night, I held classes for young adult and adult actors. On weekends, I taught workshops for kids and teens. I worked every day to build up my courses, my student enrollment, my studio reputation, and my presence in the industry.

Because I had worked in commercial casting, I replicated their pricey TV casting studio setup with professional lights, camera, sound, blue backdrop, and the best technology of the time, including 3/4 inch and 1/2-inch recorders. It was the single biggest investment I made. I was the first theatrical acting coach in Los Angeles to have a camera in their acting studio.

Other acting teachers at the time thought it was somehow sacrilegious to have a camera in an acting class. They called me a hack. I understood their concern of having actors watch themselves on playback while in the process of rehearsing a scene from Chekhov's *Three Sisters*. But I didn't teach scene study, and I didn't use plays as scenes for my acting class. I taught audition technique, and I used "sides" from TV shows and films.

Therefore, I felt it was important to have a camera in the room. I still teach my On-Camera Audition Technique Class.

I was the teacher actors came to *after* they did their foundational acting and scene study classes and were ready to start booking TV and film work. Using my acclaimed "WOFRAIM" technique, I introduced them to more in-depth script analysis that took them to the next level. I prepared them to take adjustments in the audition and "win the room."

A few years after opening my studio, other acting teachers started putting cameras in *their* classes. So, in order for this "hack" to stand out from the competition, I had to create something else, do something different. I had to pivot.

I always had a love for comedy (sitcoms, in particular), so I developed a comedy technique now known as The Sedita Method to teach actors how to work and act in half-hour comedies. I eventually wrote an internationally bestselling book based on my method called *The Eight Characters of Comedy: A Guide to Sitcom Acting & Writing,* which has already seen multiple editions and printings.

Not only have I traveled the world teaching my sitcom comedy method, but the book has also been translated into multiple languages, become a textbook in more than a hundred colleges and universities, and is used as a go-to guide in the writer's room and on set. It's considered a "bible" among comedy writers, showrunners, and directors.

Twenty-five years later, SSAS has a reputation as one of the leading acting studios in world. My staff of six coaches and I teach hundreds of students a week in person and virtually. SSAS alumni include Chace Crawford, Josh Duhamel, Lana Candor, 50 Cent, Michael Weatherly, Haley Bennett, Charles Melton, Haley Lu Richardson, Marisa Ramirez, Brandon Routh, Holly Taylor, Paula Abdul, Sydney Sweeney, Ross Butler, Joseph David-Jones, Meagan Tandy, Cameron Monaghan, Matt Lanter, Kellan Lutz, Nadine Velazquez, Ashley Greene, Stephen "Twitch" Boss, Jeff Pierre, Adam Senn, Benjamin Patterson, Chris Coy, Kym Whitley, Angela Sarafyan, Ego Nwodin, Curran Walters, Shakira Barrera, Quincy Fouse, Claudia Doumit, Rochelle Aytes, Amanda Schull, Jordan L. Jones, Caitlin Carver, Crystal Reed, Sal Stowers, Frank Grillo, Victor Webster, Arden Cho, Emerson Brooks, Tyler Ritter, Thomas Q. Jones, Jason Thompson, Kate Mansi, Kevin Alejandro, Charlie Carver, Max Carver, Bayardo De Murguia, Jeanine Mason, Jessica Stroup, JT Neal, Katelyn MacMullen, Jeannie Mai and Lukas Gage, to name (more than) a few.

At the time of this printing, Scott Sedita Acting Studios has more than sixty-five students and alumni in series regular roles. And that number is always growing. I continue to see many more potential stars walk through my studio doors every day. That, to me, is more exciting and satisfying than anything I've done in the past.

All my talent, confidence, and perseverance, as well as my experience following my various passions through the years, has paid off. I'm a successful acting coach with an award-winning studio. I have authored several books, designed my own acting app, given seminars all over the world, consulted for networks, and best of all, I get to work with actors on a continual basis.

I feel very fortunate that I've been able to explore several avenues of this business, and that I've been able to experience what it feels like to act, write, direct, agent, cast, and most of all...coach.

It's the choices you make on your journey—and the conflicts, joys, sorrows, successes, failures, and possibilities that accompany them—that form your life and your work and will eventually tell *your* story.

A CAUTIONARY TALE

And now...it's three years later

At the Larchmont Deli, a few blocks from my acting studio, I ran into a former student. I'll call him Brent.

INT. – LARCHMONT DELI - HOLLYWOOD – DAY

As Scott stands at the counter ordering an over-stuffed gyro, Brent, a twentysomething good-looking actor, approaches him.

BRENT: Hey, Scott!
SCOTT: Hey, Brent!
BRENT: Good to see you!
SCOTT: Good to see you, too!

At this point in the conversation, I would usually ask an actor I hadn't seen in a while, how their acting career was treating them. But something inside—an instinct perhaps—led me to rephrase the question.

SCOTT: So, how's life treating you?
BRENT: Good. Life is good. Very good! *(pause)* Except I've been down ever since I took a break from acting.
SCOTT: Well, that's not good.
BRENT: I was there, you know? I was on my way, and then I just...let it all go.

A little backstory: When Brent first came to my acting studio, he was a very charismatic young man with talent and an agent who was grooming him for stardom. All Brent needed to do was study his craft and stay motivated and he'd be on his way. And that's what Brent did...for the first year.

Soon after, Brent's commitment to his craft and career started to wane. Even though he booked some small acting gigs, he started to come to class unprepared or show up late, or he'd just miss class altogether. He even began missing auditions! Brent's life was full of distractions, which took him off his career path and put him on the *path of self-sabotage.*

When I confronted him, he had a million excuses: family obligations, relationship drama, money issues, etc. You name it, Brent had an excuse for it. The stories Brent wove around his excuses became his only opportunity *to* act. Eventually, Brent dropped out of class and his agent dropped him.

Nikko, the guy behind the counter, hands Scott his over-stuffed gyro. Scott takes a big bite as Brent talks.

BRENT: It's funny bumping into you because I thought about you the other day.

SCOTT: *(with mouth full)* Mmm?

BRENT: I woke up one morning and it was three years later.

Scott swallows and nods knowingly.

This might sound like an odd non sequitur, but for those who've studied with me, it makes perfect sense. I frequently remind my actors that they must "stay on course and keep focused." Otherwise, they may wake up one morning, three years later, and realize they've been wasting time, paralyzed by fear, wondering, "Why haven't I been pursuing my dream?"

Brent looks out the window, deep in thought.

BRENT: ...Which made me realize, I'm not doing what I came to L.A. to do...to be an actor. *(turns to Scott)* Instead, I let a lot of stupid stuff get in my way. And now... it's three years later.

Although Brent's story is specifically about an actor who took a break from acting, it's really about fear. It's about the fear that led Brent to do "stupid stuff," which derailed his career. That fear is universal to every actor.

Brent takes a deep breath and then...

BRENT: Guess I should get back in the game.
SCOTT: Yes, Brent, I think you should. And now you know what not to do.
BRENT: That's for sure. I could write a book!

SCOTT: *(smiles)* How about I write the book and you concentrate on your acting career?

And that's exactly what we did. After the first printing of this book, Brent did get back in the game and he became a very successful working actor.

This book is a "call to arms" to all those dreamers who want, wish, hope, and pray to have a career as an actor. This book will not only help you find *success* in your acting career, but it will also help you *rebound* from any setbacks and get you back on your feet.

Start now! Get moving. Don't just dream it. Do it!

I will be your guide, navigating you on your road to success. I will also show you how to avoid the many potholes on your path. As your tough love mentor, I will hold your hand on one page and kick your ass on the next. No matter where you are in your career, no matter what has happened (or hasn't happened) in the past, it's all about the present. It's about what you're doing *now*. And now is your time to make it happen!

The journey to a successful acting career is a marathon, not a sprint. It's like training for and competing in the Olympics. There's the thrill of victory as well as the agony of defeat. But if you want it, if you *truly* want it with your heart, mind, body, and soul, you can have it. Let me show you how.

AN ACTOR'S GIFT

We are all born with various gifts: innate abilities, skills, and talents. What we do with our gifts will define who we are and who we become.

This book is a manual for all those born with the gift to act and the desire to turn that gift into an acting career.

This book is a roadmap to help you fulfill your dreams, your destiny, your life's work.

This book is your guide to becoming a successful actor.

Your journey begins now…

THE JOURNEY OF LOOKING INWARD

What's your backstory?

A sign of a great actor is their ability to bring to life an interesting, authentic, complex character.

A way to achieve that is for the actor to create their character's "backstory." A backstory is based on the given circumstances in the script. It asks the actor to write a basic overall history of their character, including their family dynamic, religion, relationships, etc.

Most importantly, a backstory asks the actor to become very curious about their character's internal life: their emotional struggles, desires and motivations. It asks them to take a deep dive into their character's *psyche*, asking questions of their character, like, "Who am I? What do I want? What am I feeling? *Why* am I feeling this way? Why do I do the things I do?"

The problem is that many actors don't take the deep dive to analyze what makes their character tick. Instead, they choose to shy away from the psychological aspect of their character's internal life, thus leaving out what makes their character interesting, authentic and complex.

Let me introduce you to my acting technique called "**Looking Inward**." This acting tool consists of a series of questions that will help you discover the inner workings, the emotional life and the psychology of the character you're playing.

To practice the Looking Inward technique, you'll first need to ignite the curious part of yourself, the part of you that's interested in exploring and discovering what makes people do what they do. Second, you'll need a "subject." Instead of using a fictional character, let's practice Looking Inward on a real live human being, someone who is open, emotionally available, and game to learn. Hmm, but who? Oh, I know...

You!

It's easy. I will guide you through it. To begin, walk over to the mirror, close your eyes, take a deep breath, and exhale. Then, open your eyes and look at your reflection. You need to really look at yourself as if it's the first time. Stare deeply into your eyes, connecting with your inner self, and simply ask, "Who am I?" You might have to ask a few times as your "reflection" might be a little resistant to playing along. Try to come up with as many adjectives as possible to finish this statement:

I am_____

Examples could be: "I am sensitive," "I am strong," "I am impatient," "I am compassionate," "I am insecure," "I am judgmental," "I am angry," etc.

As you can see, these responses could be either positive or negative or both. The important thing is that you be honest with yourself. Take a moment to write down at least ten adjectives that best describe the *real* you. No one needs to see what you've written.

Then, when you're ready, continue asking yourself questions you would ask your character: "What do I want? What am I feeling? Why am I feeling this way? Why do I do the things I do?"

By posing these questions to yourself, you are beginning the process of Looking Inward for *you*; a self-examination that will reveal who *you* are and what makes *you* tick. This journey inward will help you grow emotionally as well as spiritually. You'll start to become more self-aware and, from there, more aware of others and what makes *them* tick.

Looking Inward helps you become more curious, compassionate, and patient… not only with yourself but also with others.

And yes, Looking Inward is more than just my trick to get you to look at your inner self. This technique also translates well into your acting work as a valuable tool to help you look inside your character and create a substantial character backstory.

From this moment on, I invite you to look inward, to "go there," to allow yourself to be open, vulnerable, and honest with yourself.

Throughout this book, you'll get an opportunity to answer various questions regarding your personal backstory as it relates to your acting craft and career. Just as you need to take a non-judgmental look inside your *character's* psychology (the good, the bad and the ugly), for your craft, you'll also need to take a non-judgmental look inside *your own* psychology (the good, the bad, and the ugly) for your career.

When you begin Looking Inward, it will also take your artistry to a deeper level. The more work you do on yourself, acknowledging who you are and your strengths and weaknesses, the more inclined (and able) you'll be to do that for a character.

Simply put, taking the Journey of Looking Inward will make you a better actor and human being.

Are you willing to begin that journey?

SECTION

ONE

> *"The struggles along the way are only meant to shape you for your purpose."*
> -Chadwick Boseman

THE WANT

What do you want?

I like the word *Want*. It's a simple enough word and by simple, I mean clear and specific. When used as a verb, it means to feel a need or desire for something as in, "I *want* to read this book." It also can be used as a noun as in, "What is my *Want*?"

I even developed an acting tool called "The Want" that I use in my classes. It's also the "W" in my script analysis technique WOFRAIM, which you'll read more about later. I always ask my actors, "What is your Want?" I ask them what they, as their character, want in the scene from the other character. Do they want to change their opinion, acquire an object, gain their affection, complete an urgent task? What is driving their character in the scene?

Many acting teachers use the word *Objective* to specify the character's need, as in "What is your character's objective?" For me, the word objective is too cerebral, too heady. We rarely use that word in our everyday life. I mean, when seducing your partner, you don't say, "My *objective* is to make love to you." You say, "I *want* to make love to you."

The word *Want* is primal, visceral, and raw. It's aching; it's a plea, a void that needs to be filled. We use it every day to express our most basic and most passionate needs, urges, and desires: I want to eat. I want to sleep. I want a raise. I want to leave. I want *you* to leave. I want you to love me. I want. I Want! I WANT!

The next time you approach a scene, first define your character's Want. Then say it out loud. For example, *"I want you to trust me."* Repeat this sentence as many times as possible with several different intentions (to plead, to shame, to seduce, to crush, etc.).

Watch what naturally happens inside your body during and after this exercise. You will instantly come alive! You will feel energized. You will feel strongly about your desire and your intentions. You will feel empowered because you know what *you* want.

Repeating your Want is an effective technique to use before entering any scene, or right before "Action" on your next self-tape. I call it "revving your engine."

> *"Nothing is impossible;*
> *the word itself says, 'I'm possible!'"*
> -Audrey Hepburn

Knowing Your Want

Discovering the Want of your character and achieving that Want is a powerful tool in your acting craft. It helps you uncover and tap into your character's true desire. It's the basis for a strong performance.

Likewise, using the Want is equally as empowering when you apply it to your acting *career*. One thing I've realized in my many years in this business is that actors who know what they want in their scene work— and use powerful tactics and intentions to get their Want—are more apt to successfully apply that same approach to their acting careers.

The truth is, knowing your Want is vital to becoming a successful actor. You have to know your Want and work to achieve your Want fearlessly, passionately, and consistently to open the door to making it in Hollywood and any other Industry City.

Let's start by getting *you* revved up to get your Want - becoming a successful actor.

THE WANT: WORKBOOK SECTION

IGNITING YOUR WANT

I want to be a successful actor

To further help you grow in your craft as well as your career, I have developed a **Workbook Section**, a series of Acting Craft and Acting Career Exercises which can be found in the back of most chapters.

These Workbook Sections are designed to enhance your understanding, application and practice of the material covered in each chapter. When it comes to both your craft and your career, the learning, the practice, the work never stops. You must always be moving forward, building on and building up your skills as well as your experience.

Think of these exercises and activities as calisthenics for your acting life. Some of them might seem basic and others might seem difficult (remember, "no pain, no gain"). In all these exercises, you must be willing to open your heart, mind, and body for them to be effective. Remember, you must always be willing to "go there."

These first three exercises are designed to help you Ignite, Declare, and Visualize your Want.

Exercise #1: **Ignite Your Want**

To get started, find a chair and get comfortable. Sit up straight, with both feet on the ground and close your eyes. Say the words, "I want" softly to yourself. Without any intention or intonation, let those words effortlessly leave your lips. Then, say them again, this time in your full speaking voice, and see how it feels.

I want.

Now, begin to say "I want" with as much passion and feeling as you can muster. Take a deep breath, reach inside yourself, and feel the words form in your gut, rise through your chest, enter your mouth, and come out through your lips.

(PASSIONATELY)
I WANT!

(MORE PASSIONATELY!)
I WANT!!

(EVEN MORE PASSIONATELY!)
I WANT!!!!!

If you are fully committed to the exercise, you should feel invigorated! You dug deep, released something strong and powerful, and verbalized some great need and desire. You opened yourself up to the prospect of wanting something, voiced it, and put it out to the universe.

Just speaking the words "I want" out loud organically *ignites your Want*. It sends an active message from your brain to your body. It triggers your survival instinct, your "fight or flight" response, which releases a vitality inside of you that prepares you to get what you want against all odds. It pumps you up and heightens your senses. You feel alive, grounded and self-assured. Voicing your Want is as primal as a baby's cry. When infants cry, they're saying, "I want to be held, I want to eat, I want to be changed...now!"

As adults, many of us feel we don't have the right to state what we want. We have been conditioned through our upbringing and life circumstances to refrain from saying what we truly want for fear of rejection, humiliation, or abandonment. We say "yes" when we really mean "no." Therefore, we can become angry, passive-aggressive, whiny, or depressed, and not even realize why. This all comes down to fear, which I'll address later.

For now, embrace that feeling that comes when you ignite your Want and carry that into this next exercise.

Exercise #2: **Declare Your Want**

You have just opened yourself up to the prospect of wanting something, voiced it, and put it out to the universe for all to hear. Let's take it to the next level.

You must feel that you can not only *state* what you want but also *get* what you want. But first, you need to be clear about what it *is* that you want.

So, what do you want in your acting career? Take your time to think about it. Be specific. You could write *I want to*... "be a film star," "work on a sitcom," "win an Oscar." Think about it and write it down below:

I want to... _____

Whatever you wrote down includes the same basic desire...to be a successful actor. For right now, fill in the next blank with: *I want to be a successful actor.*

Write it down below:

_____

Now that you've written it down (perhaps for the first time), it's time to *declare your Want.*
Say it out loud:

I want to be a successful actor.

Great! For many of you, this might have been the first time you heard yourself say it out loud. Good for you! You've just specified and identified what it is that you really want in your career.

Let's put it out there again so you can truly acknowledge it and embrace it. First, say it softly to yourself three times: *I want to be a successful actor. I want to be a successful actor. I want to be a successful actor.*

Now, say it out loud in your full speaking voice for the universe to hear. **I want to be a successful actor.**

Say it three more times, each time louder and more passionate than the last. Declare your Want!

I want to be a successful actor.

I want to be a successful actor!

I WANT TO BE A SUCCESSFUL ACTOR!

Congratulations! You've just stated your need, your desire, your purpose! You put your Want out there and the universe has officially heard you...and so have your neighbors. Let's take it one step further.

Exercise #3: **Visualize Your Want**

You have all fantasized about what it would be like to be a successful actor. You've already visualized working on a set, pulling into Paramount Studios, being on *The Tonight Show,* or winning an Academy Award. Visualization is not only important to realizing a dream, but also empowering and vital to fulfilling that dream. When you *Visualize your Want,* you put both your conscious and unconscious mind to work at manifesting your vision and making it come true.

Once again, get comfortable in your chair, close your eyes, take a deep breath, and clear your mind. Imagine yourself on a film set. You have the lead role. You've just finished a scene; the director yells "Cut!" and you feel amazing.

The adrenaline of your performance is still pumping through your veins. The director comes over, gives you a hug, and tells you what a pleasure it is to work with you and what a great talent you are. The extras are looking at you with awe and admiration while your co-stars pat you on the back. The assistant director talks to you about tomorrow's shoot as they walk you back to your trailer.

Once inside your trailer, you take a deep breath, letting the adrenaline ease away into a feeling of great satisfaction. You've done what you set out to do; you've become a successful working actor and you feel proud, excited, and ready to do it all again.

Igniting, visualizing and declaring your Want and working to achieve your Want will start you on your path to success.

Now that you know your Want, you need to pledge to always stay *committed* to your Want, your destiny. You need to sign a contract with yourself which will hold you responsible and accountable for your career.

> *"Whatever you want to do, do it now. There are only so many tomorrows."*
> *-Michael Landon*

YOUR ACTOR CONTRACT

I, _____, pledge to do all that I can to achieve my Want. I promise always to work hard, take advantage of all opportunities, appreciate the experience and enjoy the journey. I promise to go after my Want passionately and diligently and to stop at nothing in reaching my dream of becoming a successful actor.

_____

Sign and date

THE
THREE STEPS
TO
SUCCESS

TALENT

CONFIDENCE

PERSEVERANCE

THE THREE STEPS TO SUCCESS

Talent, Confidence, Perseverance

Through my many years in this business as an agent, casting director, and acting coach, I have witnessed first-hand how Talent, Confidence, and Perseverance play a crucial role in the success of an actor. That is why they are your... **Three Steps to Success.** You need these Three Steps to Success not only to start your acting career but also to help you maintain it and stay in the game.

These three steps create momentum, a positive cycle of success, which helps you reach your fullest potential as an actor. You can't take any of these steps out of the equation. When you combine your Talent with Confidence and Perseverance, there will be no stopping you from achieving your Want. There will be no stopping you from making it in Hollywood or any other Industry City. There will be no stopping you.

Can't stop. Won't stop.

TALENT

Acting is your calling

Of the Three Steps to Success, **Talent** is most important. Without talent, you won't go far.

While the other two steps—Confidence and Perseverance—are vital to being successful, neither will put you in the game if you don't have talent. More specifically, a talent to act.

Having talent means you have an innate ability to do something well and the potential to do something great.

We can all watch a movie or TV show and recognize acting talent. For the most part, we can all agree on great actors. We can appreciate the work of the modern-day masters like Meryl Streep, Tom Hanks, Julianne Moore, Viola Davis, Javier Bardem, and Denzel Washington; and their comedic counterparts like Eddie Murphy, Julia Louis-Dreyfus, Allison Janney, Jean Smart, Steve Carell, and Constance Wu.

All these celebrated actors have that instinct, that intrinsic ability to act…and they *choose* to use that talent to its fullest. To be a successful actor, you not only need the talent to act, you also need a great desire to work your talent and to *show it off.*

Where Does Your Talent Come From?

Throughout this book, I will frequently discuss how our individual genes impact who we are and inform what we choose for our "life's work." Genes are specific sequences of DNA that can be found in each cell in the human body. When we talk about our genetic makeup, we usually think about the physical attributes that were passed down to us from our family tree: "I got Mom's freckles," "Dad's curly hair," or "Grandpa's stocky build."

Scientists are now able to specify that certain types of genes passed down to us from our parents and grandparents go beyond just physical characteristics and into medical conditions, mannerisms, moods, personality traits, and yes, even talents.

I have always believed that actors (and painters, singers, dancers, writers, and other artists) are predisposed to a specific gene that gives them their unique talent(s). For actors specifically, it's their innate ability to pretend, to perform, to act.

I have named this inherited cluster of DNA…

THE ACTING GENE

The Acting Gene is where your artistic instincts reside. If you have the Acting Gene, it means you were literally *born to act.* Wherever you think this gift came from—God, the Universe, your Aunt Shelly—it's important to first acknowledge this gift and realize that it is truly a blessing. Having the talent to act is not something you can buy online, or have DoorDash deliver. You either have it or you don't.

"What if I don't have the Acting Gene?"

I'm afraid you will never be an actor.

"What?!"

Well, at the very least, it'll be very difficult to sustain a *career* as an actor. I speak from my thousands of encounters with thousands of actors over what seems like thousands of years, and the reality is…not everyone is born to act. I mean, what kind of world would it be if everyone had the Acting Gene?!

It's just like singing. If there's an Acting Gene, there must be a Singing Gene, right? And apparently, many folks think they have that gene. If *American Idol*—which has launched the careers of many singers—has taught us anything, it's that if they can't sing…*they can't sing!*

No advice, loving support or scathing criticism from a celebrity judge will ever make them singers. They can practice all they want. But if they don't have an innate ability to sing, they will never become professional singers.

Furthermore, you may be blessed with model good looks, a winning personality, or "family connections," but that does not also mean that you are blessed with the Acting Gene. Those attributes may certainly help get your foot in the door, but that's it. And just because you're a YouTube star, have millions of TikTok subscribers, or did a stint on *The Bachelor*, that alone does not make you an actor. You might get your fifteen minutes of fame, a branding opportunity, or maybe a career as a "celebrity," but it's the talent to *act* that makes you an *actor*.

> *"Acting is behaving truthfully under imaginary circumstances."*
> -Sanford Meisner

Were You Born to Act?

At its most basic, the talent to act asks you to pretend. That is what acting really is: pretending. So, growing up, did you often pretend? Could you be truthful under imaginary circumstances?

The best way to measure your innate talent is to first look to your childhood. I am going to ask you to look inwards; examine your youth to see what instincts you came into this world with and how your upbringing influenced them, for better or worse. By looking back on your childhood, you can see how you were naturally and instinctually guided to do something before fear, obstacles, and the pressures of life came into play.

Self-Evaluation Scale: Talent

In each of the Three Steps to Success you will find a fun **Self-Evaluation Scale** to help you determine how much talent, confidence, and perseverance you were born with, as well as how much you accessed and showcased it through your late teens.

If you're having trouble remembering, ask your parents, grandparents, siblings, or whoever raised you. Sometimes your own early memories can be blurred or distorted, so family can be a valuable resource for helping you examine your childhood history. Don't be afraid to be curious about yourself; it's part of the Journey of Looking Inward. Think of it as "creating" your own personal backstory.

Using this Self-Evaluation Scale, rate how much **Talent** (your Acting Gene) you accessed in *Your Instinctual Years* on a scale of "1-3," with "3" being the most brimming with raw talent.

Your Instinctual Years (birth - five years old)

1 Rating: You did not engage your Acting Gene or pretend very much. You were more practical. Even as a toddler, you took things at face value and focused on what was in front of you, whether it was an object, a task, a toy, a game, etc. You didn't drift off into a fantasy world or have an active imaginary life. You didn't wonder.

2 Rating: You frequently engaged your Acting Gene. You had your own imaginary worlds that you could escape to along with imaginary friends. You played dress up, cops and robbers, held make believe tea parties, or played with Barbies, G.I. Joes, Matchbox Cars, etc. You had a desire to perform, to entertain. You were naturally curious. You could take any object and keep yourself amused with it because you used your mind, your imagination. There was awe and wonder in your eyes.

3 Rating: At a young age, your Acting Gene was bursting with talent. You showed early signs of being a child prodigy in the field of acting. You walked and talked at a very early age. You were a quick learner and took direction very well. You had a vast imaginary life; you loved to pretend. You enjoyed being the center of attention. You were always "on." You may have even worked professionally in commercials, TV, and film (think the Olsen twins, Mary-Kate and Ashley).

At this early age, it is primarily your instincts, your Acting Gene, that plays a major role in determining where you would fall on the scale. But that all can change as you grow, especially during *Your Formative Years.*

There are some people that start off as little performers and then, as they grow, they become shyer and more reserved. They move away from their acting talent and into more practical, physical, and intellectual pursuits. There are others who start out shyer and more reserved, and suddenly break out of their shell to become performers.

Once again, using the Self-Evaluation Scale, rate how much talent you accessed in *Your Formative Years* on a scale of 1-3.

Your Formative Years (six years old - late teens)

1 Rating: The Acting Gene was a bit more active as you knew you could pretend and even act, but you rarely practiced it. You enjoyed watching actors on TV and film, but you pursued other activities. You might have appeared in a school play or two, but you rarely utilized or took advantage of your talent until adulthood.

2 Rating: You put on shows in your living room and backyard for your family, friends, and neighbors. You enjoyed being the center of attention, perhaps even being the class clown. You developed an interest and appreciation for the Arts. You acted in school plays, community theatre, and may have even become professional, having moderate success in commercials, TV, and film. You knew at an early age that you wanted to grow up to be an actor.

3 Rating: Much like child prodigies in music, math, science, and spelling, you were able to translate your raw talent into a career in acting. Talent was pouring out of you so much that you *had* to act. You were a child and/or a teen actor with a remarkable ability to pretend at an early age. Jodie Foster, Mayim Bialik, Jason Bateman, Sarah Jessica Parker, Anna Paquin, Nicholas Hoult, Jennifer Lawrence, the Fanning sisters (Dakota and Elle) and the cast of the *Harry Potter* films and *Stranger Things* series are all "3's."

Where do you fit on the Formative Years scale and how did that change from the Instinctual Years scale? Did you start out as a 2 on the Instinctual Years and drop to a 1 on the Formative Years? Did you move up or did it stay the same?

Why does your talent change? Because your talent is only part of the equation. As you grow up, there are several other factors and influences that affect not just your acting talent but also how much you used it.

Did Your Upbringing Affect Your Talent?

Whether you come from a supportive family or a dysfunctional family, or had to deal with loss, abuse, or abandonment in your youth, you could discover and develop your talent just the same. After all, many great performers have come from challenging backgrounds.

But, as with most talents, there is something to be said about creative encouragement. Having a healthier upbringing with parents or guardians who applauded your ability to act, pushed you to explore it further, and rewarded your successes may have made your talent development a little easier.

That said, looking back on how you were raised can help you take stock of what you have now and assess how developed your talent is at this point in your life.

Are you ACTOR A or ACTOR B?

ACTOR A: Did you have parents or guardians who not only acknowledged your innate ability, but also encouraged you to use it? Did they let you explore your imaginary life? Did they give you the positive reinforcement you needed to bolster your creativity? Did they sign you up for classes in the arts? Did they come see your plays, recitals, and concerts?

Or

ACTOR B: Did your parents or guardians, because of their own life circumstances, not spend as much time with you, or support you and your creative nature—physically, emotionally, or even financially? Were they unable to inspire and reward you for your creativity? Did they discourage you from participating in the creative arts? Did they look down upon acting as if it wasn't even an option for a career?

If you identified more with ACTOR A, you're more familiar with accessing your Acting Gene...or at least you feel comfortable with where you are in your acting ability. You probably spent your childhood exploring the actor in you and you're not emotionally blocked or afraid to perform. You have explored your talent and you look forward to creative challenges.

If you identified more with ACTOR B, you may have a great deal of talent, but it might be harder to uncover and break out of its shell. Although you might be excited to explore your talent, it's still foreign, unfamiliar, maybe even scary to you. Accessing your talent may be a bit tougher because you haven't gotten a chance to experiment, to play, to act. Therefore, you may have some fear connected with it that you haven't worked through yet. You will have to work harder to break through that fear and tap into your creativity, your Acting Gene.

Some actors may have had that constant celebration of their talent while some may have had the complete opposite. Whether you're ACTOR A, ACTOR B, or somewhere in between, you need to know that if you have the talent to act, you can have a successful acting career. Regardless of where you have come from and where you are now, if you have the Acting Gene, you can be a professional actor.

First, you have a big choice to make…

To Act or Not to Act?

That *is* the question. Do you want to use your talent to pursue a career?

That's a big decision to make. As I stated earlier, acting is a gift. You have the choice of whether to use that gift. Keep in mind that the life of a struggling artist is not an easy one. It can be a life filled with hard work, rejection, and disappointments. That's not to scare you, it's simply the truth.

So, you could say, "While I acknowledge and appreciate this gift, I choose not to use it. I choose not to act." Let me tell you, there's nothing wrong with that choice. We all know someone—friends, family, neighbors, co-workers—who have the talent to sing or act but never pursue their gift as a career.

Think back to any community theatre show you saw as a kid. There was always someone in the cast who really shined. They either had a phenomenal voice or terrific acting instincts or both. But they were not *professional* actors. Rather, they were executives, accountants, teachers, doctors, stay-at-home-parents, etc. They might have dipped their toe in the performing arts, but they never leapt in with both feet. They probably could have had a professional acting career, but they chose not to for whatever reason. Just because a person has a specific talent doesn't mean that they necessarily need, want, or have to make a career out of it.

For many of you, the choice of whether to act is a simple one. *You have to!* There is nothing else you can do or think of doing other than acting. You feel it in your heart, your soul, your bones. Acting is your calling.

> *"Acting is not about being someone different. It's finding the similarity in what is apparently different, then finding myself in there."*
> -Meryl Streep

Acting IS a Craft

That's right! Just like any other craft (carpentry, painting, music, dance) or any sport (soccer, basketball, golf, baseball), acting needs to be learned, studied, practiced, and mastered. You need to put your time, energy, and passion into nurturing that acting craft, personalizing it, and performing it to the best of your ability. That work never stops, even as you achieve success. Many of today's most accomplished actors still work with an acting coach. The point is, you only *begin* learning, you never *stop* learning.

There are many people who get into this business dreaming of being a star. And that's okay; I say, "Dream big dreams!" But those actors who think that they don't need to study or work their craft are in for a rude awakening and a rough road ahead.

That's not to say that I haven't seen that rare example of an actor with innate ability and no training step right off the proverbial bus and right into an acting gig…but it does not make for a career. To be an actor, you must train, you must study the complex craft of acting. Raw talent will only get you so far.

Don't Jump Over the Craft

I know everyone wants to throw themselves into auditioning as soon as they get to Hollywood or any other Industry City, but it's my strong belief that actors should *not* audition until they have sufficient training. Auditioning is for actors who have studied and are ready to showcase their skills in a professional arena. Yes, auditioning is an opportunity to act, and you can learn many things from auditioning. But learning that you need acting classes shouldn't be one of them.

I meet many actors who haven't yet trained or studied acting but who are already auditioning. Although they may have representation and show great potential or even star quality, they are usually unprepared to tackle professional auditions…and the outcome can be disastrous. I mean, would you ski down a mountain before taking skiing lessons? I hope not!

There are many managers and agents who send untrained actors out on auditions. In their excitement, they want to show off their new find, get feedback, and even motivate the new actor. I admit that when I was an agent, I was guilty of this. That's not to say that agents haven't seen success in booking brand new actors. But in the long run, it's usually those untrained actors who have booked jobs before they were ready that suffer the consequences.

I'm an Actress Now

When I was an agent in New York City, in the shoulder pad '80s, there was a seventeen-year-old girl I discovered in a mall. I will call her Anna. Even at such a young age, Anna had a maturity about her. She knew who she was which made her self-assured and confident. She had a great look: edgy, but pretty. Even though she never had formal training, she had raw talent. After Anna did a reading for me, I could tell that she had the Acting Gene and enough self-awareness to understand the material. I decided to represent her

I took her under my wing and got her into acting class, found her a headshot photographer, and started to submit her for commercials. The first one she auditioned for, she booked. She was flown to Los Angeles to shoot a national commercial. The director liked her so much that a few weeks later, he auditioned her again and she booked another national commercial!

A film breakdown came out looking for a teenage girl who was tough, smart, and pretty. Although this was a lead film role, I pitched Anna to the casting director. I told him that Anna was a new actress with no formal training, just two commercials under her belt and a couple of acting classes. He brought her in anyway and auditioned her. He said she was "a natural." Weeks later, after a few callbacks, Anna booked the job!

It was a major Disney film. Not only did she book the movie, but the studio also signed her to a three-picture deal! Plus, the film was being shot overseas in some exotic location. It was the perfect Cinderella story.

The movie shoot went well for Anna. After filming, she came back to New York to visit me at my office accompanied by the film's lead, a popular '80s teen star who was also now her boyfriend. As Anna sat there with her head down, he told me that Anna was going to leave me to sign with his agent at ICM (one of the biggest agencies at the time). Anna meekly picked her head up, smiled apologetically, said "bye," and then they left.

After Anna's film came out to moderate success, she went on to shoot her second film. This one didn't go so well. A few weeks into the shoot, I found out she was let go. The director apparently felt she wasn't connecting to her character, she required too many takes, and that she had no real technique. It seems that the raw, untrained talent that drove her through her first film was not enough to carry her through the second. At the age of nineteen, Anna was fired and replaced.

Five years later, when I had moved to Los Angeles, I was having lunch and Anna was my server. She greeted me with a big hug. When I asked how she was doing, Anna proudly declared, "I'm an actress now." She said she was studying her acting technique, taking classes, and auditioning. A year later, I saw her again, this time as a series regular on a hit TV show.

It's Not Easy Being Green

Agents, managers, casting directors, and producers refer to untrained actors as "green." Being green means being a novice, a newbie, not a professional yet. Every actor at the beginning stages of their career is *green*. Positively speaking, it means you have potential, but you also need to study your ass off!

The problem is that too many actors don't study and they go on auditions while they're still green. They think if they go on enough auditions, they won't be green anymore. Being told that you're green on a continual basis will not only jeopardize your relationships with agents, managers and casting directors, it will also take a toll on your self-esteem and your overall confidence.

If your career is a house, your acting training is your foundation. Without a concrete, solid foundation, your house will collapse. It won't take an earthquake to bring it down; all you will need is a few tremors to make it fall. The best way to build that foundation is through study and practice.

> *"The thing I like about acting is being able to lose yourself completely in someone else."*
> -Elliot Page

WELCOME TO ACTING CLASS

For an actor, there is nothing more exciting, invigorating, and stimulating than being in an acting class. In acting class, you get a chance to study with other actors of all experience levels who share the same hopes, dreams and desires.

There are some basic acting classes that all actors should take when they're first getting started as well as classes for actors who already have some training. There are many wonderful acting studios around the world (I know, I've gotten a chance to travel and teach at them). Different teachers and techniques will offer new perspectives on developing your skills. You can find an acting studio or coach by simply doing research, be it online, asking other actors or getting recommendations from those in the industry.

Find an acting class that you feel comfortable and safe in so you can grow and feel challenged. A good acting class will help you develop your imagination, sense memory, emotions, timing, voice and speech, comedic instincts, and more, all while allowing you to create complex characters and discover new and original ways to enhance the text.

Once you've enrolled in an acting class, you must attend it on a regular basis to get the most out of it. Not showing up to class or showing up late will negatively affect you and your classmates. And just showing up to class isn't enough either. While I agree that showing up is half the battle, it still is not *playing the game*. To get the full benefit of your acting class (your investment), you not only have to show up, but you also must DO. THE. WORK.

Practice. Practice. Practice.

In my class, regardless of how talented an actor is, I can tell the difference between those who practice and put in a hundred percent from those who put in...not so much. When I work with actors that do practice, I see a commitment and a constant improvement in their work. That creates a hunger within, an incentive for the actor to work harder, therefore making them better actors.

When you do practice on a continual basis, you will reach peaks in your craft. When you reach those peaks, you "arc" in your acting work. I always encourage actors to set and reach small goals in their acting. As a coach, I watch for specific moments that mark their growth, where things start to click into place.

When that happens, you can see the actor blossom and get closer to their potential. I call this "**arcing**" (ark-ing), and it is a word that you will see throughout this book. It's important for an actor to continue to arc in their work and to be able to measure their growth.

Your acting class should be fun, but it also should be challenging, as that will help you arc. Your acting coach should be someone you respect, who you can trust, who understands and "gets" you. Find a coach who believes in your potential to be a working actor. Find someone who will push your boundaries and challenge you to dig deeper into your emotions and imagination.

There will be times when you will feel lost, frustrated, disheartened, and even overwhelmed by the class, the teacher, the workload; all the above. Rest assured, that is all part of the learning process and your development as an artist. But once you commit to studying on a regular basis and make it a regular part of your life, you will grow in your craft, and you'll have a constant desire to set your own challenges in your acting class.

You must take this same approach with *all* your acting work, including the exercises and games you find in this book. The rest of this chapter, including The Workbook Section, will provide you with practical steps and exercises you can take to improve your talent. Whether you're in the beginning stages of working your craft or an actor with some experience, I will lay out what you need to know to get started, to challenge yourself, and to keep the talent ball rolling.

First, you'll need to record all the wonderful lessons you'll be learning and experiencing. No, I'm not asking you to just press "record" on your smartphone; it'll take a little more effort than that. I am asking you to go *old school* and write it down.

If You Write It, You Will Remember It

Journaling is becoming a lost art due to technology, but as you journey through your life as an actor, it is important to write it down in your **Actor's Journal**.

You will write down all the techniques, information, discoveries, tips, revelations, and personal work you accumulate in a *notebook(s)*. This Actor's Journal will serve as a constant reference guide of all your acting work, especially class "takeaways," like notes and insights from your acting coach, specific performance feedback, and any feelings or thoughts you have about your class work.

In your Actor's Journal, you should always write down the following:

- Acting technique exercises that work for you
- Imaginary and Personal Substitutions ("As if's")
- Strong active verbs (Intentions) that work for you
- Sense memory work
- Character work, including backstories, histories, and personality traits
- Pictures of how the character might look, dress, and act like, as well as their environment

- Discoveries and revelations you find in your work
- Class takeaways or pieces of advice from your teacher that you find helpful

Your Actor's Journal is also your personal diary. You should write down any mantras, affirmations, and inspirational quotes you find. It will also be your own acting career information guide, where you will write down things like names of casting directors, audition information, contacts, and anything and everything else you learn (or need) in your pursuit of a career.

Your Actor's Journal is not only a collection of notes, lectures, and materials, it's also your intimate thoughts and reflections on your craft and career. Be prepared to go through a few notebooks a year and make sure to date and safeguard them. Think of it as creating your own special acting encyclopedia or archive.

A Little Help from My Friends

It's lonely being an actor, sometimes isolating...so form or join an acting group, or what I call a **Call To Action Group**, or **CTAG** (pronounced "Cee-Tag"). Your CTAG should consist of a small, select group of other actors that you can trust, you can be honest with, and that are hard-working and dedicated to their craft and their career. They will be your accountability partners and you will all help keep each other on track. I recommend around seven actors, including yourself.

These are peers who understand the struggles of setting up your self-tape home studio, getting an agent, the efforts (and expense) in joining SAG-AFTRA, the importance of marketing yourself, the excitement of meeting a casting director and the disappointment of blowing an audition.

Throughout your journey, your CTAG will become your practice group, your support group, your marketing group and a whole lot more. They'll also be your "acting work" group, including when doing some of the fun exercises I present in the Workbook Section and the Bonus Track. One game for you and your CTAG to play is The Want Game, presented at the end of this chapter.

10 Essential Classes for Actors

1) Basic Acting Technique: Here is where you will learn what I call "the nuts and bolts" of acting. These classes are designed to provide you a safe space and encouraging environment to explore your Acting Gene. You will be introduced to the teachings of the masters like Meisner, Adler, Stanislavski, Strasberg, etc. Acting foundation classes teach you how to access your emotions, develop your imagination, and find your acting strengths and weaknesses. You learn the value of techniques like personal substitution, sense memory, repetition, improvisation, and imagination work. These foundational techniques will be your acting core that you will build upon for the rest of your career.

2) Scene Study: These classes take your foundation work and apply it to character work from plays and films. In Scene Study class, you will learn how to break down and analyze the text. You will be given a scene and a partner to rehearse with outside of class. Then you will return to class to perform the scene with critique from the teacher. Scene Study classes help you explore a character from an in-depth viewpoint: what drives them, what makes them unique. In these classes, you will build a character, a backstory, and a relationship to other characters. The goal of Scene Study is to get you prepared to tackle any type of role.

3) On-Camera: Most actors begin their training working in a theatre or on a classroom stage. On-Camera classes will help actors tailor their acting to film and television. It will also help the actor feel more relaxed, grounded, and confident in front of a rolling camera. Beyond showing you how to "hit your mark" and work sightlines within the confines of the camera, these classes will teach you how to be "still" while having a strong emotional inner life, and specific inner thoughts. On-Camera class teaches you that good TV and film acting happens "behind the eyes."

4) Audition Technique: Auditioning should (and ultimately will) become your main job as an actor. Whether in-person or virtual, you need to be comfortable in the "audition room" from the moment you say hello to the second you say goodbye, and all the acting in between. Audition Technique class teaches you to take direction and "adjustments" as well as help you overcome obstacles and fears in the audition process. You will also learn what roles work best for you as you'll get to play different types of characters from various genres. In my Audition Technique class, you learn my script analysis technique WOFRAIM, which you'll find a condensed version of in The Bonus Track at the end of this chapter.

5) Sitcom Comedy: The art of comedy is considered the most difficult of all the genres, but if you do it well, you will have an advantage. Sitcom Comedy class will show you that comedy is much more than witty one-liners, spit takes, and running into walls. There are specific rhythms, rules, techniques, and character archetypes that make comedy work. With TV drama's integrating comedy into their scripts, Comedy classes are becoming a necessity. Sitcom Comedy class teaches you to tap into your "Funny Gene" (which is to the left of the Acting Gene). You'll learn to identify different types of jokes, including what I've named "Triplets" and "The Turnaround." For more on comedic acting, read my international bestseller, *The Eight Characters of Comedy: A Guide to Sitcom Acting & Writing,* which casting directors, writers, directors, and acting programs worldwide recommend and use as a textbook for teaching comedy.

6) Self-Tape Audition: As self-tape auditions become more prominent, especially as the *first audition,* there are now Self-Tape Audition classes offered. I have been incorporating self-tapes in my classes for many years, seeing where the industry was trending. In Self-Tape Audition class, you are assigned TV or film sides to self-tape. After you do your homework (and WOFRAIM your script) you then self-tape at home and send it to your teacher via a video delivery platform. In class, the teacher reviews everyone's tape, gives each actor critique on their performance and feedback on the technical aspect of self-taping: i.e., camera angle, sightlines, lighting, sound, backdrop, wardrobe, etc.

7) Improvisation: In an Improvisation class, there are no words, no dialogue, no script, only guidelines; no written characters, only the actors and the choices and circumstances they bring to the performance. Whether the class focus is comedy or drama, an Improv Class will help you stay in the moment, think on your feet, and feel as your character would while relying on only your own instincts. That's a good experience to have when casting directors, or even other actors, throw you curveballs in class, the casting room or on set.

8) Commercial Technique: When you first start to audition, chances are it will be for commercials. Auditioning for and booking commercials gives you confidence, an on-set experience, money in your pocket and a reputable credit. And, just so you know, many of your favorite actors got their start in commercials (I know, I was probably their agent). Commercial Technique class will teach you how to be, well, *you!* This class is a great place to integrate your look with your personality and your acting ability. This class will also teach you the specific techniques to commercial acting: how to "slate," read copy, and talk directly into the camera.

9) Voice and Speech: As an actor, your voice is one of your most important tools, and there are ways to support it and train it. Voice teachers help you to speak clearly and powerfully by teaching you diaphragm exercises to strengthen your support, tongue twisters to keep you articulate, and accent reduction exercises to lose your hometown dialect. Using renowned techniques like Linklater, Alexander, and Skinner, these classes will also teach you breathing exercises, vocal warm-ups and different ways to utilize your voice more effectively. The goal is to integrate your voice and speech as extensions of yourself.

10) Movement: As an actor, your body and presence are a major source of expression. Movement class helps you connect your body with your mind and emotions. It teaches you how to be comfortable and confident in the way you move and carry yourself. Yoga and Pilates are also two great low-impact methods of movement classes that aim to strengthen muscles while improving your posture, increasing your flexibility, strengthening your core and reducing stress and anxiety. It can center you and connect you to yourself, your breath and the world around you.

Can't Stop Won't Stop...Working the Craft

You must remember that talent either grows or dies. If you nurture your talent, it will continue to flourish, but if you stop studying, training, and working your talent, it will lie dormant or just die...and die quickly.

You can't ever simply say, "I'm talented" and leave it at that. Even if you're Kate Winslet or Christian Bale, you still need to work at your craft and keep challenging yourself. Once you decide you have learned everything you need to know about acting, then you have stopped growing as an actor.

Once again, if you're serious about acting, you need to work your craft daily. You must keep working your acting muscles or they will become limp and weak; you will feel the atrophy set in. Think of how it feels when you go to the gym three times a week and then suddenly take a few weeks off. When you get back to it, working out is a lot tougher. You feel out of shape or "rusty." It's the same with acting. You can't take class for a while and then take significant amounts of time off from class or from acting in general. You must flex, stretch, and stimulate those acting muscles as often and as consistently as you can.

You need to always strive to be the best. When it comes to acting in an audition or on set, just being good is not good enough...you need to be *great*. And if you have the talent (which you do!), then you *can* be great. The way you achieve greatness is through preparation, working your craft, believing in yourself, and practicing always.

It's just like being a great athlete. Professional athletes work every single day to make themselves better. Think of Serena Williams and how many tennis tournaments she's won. Yet she still competes as often as she can. Serena has said in interviews that she gets up early almost every morning to work out and play tennis for hours a day. She is without a doubt one of the greatest of all time, and she still works just as hard as she did when she was starting out.

That's what you need to do. That's how hard you need to work. That's how you effectively use your gift, your talent. Work it every single day and *want* to work it even more. Once you are consistently working your talent, you are ready to go on to the next step.

"If you're meant to do this, you'll find a way."
-Richard Jenkins

ORIGINS OF THE SELF-TAPE

Since the publishing of the first edition of this book, there have been major shifts in the audition process in the TV and film industry for both actors and theatrical casting directors.

Prior to 2007, actors would rarely see a video camera present in a theatrical casting office. For a TV series or a film, actors would audition (sans camera) sitting or standing across from the casting director who was usually sitting in a chair or sometimes behind a desk. Only when actors were chosen to finally "screen test" for a role did they find themselves in front of camera. And if an actor screen tested with another actor (to find out their suitability), they were doing what is called a "chemistry read."

Only *commercial* casting directors at that time had a video camera. Commercial casting offices also came equipped with lights, sound, a blue or gray backdrop and a video tape player/recorder. They would record the actor's audition and send the tape (by messenger or FedEx) to producers and directors. But when portable mini-cameras became readily available and affordable, they started popping up in the offices of theatrical casting directors. Now casting directors could record actors and send their tapes via the internet. Soon, most TV and film casting directors had a camera setup in their offices.

The next major shift in auditioning (and the business) was the introduction of the "self-tape." The emergence of the smartphone—and its higher resolution video camera—gave actors the means to record themselves. So, when casting wanted to see an actor who was unavailable, they would ask their representation to have that actor "put themselves on tape." Alas, the self-tape was born.

At first, it was only a small fraction of actors who were doing self-tape auditions. But it would soon grow. The technology of the self-tape also gave agents and managers the opportunity to peek inside their client's audition process, something they were never able to do before. They would also use it as a tool for prospective actors. If they were interested in an actor who didn't have a demo reel, they would ask them to put themselves on tape.

And then the 2020 pandemic hit and shut down all in-person auditions. Recording at home with a reader and sending it in was the only way for an actor to be seen for an audition. Self-tapes became the new normal.

Suddenly, every auditioning actor needed a functional home studio setup with an industry standard camera, lighting, sound, and backdrop. Actors took on the additional job of being their own producer, director and editor. They had quickly become savvy about the technical aspects of editing, graphic design, and sending the correct sized files to casting.

Most actors have mixed feeling about the self-tape process. Some love it, some hate it. Either way, self-tapes are here to stay, at least for the first audition. Self-taping is now just another aspect of being an actor. You need to master this new format and add this new tool to your actor's toolbox.

TALENT: WORKBOOK SECTION

THE WANT GAME

A way to get out of your head

I developed this game for actors in 1998, and since the first edition of this book was published, many colleges and university acting courses have put it in their curriculum, too. Let me introduce you to my acting exercise, **The Want Game.**

The Want Game helps you access your talent and use your training while giving you a sense of what real acting is like and how powerful it can be. It encompasses a variety of acting tools from my script analysis technique WOFRAIM. It is centered on the fundamental core of acting: the character's Want. However, I also designed the game to touch upon other WOFRAIM elements, including Obstacles, Relationship, As If, and Intentions. Playing The Want Game allows you to be in the moment which, in turn, gets you "out of your head."

To play The Want Game, you start by meeting with your Call To Action Group (CTAG) someplace that's comfortable and offers some privacy and room for two actors to perform. Set up two chairs facing each other a few feet apart in the middle of that space. All the other chairs should be set up to face the two chairs in the center.

Everyone in the CTAG will get to play The Want Game. Each game takes about fifteen minutes. Three players will participate at the same time. Two will play the game while a third will act as the Moderator.

The Want Game comes in four "Acts."

Act I starts with two players (Actor One and Actor Two) sitting in the two chairs across from each other. The Moderator will give each Actor a Want from the list below. Notice that the Wants come in pairs. Work with one of these five sets of Wants for the best results:

WANTS:

#1
ACTOR ONE: *I want you to love me.*
ACTOR TWO: *I want you to leave.*

#2
ACTOR ONE: *I want to borrow money.*
ACTOR TWO: *I want you to get a job.*

#3
ACTOR ONE: *I want you to tell me the truth.*
ACTOR TWO: *I want you to believe me.*

#4
ACTOR ONE: *I want you to help me.*
ACTOR TWO: *I want you to grow up.*

#5
ACTOR ONE: *I want you to take care of me.*
ACTOR TWO: *I want you to back off.*

I will use #1 as an example. Actor One will have the first Want (*I want you to love me.*) while Actor Two will have the second Want (*I want you to leave.*). Once the Moderator assigns the Actors their individual Want, they should take a few moments to breathe and relax. When they are ready, each Actor should sit up straight in a comfortable position and make eye contact with the other Actor. When it looks like they are both ready, the Moderator will have them begin with Act I.

Act I: Repetition

In Act I, the Moderator will only serve as an observer. This game starts very similarly to a basic Meisner activity of Repetition. Both Actors will take turns repeating their individual Wants back and forth to each other. There is no acting in this first part. The Actors should simply state their given Want with no intonation, intentions, facial expressions, or body movements. They shouldn't think about what they're saying.

The two Actors maintain eye contact with each other and simply speak the words to each other. They should keep repeating their Want until it becomes second nature. It may feel a little strange and tedious at first but each Actor should do their best to connect with the other Actor and let the words flow from their lips. Don't think, just speak.

As an example:

ACTOR ONE	ACTOR TWO
I want you to love me.	*I want you to leave.*
I want you to love me.	*I want you to leave.*
I want you to love me.	*I want you to leave.*

After a few minutes of this repetition, each Actor should allow themselves to slowly pick up on what the other Actor is sending to them. Gradually pick up on each other's intonation, body language, attitude, speech pattern, facial expressions, etc. They should allow what they observe to affect them. Don't think about it, simply react to it. Each Actor connects with their partner and sees what organically happens when they allow themselves to work off each other. Don't force it. The Actors just keep repeating, while being observant and finding the truth in what they're saying, to see what naturally occurs.

Act II: Intentions

As the Moderator observes the two Actors staying in the moment, truly connecting with their Want and each other, the Moderator will then add Intentions. These Intentions will give the Actors something active to *play*, tactics to help them achieve their Want. If the Intention is "to seduce," the Actor's job is to make their partner feel "turned on."

These active verbs will make the interaction between the two Actors deeper and more challenging. Using and playing active intentions (for the *other* Actor to feel something) will get the Actor out of their head and into their body. This type of activity produces a more interesting scene not just for the participants, but also for the observers. Some will only need two or three

Intentions to propel them into the scene, while others may need more. The Moderator will choose a few Intentions from this list and have them ready to give to the two Actors as they continue with the exercise.

INTENTIONS:

Actor One	>	<	Actor Two
To Attack	>	<	To Challenge
To Charm	>	<	To Demand
To Crush	>	<	To Entice
To Mock	>	<	To Plead
To Seduce	>	<	To Threaten

The two Actors will continue repeating their Wants to each other as the Moderator will call out Actor One's name and give them an Intention (to charm). It is the responsibility of Actor One to keep stating their Want while putting an Intention behind that Want.

After Actor One starts to incorporate his or her Intention into their Want, the exercise will shift as Actor Two will organically respond to Actor One's Intention. Then, after a few rounds, the Moderator will give Actor Two a different Intention (to crush). Actor One's Intention (to charm) will start to organically change as they react to Actor Two's Intention (to crush).

The participants should let this process naturally evolve. Again, don't try to force these Intentions into the acting. The Actors should just keep speaking and reacting until they come naturally.

The Moderator should allow the interaction to unfold until they observe the scene is getting stuck or that they have exhausted that Intention. At that point, the Moderator will then change that Actor's Intention by shouting out another one from the list. This also ensures that the Actors won't get trapped playing their Want only one way. As the Moderator, feel free to make drastic changes to the Intentions. If Actor One is playing "to charm," change it up and give them "to threaten." If Actor Two is playing "to crush," give them the opposite Intention, "to plead."

At some point during this phase of the game, the Moderator will ask both Actors to stand up, giving them more space as they continue to repeat their Wants and Intentions. This will lead into Act III.

Act III: Improvisation

As the two Actors stand, repeating their Wants, the Moderator continues to throw out new Intentions. As the scene builds and the Actors absorb these new Intentions, the Moderator will yell out, "Improvise!"

What I mean by improvise is that both Actors continue with their same overall Wants, but they are now free to say whatever they like to achieve that Want. As the game progresses to this point, chances are a scenario has formed in each Actor's mind. By the time they are on their feet, there is a natural connection to each other, as well as the Want and the scenario that has developed. Allowing them to improvise at this point will often unfold a powerful scene.

Just like with any of the other Acts, the Actors shouldn't push or force anything. They should try to stay out of their head, just say what comes naturally. If they can't think of anything to say, they simply go back to repeating their Want (*I want you to love me*) until something naturally comes out in the moment. Also, remember a basic rule of improvisation is to never negate what your partner is giving you. If Actor One *first* defines Actor Two as their friend, lover, or boss, then they become that person.

The Moderator allows the two Actors to work with each other and play out the improvised scene for a short time. The Moderator then ends the game by shouting, "Scene!"

Both Actors should take a few deep breaths, let the work they were just doing ease away, sit back down in their chairs, and answer the questions in the final Act.

Act IV: Reflection and Discussion

Here's a list of questions the Moderator could ask the two Actors:

- How did the overall exercise feel?
- Did you feel a connection with your partner, and how did you feel that connection deepen as the scene progressed?
- Did you feel that your Intentions heightened the scene? How did they help you achieve your Want?
- Did a specific scenario, real or imaginary (As If), play out in your mind? What was it?
- At the end of the exercise, how did you feel? Did you feel excited, invigorated, and exhausted?

Take a few minutes to discuss these questions. Then one of the Actors who performed will now take over as the Moderator and two new Actors will take a seat up front and get ready to play The Want Game.

The Acting Zone

The Want Game also gives actors an opportunity to enter what I call **"The Acting Zone,"** a place where nothing matters except for what is happening in the moment between you and your scene partner. This is what good actors feel after performing well in a scene on a professional set. The Acting Zone is where you want to be.

The Want Game is a microcosm of everything that good acting encompasses. It's an experience, a chance for you to get into the Acting Zone. It's also a way for actors to feel like they are listening and reacting organically while staying focused on their Want.

It's not easy, but this experience is what makes acting so challenging, thrilling, and ultimately satisfying. And it shows you exactly why it's important to keep working at this craft, keeping it fresh and alive.

BONUS TRACK: TALENT

WOFRAIM It!

Acting homework made easy

In 1998, I developed a script analysis technique that is used by thousands of actors all over the world. It incorporates various acting methods to help you quickly, easily, and efficiently break down your class assignments, audition sides, and TV and film scripts. I call it by its acronym: W.O.F.R.A.I.M. It is your acting homework, made easy.

Here is a condensed version of my technique. For the full version of WOFRAIM and much more, please download the Actor Audition App, the first of its kind, which can be found on all the major app platforms.

There are two things you need to do before you "WOFRAIM It!"

1) Read the **Breakdown.** The breakdown is a separate sheet of information about the film or TV project for which you're auditioning. The breakdown includes a short synopsis of the storyline and vital production notes: shoot dates, name(s) of producer(s), writer(s), casting

director, etc. Most importantly, it provides a "breakdown" of your character with important details like age, personality traits, relationships and backstory.

2) Download your **Sides**. Sides are specific audition scenes selected from the script for co-star roles to series regulars to leads in a film. The industry term "sides" refers to either one scene or a set of various scenes. The chosen sides showcase the character and carry a certain weight and complexity to the scene, especially for lead and supporting roles. Ultimately, sides help the casting director determine if the actor has the look, essence, and understanding of the character to book the role.

To WOFRAIM your audition sides, answer these questions as your character:

WANT: What do you **Want**? What do you Want the other character to say or do? What are the stakes involved if you *don't* (or *do*) get what you Want? Specify at least three high stakes.

OBSTACLE: What is your *External Obstacle(s)*, that *person, place* or *thing* that's stopping you from getting your Want? What is your *Internal Obstacle(s)*, that *inner conflict* you carry?

FEELINGS: What *Feelings* are you exploring throughout the scene? Choose three emotions, making one positive.

<u>R</u>ELATIONSHIP: What is your *Relationship* to the other character(s)? How do you feel about the other character(s) and why do you feel that way? Write a brief history.

<u>AS IF:</u> What is your *As If,* your personal and/or imaginary substitution? How do you, the actor, relate to the emotional experience of your character's circumstance and Want?

<u>INTENTIONS:</u> What are the *Intentions*, the actions, the tactics, you implement to achieve your Want? What active verbs will you attach to the dialogue to change the other character's emotional and/or physical state?

<u>M</u>OMENT BEFORE: What is the *Logistical Moment Before,* your environment when the scene begins? What is your *Emotional Moment Before,* the single strong emotion you feel as the scene starts?

CONFIDENCE

I believe in myself

You just learned that the first of the Three Steps to Success was Talent, that precious innate ability that—when combined with technique, training, and practice—will put you on your journey to becoming a successful actor.

Yes, talent is the foundation, but if you don't believe in yourself or your ability to succeed, you won't make it. If you *do* happen to make it, it won't be for long. To truly realize your potential, you need the second of the Three Steps to Success: **Confidence**.

Having confidence is having total faith in yourself even when others don't. You trust in your abilities and believe that you will be able to achieve your goals and fulfill your dreams.

Confidence and talent go hand in hand. No matter how talented you are, your confidence level—your "C-level," as I call it—will always be challenged. Having self-confidence, along with your talent, will help you get through those challenges. You'll need this dynamic duo in your corner whether you are performing scenes in acting class, filming a self-tape, meeting a casting director, or working on a television or film set. You need both working in unison as you continue to learn this craft and tackle this career.

Confidence is More Emotional

Of the Three Steps to Success, confidence is the most emotionally based, meaning it applies directly to you, your belief in what you're capable of, and your feelings of self-worth. That's what makes it tricky. The way you feel about yourself, present yourself, and the energy you put out to the world are key ingredients to your success. Only those who feel sure about themselves, their talent, and their intentions will be successful.

Unlike talent, confidence isn't something you have to be born with to possess, although there are those entering this world with a higher level of self-esteem and self-worth. For the most part, confidence is something that is *learned*. Many learn it as kids growing up while others learn it as adults.

Either way, building confidence and sustaining it is not always easy, especially in a business where you deal with rejection, disappointment, and second-guessing on a continual basis.

No matter how much talent you have, you will experience a lot more rejection than you will success, at least initially. That rejection will often feel personal, and you will *take it* personally. It will make you feel sad, angry and defeated. Confidence in your ability to act will help you deal with that rejection and those feelings and keep you and your career moving forward.

However, the confidence you need isn't something that just magically appears. Building self-worth is something you need to work at *daily*. The best way for an actor to find confidence in their talent is to do the *work*. Confidence in your talent and your potential to succeed is found in both accomplishments and disappointments. We learn confidence through our achievements as well as our failures.

Where Does Your C-Level Come From?

You'll see that your C-level comes from a mix of nurture/nature: what you're born with combined with your upbringing, with some other factors mixed into the pot.

If our DNA determines everything from hair color to disposition to personality traits to specific talents, then it probably also influences our initial level of self-worth. Therefore, some children are born a little more outgoing while others enter this world a bit more reserved.

<u>Self-Evaluation Scale: Confidence</u>

Once again, using your **Self-Evaluation Scale**, rate your C-level by determining how much confidence you were born with, how much you have now and where you need to grow. Remember, if you're having trouble looking back, don't be afraid to ask your parents or whoever raised you for help.

Rate your **Confidence** in *Your Instinctual Years* on a scale of "1-3," with "3" being the most brimming with confidence.

Your Instinctual Years (birth – five years old)

1 Rating: You had very little instinctual self-assurance. You were quiet, shy, and reserved, perhaps even a loner. You were hesitant to play with other children or to take part in activities. You had to be pushed to participate or encouraged to complete tasks.

2 Rating: You were outgoing, the first one to run over to the other kids on the playground. You were more curious and that made you more daring. But you were also content to keep to yourself at times. You learned how to walk and talk, maybe slowly, maybe quickly…but you were proud of yourself for each accomplishment. You were not afraid to take initiative in whatever you were doing.

3 Rating: You were a born leader. You excelled at activities because you were confident in your abilities. You took pride in your accomplishments. Even as a toddler, you were the dominant one in the group. You walked and talked early, showed signs of being decisive, bold, and always curious. You could be stubborn and precocious, but you believed in yourself and what you were doing.

As with talent, how much confidence you have as a small child can change (sometimes significantly) as you go through childhood and into your teenage years. Once again, use the scale to assess how much confidence you had in *Your Formative Years.*

Your Formative Years (six years old – late teens)

1 Rating: You were shy around other kids and were more content to be on your own, and you found comfort in that solitude. As a teenager, you were the loner or the outsider of the group. You perhaps lacked the belief in yourself to make friends. You might not have had a desire to participate in school activities because of your shyness.

2 Rating: As a child, you were outgoing enough to follow the pack, but not necessarily lead. As a teenager, you found a small group of friends and got involved in some activities, perhaps to fit in. You went to dances, played sports, performed in school plays, and even had a job. The more you got involved and participated, the more your self-worth grew. You didn't necessarily stand out, but you were confident enough with yourself to pursue your dreams and goals.

3 Rating: As a child, you felt self-assured. You made friends easily. You loved to work. You ran lemonade stands, had a paper route, organized neighborhood games and clubs. As a teenager, you were the star of the football team, head cheerleader, president of the student council, voted "Most Likely to Succeed." You not only starred in but also directed and produced school plays.

Those with a real high dose of confidence also may have found some limelight in the arts. You were child actors, dancers, singers, artists, musicians. You didn't really care how you were perceived by others because you were completely and totally confident in yourself and what you did.

So once again, what were your ratings? Did you move up or move down when growing up? Were you a 1 on the Instinctual Years scale that grew into a 2 on the Formative Years scale? Were you a 2 that grew into a 3? Or were you born a 3 on the Instinctual Years scale that slipped down to a 2 on the Formative Years scale?

The even bigger question is *why* you moved up or down that scale. There are many things throughout your life that will affect your C-level. Life constantly presents challenges as well as opportunities that will significantly impact how much confidence you have. Whereas taking risks and accomplishments will boost your confidence, medical misfortunes, negative events, and personal traumas can drain that confidence.

Like talent, how your confidence is initially shaped, and how you maintain your self-assurance throughout your life, is mainly influenced by your upbringing.

Did Your Upbringing Affect Your Confidence?

Even if you were born confident, with a high C-level, that can be suppressed by family circumstances and influences. The opposite is true as well; a shy child can come out of their cocoon with the right guidance, support and encouragement. How our parents or guardians raised us and what they instilled in us (or didn't instill in us) gives us a pretty good idea of where we stand now and how we need to grow.

Are you ACTOR A or ACTOR B?

ACTOR A: When growing up, were your parents or guardians nurturing and supportive? Did they instill in you a strong sense of self-worth? Did they teach you to believe in yourself? Did they encourage you to take risks and try new things? Did they reward you for accomplishing goals? Did they ask you what you learned from your mistakes and failures?

Or

ACTOR B: When growing up, did you have parents or guardians who, because of their own life circumstances, couldn't be there for you? Did they lack the time, the know-how, the parental skills, or the energy to support you? Or did they simply not know how to instill in you a feeling of self-worth?

If you picked ACTOR A, you probably have a high C-level. You are very fortunate. The people who raised you have given you a solid foundation. It's a blessing that needs to be recognized. Those of you entering this business with a higher level of confidence usually have less fear. You are often self-assured, daring and direct about your potential. You usually have the courage to risk embarrassment because you believe you will ultimately achieve success. And that's a good beginning.

If you picked ACTOR B, you probably have a lower C-level. You might feel hesitant, more reserved and insecure. You tend to have a lot of self-doubt about achieving your Want and you become fearful of taking risks. When you do take risks, you endlessly question your decisions. Growing up, you didn't get the support you needed and that's unfortunate.

The good news is, as adults, you can *change*. You can improve your feelings of self-worth. You can raise your self-esteem. Just knowing that you want to be an actor, declaring it and moving to an Industry City is the sign of a courageous person. And with courage comes confidence. And that's a *very* good beginning.

Acting With Confidence

You should now have at least an idea of how much confidence you possess. When it comes to confidence in your *talent*, however, there's a catch. Regardless of whether you're ACTOR A, ACTOR B, or somewhere in between, you will need to work on a specific type of confidence, what I call **Acting Confidence**.

Acting Confidence applies specifically to your creative instincts, training, artistic inspiration and the feelings you have about your art and your abilities. Confidence in this ability (or the lack thereof) also translates to your career as an actor.

You are embarking on a professional career, an artist's path where anything can and will happen, where you must expect the unexpected. No matter how confident you are as an actor, you *will* face new situations and experiences that will test both your acting abilities and your belief in those abilities...like getting a same day callback with all new sides and finding out later you didn't get the job. You will need to first establish and then maintain your C-level to get you through these acting career challenges.

Just like building your talent is a constant daily process, so is building and sustaining your Acting Confidence. In the rest of this chapter, as well as its Workbook Section and Bonus Track, I will give you specific exercises to help you gain and sustain your self-confidence and, more specifically, your Acting Confidence.

> *"It's insecurity that is always chasing you and standing in the way of your dreams."*
> *-Vin Diesel*

You Can Do It!

Whether your C-level is high or low, or somewhere in between, you will hit a roadblock on your career path that will challenge your self-worth, and you will need to know how to combat that. I will show you how.

When it comes to building your self-worth, it all starts with *you*. You are the one who will ultimately decide if you are worthy enough to have a career. You are the one who has the control over your self-esteem in both your life and your acting career. You are the one with the power to lift your confidence.

For those entering with a higher C-level, the work in this chapter will not only reinforce your Acting Confidence but also heighten your overall self–esteem. For those entering with a lower C-level, you will start building upon what you have from the ground up and learn how to preserve your confidence on your career path.

For those that struggle with very low self-esteem and low self-worth, I suggest to first seek help and guidance through therapy and counseling. A therapist is like your personal guide on the Journey of Looking Inward. Therapy can make you more enlightened, self-aware and evolved, which makes for a better actor and a better human being.

One big thing that will help your C-level is feeling *comfortable*.

FINDING YOUR COMFORT ZONE

Moving to Hollywood or any Industry City is an overwhelming adventure, to say the least. Many actors get through these initial stages of setting up their new life through sheer excitement and adrenaline. They have such hope, desire and optimism as they embark on this journey that their first three months is a whirlwind: a blur of emails, texts, calls, driving around, learning public transportation and shopping at Target, Ikea, and Costco. It's thrilling!

It can also be terrifying. Many actors uproot their lives and move without really knowing anyone. Many don't even have a place to live or, at best, they have a *temporary* place to live. For the most part, they have left behind their schools, their jobs, their family, their friends...all that is familiar to them. They might not have a support group or that wiser, more experienced person that they can trust. They are trying to take on a new city, a new job, a new career...a whole new life and they are often going into it blind, without the security and stability of their **Comfort Zone.**

Finding your comfort zone within the first three months in any Industry City is important to getting settled, staying positive, and preparing to embark on your new journey. It is also vital to maintaining your C-level. You need to feel comfortable, to find your new comfort zone as quickly as you can.

Here are eight essentials that will help you begin a new life as an actor in Hollywood or any Industry City.

8 Easy Ways to Find Your Comfort Zone

1. Get a place to live. More specifically, find a place you can call *home*. Get a place that is safe and affordable, some place you feel the most at ease. Your life in your Industry City is going to be hectic and draining at times. Whether you live by yourself or with a roommate, you need a place you can come back to in order to relax and recharge.

Your place to live will also double as home base of operations for your acting career, meaning you will need a desk, a computer and/or laptop, a tripod and a smartphone, as well as a private space where you can self-tape your auditions and do your acting work.

2. Get transportation. In some Industry Cities, like New York and Chicago, you will *not* need a car. But you will need to be familiar with public transportation: the subway system, trolley lines, or bus schedule. In cities like Los Angeles, Vancouver, and Atlanta, however, you will most likely need a car. Riding a bus won't get you where you need to be in the time you need to be there. These cities are spread out and you may need to go from one end of the city to the other, sometimes the same morning. And ride share costs, like Uber and Lyft, can get very expensive.

Also, take note that for many of these Industry Cities, you'll need a car to drive to the set because locations are often on the outskirts and call times are usually very early. The car can be basic: four wheels, an engine, and a warranty. You'll look back someday and remember it as your "struggling actor" car. It'll be a good reminder of your "starving artist" days.

3. Get a job. This is not a career job; it's a survival job. I'll tackle this issue more in the latter part of the book, but for now, just know that your survival job should offer you enough money to do just that...*survive*. Find yourself a job or jobs (yes, actors often have multiple jobs) that give you flexible hours so you can concentrate on your acting career.

Although I advise coming to your Industry City with some kind of savings, it won't last long. You need to get a survival job immediately, so you have enough money to pay rent, living expenses, and class tuition.

4. Get into acting class. Along with fulfilling the basic need to study your craft, acting class is a great way to meet other actors. Within any acting class, you will immediately find new friends, some who will be friends for life. You will also find other actors in class who you will work with, being each other's "readers" for your self-tape auditions. In class, you'll learn more about the business (and the city) from both newbies and actors who have been there awhile. Plus, you'll make industry connections; many actors find their agents through other actors.

Find an acting class that has sixteen to eighteen actors (smaller groups make it easier to meet folks), a class that periodically offers partner assignments (so you work outside of class together), and one that you feel like you can stay in a while and grow to help build both your comfort zone and your C-level.

5. Get a family of friends. As you tackle a whole new set of circumstances, challenges, and emotions, you need to start forming a second family, a *family of friends*. I'll grant you, finding friends in a big city isn't easy, especially finding good friends, but it's a task you need to take on. In order to find a good friend, you need to first *be* a good friend, which means someone who's honest, who listens, is curious, doesn't judge, and who wants to have fun.

Find friends with whom you can unwind, go to coffee, lunch, or go on a hike. Find friends you can laugh with, friends you can really talk to and trust. Find friends with whom you can share your life, your successes and your struggles. These friends will not only be your emotional support system, they will also be your partners as you explore this new, exciting life.

6. Get a CTAG. As discussed, find a group of actors who could make up a CTAG. Take note, this might not necessarily be the same group of actors from your acting class or your family of friends. This is a group of colleagues that you will work with on achieving career goals and that will help you deal with the challenges of the craft, the pressures of your career and the turbulent life as an actor in an Industry City. You can form these actor support groups with other people you find anywhere, including class, at your job, in your apartment complex or even Starbucks.

Find CTAG members who will be completely honest and sympathetic to you and your cause. When your C-level in your acting career is at its lowest, turn to these peers who know and understand what you're going through. Remember, you are in a town filled with actors who share your same fears, dreams, concerns, and goals. That is one of the most thrilling aspects of living in an Industry City. You can befriend the competition and help each other survive.

7. Get streaming TV services. A great way to learn good acting is by watching good acting. Watch the master actors do their work. Get a streaming TV service. Watching TV is part of your job as an actor. You need to research what shows are out there, what shows you might be auditioning for, roles you might be right for, and what types you could play.

Whether you watch your streaming service on your TV, computer, tablet, or smartphone, it's also great for your comfort zone. You will need an escape from time to time, a chance to relax and take your mind off your problems. There is no better way to lose yourself than curling up on the couch, treating yourself to your favorite snack and tuning in to your favorite sitcom, classic movie or the hottest new streaming show.

8. Get a mentor. Another way to maintain your C-level is to find a mentor. A mentor is someone who believes in you as much as you believe in yourself...sometimes more. This could be a manager, agent, casting director, acting coach or even a more experienced actor. Seek out someone whose life experiences have made them wise and compassionate, someone who might be active in their own careers but who can still give you quality time.

A mentor needs to be someone you can trust. It should be someone who's not competitive with you but who understands your journey because they have either taken that journey or a similar one in their own life. They have seen what works and what doesn't. A mentor wants to help you fulfill your destiny.

Finding a mentor will take some time, especially in establishing a personal relationship. When you do find that mentor, be grateful and appreciative for that relationship, as well as for their insight and support.

Establishing your comfort zone is a great way to lay the foundation for building and sustaining your confidence. So is the power of observation, another important tool for an actor.

OBSERVE CONFIDENCE IN OTHERS

Great artists are great observers of life. As actors, we observe people all the time. In order to create authentic, multi-dimensional characters, we model ourselves after others and integrate their personalities into our work. We adopt their speech patterns, intonations and dialects. We observe their behaviors, mannerisms, their posture, their gait and how they carry themselves. We learn about their hopes and desires, their achievements and failures as well as their insecurities. And we also learn what they are most confident about.

Who have you observed in your life that is confident? Look to your family, your friends, your co-workers. Who walks and talks with self-assurance? Who is direct, decisive, and even fearless? Is it your father, your mother, your older sibling, your boss, your best friend, your acting coach?

Make sure you are observing someone who is actually *confident* as opposed to *arrogant*. There's a big difference between confidence and arrogance. People who showcase their self-importance and contempt for others are usually masking insecurities and overcompensating for them by *acting* superior. They are full of false pride, full of bravado, full of themselves. Those with a real sense of confidence know what they want and work hard to get it. That's the kind of person you want to observe.

Think of a person in your life who is the most confident. Believe it or not, you have consciously or unconsciously studied this person. So, think about what makes them confident? What qualities about them do you admire? Most likely, these are folks who are successful in whatever they do, so how did they achieve their success? Often these are people that have a specific talent, ability, or skill that makes them successful. You're noticing their talent as well as their confidence in their talent.

There are some things to look for that confident people possess. These are not only personality traits that identify a confident person, but they are also personal proactive challenges that you can work on to help build up your own C-level. Plus, they'll help you in your acting work. The next time you play a character who's confident, use these personality traits to build their backstory.

What Is a Confident Person?

A confident person...
- Is open to criticism.
- Sets goals they can attain.
- Will work to accomplish those goals.
- Expects good things to happen.
- Is open to new challenges.
- Is willing to take risks.
- Gets involved.
- Is comfortable in their own skin.
- Speaks authoritatively.
- Experiences their fear and overcomes it.

Understanding and embracing these personality traits will help you become a more confident person. Each day, work on implementing these characteristics. Be more authoritative, set goals, challenge yourself and expect that only good things will happen.

Also, don't be afraid to be a little shameless. In this industry (and life), gaining a bit of "benign" shamelessness will help you care *less* about what others think about you. The less you care about what others think, the more apt you will be to express your true, authentic self.

But most important, being a confident person involves believing in yourself. And to do that, we all need a little affirmation.

> *"It all has to do with how you feel about yourself-it's about projecting the attitude, I'm happy with who I am. "*
> -Jennifer Lopez

THE POWER OF AFFIRMATIONS

From the very start of my career as an agent in New York, I found that many of my clients lacked the confidence they needed to book the job. Even though they were trained actors, something inside them (some negative voice or event) made them second-guess themselves, which interfered with their acting work. As much as I told them to believe in themselves, the seeds of self-doubt kept creeping into their conscious minds. I taught them the **Power of Affirmations.**

Affirmations are positive thoughts you speak out loud. They are designed to alter the way you think and feel about yourself. Affirmations invigorate you, encourage you, and pump you up when you feel uninspired, deflated, or defeated. There's a lot of power in thoughts, positive ones and negative ones. Before I get to the positive ones, let me address those destructive negative thoughts that attack your C-level and show you how to get rid of them.

Negative thoughts begin in your subconscious. They were planted there by past negative experiences or events. You could say your negative thoughts are a byproduct of your negative experiences. These negative thoughts are formed into damaging statements that you say to yourself or speak out loud, sometimes in front of others.

Do any of these negative thoughts or statements sound familiar?

> *"I'm not good enough."*
> *"I'll never be happy."*
> *"I look ugly."*
> *"I'll never be a good actor."*
> *"I'll never succeed."*

The problem with these statements is, when said often enough, your unconscious mind believes them to be true. They *become* true only because you consciously believe them to *be* true. That's how the vicious cycle of self-doubt begins and never ends. Not only that, but you may also begin to find a certain comfort in these negative phrases you express to yourself. It is these negative thoughts that prevent you from achieving your career goals.

3 Ways to Rid Yourself of Negative Thoughts

1. Stop planting them. You need to consciously stop putting those negative thoughts in your mind. When a negative thought enters your mind, acknowledge it, and then take a deep breath and exhale. As you exhale, visualize blowing that negative thought out and watching as the words evaporate before you.

2. Stop giving them a voice. You need to stop saying your negative thoughts out loud to yourself or around others. Be diligent in catching yourself when expressing these negative thoughts, even if you deliver them with self-deprecating humor. Perhaps someone close to you can remind you when you say them out loud.

3. Start reprogramming them. You must reprogram those negative thoughts that have already taken up residence in your subconscious. The only way to reprogram them is to first rephrase them in your conscious mind. For example, if you say "I'll never succeed," change it to "I am succeeding." To show you how to turn your negative thoughts into positive ones, I have included several Affirmation Exercises in the Workbook Section at the end of this chapter.

While affirmations and personal growth are a great way to nurture your overall confidence, there is nothing that will help you sustain your *Acting Confidence* like working your craft.

Repetition. Repetition. Repetition.

Many actors ask me, "How can I feel more confident as an actor?" The answer is simple: Practice your craft.

Before you can feel more confident as an actor, you first need to feel more confident about your acting skills. That's another reason why acting class is so important. You need to be *constantly* practicing your acting techniques: accessing emotions, imagination work, characterizations, script analysis, etc. Repetition breeds confidence.

In class, your C-level will grow as you work on scenes and auditions. At the end of every acting class, you should feel enlightened and excited. You should leave class with a "takeaway," the one thing that impacted you the most in what you learned about acting and/or about yourself. Again, be sure to write it in your Actor's Journal. You should walk out of each acting class with a little more confidence because you practiced working on your craft.

Just as acting class will develop your talent, it will also help your confidence blossom. Acting class is really the point where talent and confidence begin to merge. Acting class pushes your creative boundaries in a safe environment. Acting class should also be a place where you feel comfortable enough to fall flat on your face and fail—only to pick yourself up and try again.

That's part of an actor's growth. The more an actor grows through their failures, finds success and arcs in class, the better they feel about their individual talent. Talent and confidence always work together, whether you're acting, singing...or playing professional sports.

Acting is Like a Game of Tennis

In my seminars, lectures, and acting classes, I talk about how the career of a professional actor often mirrors the career of a professional tennis player. The training and the entertainment aspect of both professions are very similar.

Watching two good actors perform an intense, high stakes scene is like watching a thrilling, edge-of-your-seat tennis match. The back-and-forth interplay is what makes for fascinating entertainment.

A tennis player enters a match looking to win with a specific strategy. But they also have a willingness to change that strategy based on what's happening in the match. The same is true for an actor; they enter the scene with a strong want and clever intentions to get that want. But they must be willing to change those intentions based on what's happening in the scene.

Like an actor, a tennis player is born with an innate ability, a talent. As the tennis player grows up and practices their talent, there is hopefully enough faith, belief and support from parents, coaches, loved ones, etc. The young player also learns by watching and observing the tennis greats, and builds their confidence by acknowledging their own talent, using mantras and affirmations as reminders.

The main way tennis players get better, though, is by practicing and believing in themselves. They work with a coach, take lessons and perfect their techniques: their stance, serve, hitting style, hand-eye coordination, awareness of the court and the anticipation of their opponents' shots. The more they practice their techniques, the more confident tennis player they become.

Eventually, they feel certain about what they have learned and they're ready to play the game. When they first start playing, they don't always win, but they learn from their mistakes and grow from their losses. They pick themselves up to play another game, to keep at it, to win!

When they begin to win, their C-level elevates, and they want to play more. They get a taste of success, which feeds their confidence. They start challenging better players. Their confidence drives them, pushes them to be the best they can be. As they get better, they get more confident: That's the cycle of success.

This should be no different for actors. You will train. You will practice your craft and when you are ready and feeling confident, you will play. You will be able to walk into any audition, live or virtual, unafraid because you are prepared. That's the goal.

> *"You have to believe in yourself when no one else does."*
> -Serena Williams

I *Am* a Confident Actor!

It's important to remember that all the talent in the world won't get you anywhere unless you have the confidence in yourself and in your abilities. Talent and confidence unite to mold you into a successful actor. They rely on and reinforce each other.

Some of you (in fact, all of you at some point) will struggle to keep your confidence growing. When it comes to maintaining your C-level, you must always think of the reward: a career as a successful actor. If that's your ultimate Want, then it's worth the struggle.

You have the talent. You have the confidence. Now you have to combine those two to face the most demanding of the Three Steps to Success: **Perseverance.**

CONFIDENCE: WORKBOOK SECTION

AFFIRMATIONS

I am good enough to be great

Scott's Favorite Five Affirmations:

1: *I am...*

The "I am..." affirmation is meant to uncover your negative thoughts and turn them into positive thoughts. Choose a negative statement you find yourself saying and change it to a positive statement. Start your positive statement with the words, "I am." Those two words are very powerful and serve as a command meant to lead you to a positive outcome. Then write down your positive statement either in the space provided or in your Actor's Journal.

For example, using the negative statements I mentioned earlier:

If you say, "I'm not good enough," change it to "I am good enough."

If you say, "I'll never be happy," change it to "I am happy."

If you say, "I look ugly," change it to "I am beautiful."

If you say, "I'll never be a good actor" change it to "I am a good actor."

If you say, _____ (Negative Thought)

Change it to…

I am _____ (Positive Thought)

Positive affirmations need to start with a positive declaration. Look at what you wrote and say it out loud. The more you say it, the more you'll train both your conscious and unconscious mind to believe it.

You'll need to look inward and make sure those words, and the feelings behind them, come from somewhere deep inside you. Concentrate on what you're saying and feel the negative thought leave your mind and body as you let the positive one in. Each time you say it, believe that you are truly letting go of your negative thought and the feelings that are attached to it. Believe in the positive words you are now saying.

2: *I am good enough to be great.*

Of course, remnants of your negative thoughts will still linger. Let me show you how to counter those nagging negative thoughts with an even more positive thought.

This next affirmation will be all-encompassing to your life as well as your career. Once again, write down the following in the space provided or in your Actor's Journal: I am good enough.

_____

Now clear your mind, close your eyes, take a breath, and say it out loud five times:

I am good enough.

As you repeat this affirmation to yourself over and over, some flashes of a past negative event may play out in your mind like a home movie. You might become emotional as this negative experience runs through your mind. You might see someone telling you that you're not good enough, not smart enough, not good looking enough or that you're too fat, too skinny, too small, too tall, too odd. Or the event could have been much more specific. For example, maybe you forgot your lines in a play in front of friends, family, and teachers, which left you feeling embarrassed and humiliated. It will probably be something that left a deep scar.

Acknowledge this negative event, and the thought and emotions that go with it. Exhale and let the negative thought start to evaporate. Counter this negative thought with a more passionate, positive thought. Open your eyes and say:

I am good enough.

Say it as many times as you need to wash that negative thought away. Feel it and experience it slipping from your mind. You should feel relief as you allow yourself to be rid of the negative thoughts that surround that negative event. Hear the words come out of your mouth. Listen to that single voice, that single affirmation. Say it again. Say it louder and stronger:

I am good enough!

Let's take it one step further. Now, you're going to say it directly to yourself. Walk over to a mirror, look yourself in the eyes, take a deep breath, and say:

I am good enough.

Keep saying it until the person staring back at you believes it. Once you feel it in your body and you truly believe that you are good enough, take another deep breath and say:

I am good enough to be great!

You should feel stronger, exhilarated, and more empowered. You have triggered the positive energy that you possess. You should feel a belief building in yourself. You have embraced your potential and you are ready to move forward and be great.

3: *I believe in myself.*

This next affirmation will help you believe that you *are* good enough to be great. Once again, write this down below in the space provided or in your Actor's Journal: I believe in myself.

Say it quietly to yourself.

I believe in myself.

Then take a breath and say it out loud:

I believe in myself!

Feel it, own it, and live by it. This should become your mantra, part of your morning ritual. Before you brush your teeth, drink your coffee, or pick up your cell phone, you need to look in the mirror and say "I believe in myself" three times.

You will immediately see a difference in yourself. You will gain a stronger desire to achieve your Want and you will be more positive about your prospects. Incorporate your mantra into your daily life. Say it to yourself three times before you go to class. Say it before you go into a meeting with an agent. Say it after a rough day before you go to sleep.

I believe in myself.

This affirmation is especially effective before all types of auditions. It will counteract any prior self-doubt and negative thoughts and statements about failing such as "This self-tape is too hard to do" or "I'm going to screw up this audition." It's equally as valuable after auditions to block any negative thoughts from re-entering your subconscious like "I just screwed up that audition."

4: **Visualization (***I believe in myself.***)**

To complement the previous affirmation, try the following visualization exercise while sitting at home or in your car before any Zoom or live audition:

Once again, relax, take a deep breath, and imagine the inside of the casting room. Imagine yourself standing in the middle of the room performing your scene with focus, energy, passion, and the confidence that comes with being fully prepared. Picture a casting director, writer, producer, and director all sitting across from you, smiling, interested, taking notes and circling your name on their call sheet. As you finish your audition, visualize them smiling, thanking you for your work, and telling you with a wink that they'll be in touch. See yourself leaving the audition with your shoulders back and your head held high, proud and satisfied with your audition, confident that you did your best.

Visualizing a positive outcome will fuel you with confidence.

5: *I am a confident actor.*

In this final affirmation, I am going to build upon your C-level. I'm going to help you find something you're confident about and translate that into your acting. I'm going to help you accept that you can be a confident actor.

First, let's find out where else in your life you feel the most confident. Steer it away from acting. Think of something you know you are good at, something that you believe you can do and do well. We all feel confident about something. Do you feel most confident about your relationships, at your survival job, playing a sport, cooking, making love?

Where are you most confident? Write it down below or in your Actor's Journal:

I am very confident when I _____

Let's say you wrote down, "I am very confident when I am driving." That doesn't mean you have to be an expert or a professional race car driver. It just means that driving is something you feel sure of doing.

In other words, when you drive, you are not fearful of the road or other motorists. You feel relaxed, yet in control. When driving, you are cautious even when you're talking to your passenger, singing along to SiriusXM, or listening to a podcast. You feel free, at ease, your thoughts flowing. You feel self-assured and the confidence surges through your body.

Well, that's how you should ultimately feel about your acting, whether it's in class, in auditions or on set. You should feel comfortable with the material. You should feel at ease in the room. You should feel strong about your intentions. You should feel confident. You should feel like you are a good actor.

I want you to think about that activity, the one that makes you feel confident. Picture yourself doing it in your mind and feel the confidence rise in you. Attach that powerful feeling to the following words. Write them down and say them out loud three times:

I am a confident person!

Carry that feeling and that positive thought into the classroom, meeting or your next self-tape. Experience the difference it makes. Translate those feelings of confidence into your acting. Say it out loud:

I am a confident actor!

As you work on your confidence in and out of acting class, this mantra will ultimately become your personal truth.

Now you have several affirmations to work with in gaining confidence and sustaining it daily. Take these affirmations and write them on a Post-it Note. Put the Post-it on your computer, your bathroom mirror, your dashboard, your phone at night (it'll be the first thing you see when you wake up), or put it in your wallet to always carry with you as a reminder.

BONUS TRACK: CONFIDENCE

KNOWING YOUR TYPE

Who Am I?

There's nothing more powerful than an actor who knows who they are and embraces it. When I meet an actor with a great sense of self, they immediately capture my attention. They show me something that intrigues me, makes me want to get to know them, to see more. There is a power in self-awareness.

Your self-awareness will permeate everything you do, and that's important in your acting as well as your career.

Once you know who you are, then you can begin the process of discovering and identifying what kind of characters you play best. Knowing your type, embracing it, and playing it to the fullest will give you the confidence you need in your auditions and meetings. More importantly, it will get you the job. It will help you continue to market yourself in this competitive industry. Knowing your type (or types) is another tool in an actor's toolbox. The more tools to draw from, the more confident you will become.

Know Who You Are

We all know the basic types of characters in films and television: the All-American Guy, Gal Next Door, Corporate Lawyer, Computer Nerd, the Everyman, etc. And now, when it comes to playing these archetypes, casting offices are more inclusive, opening their doors to all ethnicities, genders, sexualities, religion, and even ages. As such, whether you're doing comedy or drama, film or television, you must know *your* basic type: which type you most naturally fit into, what you are presenting to the industry.

It starts with your appearance, your "look." Determining your look and the type that is attached to that look will help you get auditions. This is especially true in commercials and print work. If you look like a fresh-faced All-American Guy or Gal Next Door, you'll get called in for *those* auditions.

Film and television roles, however, are more multi-dimensional. It's not only your look, but also the complex personality traits that go along with your look that create authentic characters. Even though your appearance is significant in getting a part, what's equally important is knowing your essence, what personality traits you possess that you can tap into to bring to a specific character.

For example, a casting director might bring you in because you look like the All-American Guy, but the character you're auditioning for is angry and defiant. So, do you have the personality traits you need to relate to that character's frustration and rebellion? Or if the role asks you to be the kind, sweet Gal Next Door who gets pregnant, can you understand her innocence, her naivete, her fear? Could you play an ambitious and aggressive Lawyer because you have the essence of someone who gets things done? Could you play a Computer Nerd because you identify with their attention to detail and social awkwardness? Could you play the Everyman who is secretly a serial killer because you can tap into the dark side of your essence and/or imagination?

These TV and film types can be played many different ways. It's your look merged with your personality that will make them different. Your best chance to get the job is to play characters not only close to your look, but also close to your essence, your life experience, your emotional depth, and your imagination.

Know Who You Aren't

For many actors coming to Los Angeles or any other Industry City, especially those of you who have graduated from formal acting programs, I'm sure you have played many different characters in your acting classes and staged productions. Acting class is where you take creative risks, push your boundaries, play a broad range of characters, and make wild choices. While that will make you a well-rounded actor, it may also give you the impression that you could book any role, no matter how against your type.

For example, in a traditional scene study class, a twenty-year-old actor can play an eighty-year-old character in a scene. They can even perform that older character on stage in a full-length play. But they would never be cast to play that role on television or film. The casting director will get a *real* eighty-year-old actor…as they should!

When you're doing stage work, you can put on makeup, a wig, alter your appearance. You can change your voice, your costume, your gait to become the "character." On a stage, where the audience is slightly removed, you can get away with that, but not with the intimate close-up of a television or film screen.

Unless you are a crafted, experienced, professional actor like Daniel Day-Lewis, Cate Blanchett, Tilda Swinton, Benedict Cumberbatch, or Jared Leto, chances are, especially at first, you are going to play someone who pretty much resembles *you*. Playing someone you are familiar with inside and out will automatically instill confidence where you need it most: in the casting room.

Casting Directors Know You

Casting directors are people watchers. They study people, and they are very insightful. A good casting director has the gift to see beyond an actor's look and into that actor's *essence*.

When a casting director is looking to cast a role, they put out breakdowns to agents, managers, and sometimes acting sites looking for actors. They will ask an actor to self-tape an audition or call them in directly based on their look, experience and an agent or manager's recommendation. From the moment a casting director sees the actor's self-tape audition, or the actor walks into the casting room, the casting director begins to evaluate whether they're right for the role. They make their initial judgment based on the actor's look and the way they carry and present themselves.

What the actor does when they audition will either change the casting director's mind or validate their initial assessment. When the actor reads, the casting director will decide if they are right for the role. Casting directors are looking for a certain "connection" that the actor has to the material, the character they're reading for. That connection comes from the actor's understanding of the nature of the character and what they instinctually and organically bring to that character.

Actors feel that focusing on only a certain type will limit their audition opportunities. The truth is, defining your type and knowing your niche will make you stand out more and heighten your C-level. *That* will set you apart from other actors. You'll get more auditions that you're right for, and ultimately…you'll work more.

So, Who Are You?

That's the question you will need to ask yourself. Please understand that the concept of discovering your type is complex. It's a process and it takes time. But I have a way to help you.

First you need to know who you are as a person and that's not always easy to see. It's difficult to stand back and objectively observe yourself. But if you've been doing your Looking Inward work from the beginning of the book, this may be easier as you've already begun compiling a list of your personality traits. Otherwise, I need you to consciously take note of certain personality traits you possess, traits that make up the essence of *you*.

Let's start there. Write down in your Actor's Journal five adjectives that you think best describe you. Be as honest with yourself as possible. For example, you could write down:

Eccentric,
Exciting,
Unpredictable,
Funny,
Moody

The catch is that who you think you are and what you put out to the world can be two different things. In the following exercise, you are going to see if others agree with your specific character traits or if they perceive you differently.

THE TYPING GAME

As a casting director back in the '90s, I developed a game as a way for actors to have a better understanding of who they are, how others in the industry perceive them, and how to market themselves. I've been playing this game for years in my acting class with amazing results. I call it **The Typing Game**. The game effectively helps actors *begin* the process of identifying and embracing the type(s) they can play. To play The Typing Game, it's once again time to meet with your CTAG.

Find a relaxed, safe environment. Let's say there are seven members attending. All CTAG members will play the game. You will need a timer and enough pens and copies of the *Typing Game Results Sheet* (found at the end of this game description) for everyone. Only one member plays at a time. Players will be referred to as "Actor" and the rest of the players will be referred to as the "Group." Each Actor will sit away from the Group and be the only one speaking.

Let the game begin! First up, Actor One leaves the room for a minute. At this time, members of the Group will get their individual Typing Game Results Sheet and write down the first name of the Actor. When the Group is ready, Actor One will be called back into the room so they can see him or her with a fresh eye as the Actor walks in. The Actor then sits silently in a chair in front of the Group.

The timer is then set for five minutes.

Without conversing, using their Typing Game Results Sheet, the Group will study the Actor and immediately circle Actor One's "Age Range." Actor One continues to sit in silence for another ten seconds, as the Group now circles the *first* adjective from the *Personality Traits List* that they think best reflects the Actor. While I encourage you to use the strong adjectives I provided, you should also feel free to come up with your own.

Actor One then picks a random question from the *Typing Game Questions for Actors* to answer about themselves. They begin to talk to the Group, answering the question. They may never get through all the questions (in fact, they may only answer one). That's fine. Actor One should simply use these questions as a guideline to share something about themselves with the Group.

Within the five-minute period, the Group will silently circle *four* other adjectives they observe about the Actor from the Personality Traits List, or write in their own. When the timer goes off, Actor One stops talking and the Group stops writing. Actor One will collect their Typing Game Results Sheet, paperclip them, and put them aside. NOTE: Actor One should not look at their Typing Game Results Sheet until after the whole game is over.

Actor One takes a seat and becomes part of the Group as Actor Two now leaves the room. A new set of Typing Game Results Sheets are handed out and everyone writes down the name of Actor Two at the top of page. Everyone clears their mind for a minute, preparing for the next Actor to enter. They then follow the same steps.

After every player has participated and all Typing Game Results Sheets are collected, the game is over. Take a moment to decompress. Don't discuss the specifics of what was written but feel free to talk about what the exercise felt like. As a reminder, you are not to look at these sheets while you are still together in a group.

When you are alone, take all your Typing Game Results Sheets and spread them out on a table. In your Actor's Journal, write down all the adjectives that you got from the Group. Begin to tally the age ranges and the characteristics. Write down each specific adjective and then count and mark how many times the other players used that adjective. You will then take those adjectives and write yourself a character breakdown incorporating as many of those character traits as possible.

Here are examples from three of my students—Jim, Max and Katie—followed by my assessment of each:

Jim

Age:
20-25 (1), 25-30 (5)

Adjectives:
Optimistic (6), Charming (5), Funny (5), Good-natured (4)
Hopeful (4), Jolly (4), Attractive (1), Talkative (1)

Breakdown: Jim is an attractive, good-natured guy in his mid-twenties, who is sometimes jolly. He is hopeful and very charming to talk to and he has a funny, optimistic approach to life.

Assessment: Having all very similar characteristics appear on your Personality Traits List, like Jim (optimistic, charming, funny) is certainly helpful because it's clear what you're putting out there. Jim could get work in commercials. What Jim lacks is depth in his character. I told him he needs to find and work material in class that will help him uncover and unleash the other side of his personality. He needs to expose his flaws and vulnerabilities (insecure, sad, frustrated) to get work in TV and film.

MAX

Age:
25-30 (1), 30-35 (2), 35-40 (3)

Adjectives:
Shy (3), Outgoing (3), Aloof, (2), Desperate (2), Frustrated (2) Insecure (2), Awkward (2), Self-assured (2), Smart (2), Aggressive (1), Anxious (1), Caring (1), Enthusiastic (1), Judgmental (1), Lovable (1) Perfectionist (1), Positive (1), Responsible (1), Tough (1)

Breakdown: Unable to do the exercise.

Assessment: Max was unable to write a character breakdown. As you can see in his adjective list, Max had a lot of varying characteristics (shy, outgoing, insecure, self-assured) as well as many single adjectives, "1's."

Having a lot of "1's" on your Personality Traits List signifies that people don't know how to perceive you.

That's why Max couldn't do the assignment or build a character breakdown based on the adjectives given to him. Immediately upon seeing his Typing Game Results Sheet, Max knew that it was difficult to put these varied characteristics into a character type. Max wasn't surprised. He told me, "My friends *always* have trouble figuring me out." Well, if Max's friends are going to have trouble figuring him out, an agent, manager, or casting director most certainly will. Having such a scattered range says to the industry, "I don't know who I am, and I don't know what type I am."

I told Max that he needs to understand that he's in the process of discovering himself. He needs to work on figuring out who he is as a person as well as an actor. The best advice for Max is to work on different types of scripts in various genres until he finds characters that naturally fit and best showcase the strongest sides of his personality, and then build from there.

KATIE

Age:
17-22 (3), 20-25 (3)

Adjectives:
Attractive (4), Bright (4), Charming (3), Grounded (3), Reserved (3), Over-achiever (3), Vulnerable (3), Daddy's Girl (2), Thoughtful (2) Unsure (2), Troubled (1)

Breakdown: Katie is an attractive, bright overachiever who strives for excellence in all she does. Her upbringing keeps her grounded and a tad reserved. She is extremely thoughtful of others and a bit of a daddy's girl. At times she can be removed, vulnerable, and unsure, but would never let you see it. Beyond her charming demeanor and well-put-together exterior is a world of sadness from her troubled childhood.

Assessment: Great characterizations are layered. Finding the characteristics within those layers that you naturally identify with is how you really begin to find your type. The best kind of response in The Typing Game is to have very specific characteristics along with opposing characteristics on your Typing Game Results Sheet like Katie. Her personality list shows that she is "grounded" but "vulnerable," "charming" but "troubled."

Some might be surprised to see some of these "negative" adjectives. However, having what one might consider negative personality traits is human; it's universal. It shows you are flawed, which is important. Those negatives are positives to the inner life of a character…if you can embrace them. Katie's not afraid to show depth in her personality and her work, which will serve her well in the casting room. She has a better opportunity to book. I told Katie to keep exploring and infusing her depth into her work.

After playing The Typing Game, you might not like your results, the traits that were written down about you. You may disagree, not understand, or feel that your peers perceived you incorrectly. First, remember, it's just a game and second, I designed this game to help you understand what TV or film "type" characters others saw you as (using a list of adjectives). That's all. Most actors who play The Typing Game usually agree with the traits given to them by their peers. But that's only part of it; you also need to make sure those personality traits are pairing well with your look...or vice versa.

You Need to Give Up a Little of Yourself

This is very difficult for many actors to accept, especially those new to the business. It's important to understand that your "look" is a huge factor in the roles for which you'll audition. Sometimes you need to give up a certain look to play a character type that best fits your personality.

As an example, a student of mine (I'll call her Sharon) went through a mini-metamorphosis after playing The Typing Game. Sharon didn't know her type. She complained that the industry didn't know who she was either. When meeting with prospective agents, they thought she could act, but they had vague, conflicting opinions of what characters she could play. The good news is that after playing The Typing Game, she found her *true* character by taking a hard, objective look at herself...and then being willing to make a change.

On social media, Sharon presented herself as a "glamour girl," going for that chic, club look...a Kylie Jenner type. The problem was Sharon *wasn't* a Kylie Jenner type! She was attractive, but more like the "best friend" type. She was intelligent, clever, and she had quite a bit of depth.

After Sharon did The Typing Game, she saw some similar personality traits (smart, responsible, reasonable, grounded, straightforward, nurturing). That was a stronger reflection of who she was and what she most resembled. Interestingly, of the adjectives she received in the game, only a few described her as the glamour girl she thought she was (well-dressed, stylish).

As you can imagine, it was a big awakening for Sharon. Once she was able to process this new information, she could acknowledge and embrace her true characteristics. Then, as Sharon said, after "a good cleansing cry," she decided to take a chance and change her look. Gone were the long nails and the sexy clothes. She simplified her look and emerged as an intelligent, classy, young woman with style and sex appeal. She was ready to tackle the young professional roles and she became a working actress.

The message here is to accept who you are as a person and as an actor. Search inside yourself, be open, and play The Typing Game to find out your type (who you really are), and then embrace it.

TYPING GAME RESULTS SHEET

NAME OF ACTOR: _____ —

AGE RANGE: 15-18, 18-22, 20-25, 25-30, 28-32, 30-35, 35-40, 40-45, 45-50, 50-55, 55-60, 60 and up.

PERSONALITY TRAITS LIST:

Grounded, Responsible, Charming, Sexy, Desperate, Lovable, Sweet, Attractive, Educated, Fearful, Analytical, Awkward, Childlike, Funny, Good-Natured, Moody, Enthusiastic, Innocent, Happy, Frustrated, Smart, Condescending, Caring, Tough, Talkative, Smooth, Perky, Aggressive, Judgmental, Optimistic, Insecure, Uptight, Jolly, Provocative, Anxious, Shameless, Perfectionist, Articulate, Positive, Sarcastic, Angry, Sad, Troubled, Distant, Aloof, Cynical, Shameless, Exciting, Opinionated, Shy, Compassionate.

5 TYPING GAME QUESTIONS FOR ACTORS:

1. Where did you grow up and what was it like? (Describe your city, your town, your neighborhood, etc.
2. What was your upbringing like? (Describe the relationship you had with your mother, your father, and your siblings)
3. Who in your family were you closest to growing up and why?
4. Who are you closest to now in your family and why?
5. Who are you most like now?

PERSEVERANCE

Being a Lifer

The third and final of the Three Steps to Success is **Perseverance**.

As you're working your talent and building your confidence, you must now add perseverance to this power pack to build a *long-lasting* career.

Perseverance will be the most difficult step to incorporate into your career as it requires an unshakable devotion to doing whatever it takes to accomplish your goals. Perseverance will test you more physically, emotionally, mentally, and spiritually than talent and confidence combined. It will test your endurance, your desire, and your *passion*.

Once you move to Hollywood or any Industry City, don't expect anyone to come knocking on your door and offer you a role. Don't expect anyone to call you out of the blue to offer you representation. Don't expect anyone to discover you at a gym or Starbucks and offer you a three-picture deal. It just doesn't happen that way. Perseverance is how you get work.

Just like talent and confidence, we are all born with different levels of perseverance. It is your instinctual perseverance *combined* with your upbringing that has shaped your ability to endure.

Throughout this chapter, as well as the Workbook Section and Bonus Track, I will help you define your own perseverance and show you how important it is to your career. I'll give you specific exercises, tools and tasks for what you need to do to persevere. If you have the want, the talent, and the confidence and if you're willing to commit to the perseverance, you will succeed in fulfilling your dream.

What is Perseverance?

Perseverance is your tenacity, your resolve. It is your *drive*. You will be challenged many times in your acting career, from the moment you step into your first acting class to the day you receive your Lifetime Achievement Award. Perseverance means staying the course, being strong, steadfast, and willing to make sacrifices to get your Want: to be a working actor.

Perseverance is about doing the work necessary not only to get noticed, but also to build a successful and lasting career. For the newer actor, perseverance is about doing the "grunt work," all the work needed to get your career started and off the ground.

For the more experienced actor, perseverance is often more about staying in the game, having longevity. Your perseverance is what keeps you hanging in there, keeps you going, keeps you working at your craft and career in slow times and even slower times.

What exactly does it mean to have perseverance? It means that you are and always will be involved, active and *busy*, especially when it comes to your career. Perseverance is what builds character.

Perseverance Traits

Whatever profession one's in—doctor, lawyer, acting coach, etc.—it takes great focus and effort to have a prosperous career. There are certain characteristics and attributes, or what I call *Perseverance Traits*, that define someone who successfully perseveres in their career. These traits manifest themselves in four aspects: Physical, Mental, Emotional, and Spiritual.

Physically, perseverance means:

- Waking up early to get a jump on your day.
- Working a minimum 40-hour work week.
- Setting daily, weekly, monthly, and yearly goals and accomplishing them.
- Making time to attend industry events, seminars, training workshops, etc.
- Getting daily exercise.
- Putting yourself out there…always.

Mentally, perseverance means:

- Being curious about your work and your world.
- Having a willingness to learn and perfect.
- Saying "Yes" when everyone else is saying "No."
- Being persistent in achieving goals.
- Reading the room and adjusting.
- Staying focused...always.

Emotionally, perseverance means:

- Opening your heart and being available in all your pursuits.
- Being aware of yourself and others around you.
- Experiencing your emotions and then moving on.
- Staying calm and not letting your emotions get the best of you.
- Acknowledging your disappointments and finding solutions.
- Staying patient...always.

Spiritually, perseverance means:

- Being centered, following your breath.
- Being present -in the moment.
- Being fearless, operating without limits.
- Being humble.
- Being of service.
- Being grateful...always.

You can apply all these Perseverance Traits to any actor pursuing their acting career. Perseverance, like confidence, is something that can be learned and, as Yoda would say, "Learn you must." Like talent, perseverance is something you can get better at with practice (and yes, practice you must).

Where Does Your Perseverance Come From?

Every one of us has the capacity to persevere. As with talent and confidence, we're all born with a certain amount of perseverance in our genetic makeup. There are some people who are born more driven, more predisposed to a higher level of ambition. The good news is even the least driven person has the ability and the instinct to persevere. Every one of us has the instinct to survive.

Our survival instincts include the need to eat, to drink, to breathe…to have sex! We all have the instincts that help us persevere to live. On top of these most basic instincts, we also have hopes, desires, and dreams.

So, just like we did with your talent and confidence, let's take a look at where your perseverance comes from and how it may or may not have changed.

Self-Evaluation Scale: Perseverance

Using your **Self-Evaluation Scale**, rate how much perseverance you were born with and then grew up with. Remember, this is to assess your natural ability to persevere and to see where you might need to work on your perseverance skills. Again, if you have trouble recalling, ask your parents or whoever raised you.

Rate your **Perseverance** on a scale of "1-3," with "3" being the most brimming with perseverance.

Your Instinctual Years (birth – five years old)

1 Rating: As a child, you didn't have the impetus or that early curiosity to walk and talk and so it took a little longer. You were content to play with whatever was given to you and to do what you were told, to stay in your comfort zone. You rarely asked "Why?"

2 Rating: You walked and talked at an early age. You were a little more curious. Your parents were constantly taking things away from you. You were the kid who climbed up on the counter to get the cookies, the kid who wondered what would happen if you put your peanut butter sandwich in the DVD player. You enjoyed trying to figure things out on your own and working to accomplish a task. You often asked "Why?"

3 Rating: You were the prodigy. You showed signs of having a very strong will. You were infinitely curious about the world around you. You walked at a very early age. Once you started talking, you never stopped. You learned how to ask for and get what you wanted, and you were determined to get it, no matter what. You *always* asked "Why?" You were the "Why this? Why that? Why not?" kid.

Now that you've examined how much perseverance you had when you came into this world, you must look to see how it changed growing up.

Your Formative Years (6 years old – late teens)

1 Rating: As a child, and growing into your teen years, you may have been talented and smart and showed potential, but you weren't proactive. You needed to be pushed into activities. You didn't have the curiosity or motivation to be adventurous. You didn't feel the need to be ambitious. You might have had great ideas, but you never followed through. You rarely finished a project, never stayed committed to something long enough to complete it.

2 Rating: You liked school and excelled throughout. You were very responsible. You often held jobs, whether it was a paper route, babysitting, or flipping burgers. You participated on a sports team, drama club, student council, newspaper staff, etc. You knew how to balance all you were doing. You worked hard and followed through on your work and you enjoyed the process.

3 Rating: At a young age, you had an extraordinary work ethic; you were always 110 percent committed to completing any task. Absolutely nothing would discourage you from achieving your goal. You started several programs, organized events, and managed projects. Everyone knew that you would be successful. Whether it was acting, playing the violin, singing, painting, etc., you not only stuck to it, you mastered it.

You may even have become professional or at least showed signs of achieving greatness later in life.

Once again, assess how you changed growing up. Did you move up or down from one to the next? Did you start out as a 2 and move up to a 3? Did you start as a 3 and move down a notch?

Just like talent and confidence, there are several factors that affect how much your ability to persevere changes throughout your life. Sure, it is up to each one of us to persevere in our own individual lives, no matter what our goals. How easy or difficult that is for us is determined initially by other influences, none more so than our upbringing.

Did Your Upbringing Affect Your Perseverance?

Let's examine how you were raised and how your perseverance was either rewarded or ignored. Looking back to where you were as a child and young adult will help you understand what you need to do today to persevere.

Are you ACTOR A or ACTOR B?

ACTOR A: Did you have parents or guardians who taught you the importance of setting goals and encouraged your curiosity and drive? Were they there to see you through your schoolwork, projects, and activities? Did they set goals for you, like getting good grades, and insist that you accomplish them? Did they hold you accountable and reward you when you met your goals, whether it was a gold star, a trip to Disneyland or even money? Did they teach you the core values of responsibility and working hard to get what you want?

Or

ACTOR B: Did your parents or guardians, for whatever reason, not support you, push you or hold you accountable? Did they willingly or subconsciously discourage you from developing a solid work ethic? Did they neglect to teach you the value of staying focused or committed to completing a task or project? When the task became too difficult, were you told that you didn't have to finish? Were you sheltered and coddled? Worse yet, were you left with no one to teach you how to persevere?

If you identified more with ACTOR A, chances are you have a clear understanding of what it is to persevere. You have the motivation to push through obstacles and accomplish your goals. You were rewarded for not just achieving goals, but also for the *pursuit* of those goals. That motivation, support, and discipline has probably carried over to your life today, giving you a strong work ethic.

If you fall more under ACTOR B, you're less likely to understand what it will take for you to persevere. It doesn't mean you can't, it just means that the process might be more unfamiliar and thus a bit more challenging.

"Goals on the road to achievement cannot be achieved without discipline and consistency."
-Denzel Washington

Perseverance Also Comes From...

Your Ancestry: We've talked about how our perseverance, our drive, comes from our genes, which we inherit from our parents, our grandparents, our ancestors. If you're able, you should look deeper into your family history. If you come from ancestors who are part of a disenfranchised group that dealt with oppression, repression, or persecution, then you may be part of a bloodline that *inherently* knows how to persevere.

Families who have risen above great struggles to become successful are the epitome of self-sacrifice, determination, hard work, and perseverance.

What have *your* ancestors endured? What lessons have you learned from stories of the "old days," listening to grandma and grandpa talk of struggles in their life? How has their steadfastness, their tenacity shaped and influenced your life?

Your Curiosity: To have the drive, the need, the want, you first need to be *curious*. Curiosity is the fuel that ignites your drive. Not only is curiosity instinctual, it's also intellectual. There is something in our brain that

makes us want to learn more about the world around us—
—to educate ourselves, to see different places, to hear new
stories—so we can ultimately be more in control of our
destinies.

Our curiosity propels us to move forward, inquire, probe,
and study. It also *motivates* us, drives us to do good things
(and sometimes, unfortunately, bad things). Curiosity
makes us want to know what else is out there. It makes
us want to know if we can do better. From childhood on,
there are those of us who are not content to settle for
what we're told; we want to know the reason why.
"Why?" is as important of a question as "How?" to
somebody who is curious. That perpetual curiosity is at
the core of people who persevere.

Your Passion: To persevere, you need to have passion
driving you. Managers, agents, casting directors,
producers, those in the business who have great passion
are always looking for that same passion in actors. You
need to have passion for your craft and career always
running through you.

Whether it's taking an acting class, self-taping, or
spending fourteen hours a day shooting a modified, low-
budget, SAG/AFTRA-deferred, independent, new
media web series, you must have the passion, the love for
what you're doing! Acting needs to excite you, drive you,
give you a rush that you can't feel with anything (or
anyone) else. Your passion for acting can go a long way
in helping to keep you driven.

Your Competitive Spirit: Some people are born naturally more competitive than others. Once again, think of Serena Williams. Sure, she was born with a tremendous amount of talent and confidence and had the support of her family. But there was something else that made her great, something else that pushed her to be the best.

Entertainment giants like Steven Spielberg, Oprah Winfrey, Ryan Murphy, Rihanna, Ryan Seacrest, Dwayne Johnson, Tyler Perry, Reese Witherspoon, Madonna, must have been born with a competitive spirit. These people are not content with second place. They want to be the best at what they do…and not just the best today but the very best *always*. More importantly, they're willing to do the work required to be the best because that's how you win.

You Can Persevere!

Perseverance is something that can be learned, studied, and implemented. Just like confidence, no matter how little or how much overall drive you were born with or have now, you will need to learn a whole new kind of perseverance, an **Acting Perseverance**. It is this Acting Perseverance that will directly relate to your career, to the work you will have to do to reach your *acting* goals.

In order to be successful in any career, you need to first have a goal and then a plan. The same is true when it comes to your acting career. If you want to persevere in an acting career, you must adhere to…

The Four P's of Perseverance

For many years, I have taught actors the mantra I created about perseverance:

Be **Persistent** and **Patient** in **Pursuit** of your **Purpose**.

Make this *your* perseverance mantra. Write it down in your Actor's Journal. Put it on a note to stick to your computer so every morning, when you're submitting on Actor's Access, you can see it as a reminder to keep going. This formula will define all the work you need to do to build your career as an actor. It applies to everything from accomplishing simple every day career challenges to achieving lifelong career goals. It encompasses all aspects of perseverance—physical, mental, emotional, and spiritual—to get you focused, prepared, and perpetually moving forward.

Purpose

You need to know what you want, what you're fighting for, what you're trying to accomplish. It's your goal, it's your mission, it's your **Purpose**. You already know your purpose is to be a successful actor.

A *spiritual* quality also flows through your purpose, through your art. You want to fulfill your destiny while bringing light, positive energy, compassion, and love into the world. You want to entertain, inspire, enlighten, impact, and move others with your art. It's important for you to put your purpose out there for the universe to hear, accept, love, and embrace.

Pursuit

This is about all the *mental* work required to achieve your goal. **Pursuit** is about having a plan. Pursuit is defining and strategizing exactly what you need to do to carry out that plan, thereby accomplishing your purpose. It's about drawing a blueprint, setting up a roadmap to stay on course.

For actors, there really isn't a set plan. It's not like being an accountant, lawyer, architect, or engineer, where there is mandatory schooling followed by internships, jobs, and then a career. When it comes to an acting career, the only thing that actors share is a want, a desire, a need to act.

While you may receive advice on how to approach your career, the details and the execution of any plan really depend on your individual goals. How you choose to go about working at those individual goals is how you define your pursuit.

Patience

This is about all the *emotional* work required to achieve your goal. It's accepting what you need to do to fulfill your purpose. It's also preparing yourself for the fact that fulfilling your purpose might not be so quick or easy. It's being willing to stay calm and composed about the task at hand no matter what obstacles get in your way. It's about having **Patience.**

It's the "hurry up and wait" mentality.

"Hurry up and wait" is a familiar phrase for many different artists. I believe it originated in the military, but quickly was co-opted on movie sets across Hollywood: actors would be in their trailers, preparing for their scene until the knock on the door had them "hurry" onto set...only to have them "wait" for the gaffer to fix a light or something else. When that happens to an actor on set, they need to stay in character and stay in their emotions and intentions until the director yells "Action!"

This easily translates to your career. The phrase "hurry up and wait" means landing a meeting with an agent only to wait for their phone call, rushing to an audition only to wait an hour to audition, and getting a callback only to wait to hear if you got the job.

The "wait" is about having patience.

It's about concentrating on your tasks, keeping yourself motivated, and not letting your emotions get in your way. Having patience will help you stay in the game through successful times and slow times. You need to be patient before you get your big break, in between your big breaks and so on.

Persistence

What you're doing during the time you're waiting is often most important. It's about working hard and being ready for your opportunities. **Persistence** means constantly taking the *physical* steps necessary to follow through with your pursuit.

Every actor trying to "make it" goes through a process to establish themselves, whether they're just starting their career or looking to take it to the next level. This process will consist of doing "grunt work."

What I mean by grunt work is getting headshots, updating your résumé, researching agents, managers and acting studios, doing emailings, signing up for casting websites, and so on. It's all the work that will help you build a *career* while you learn your *craft*. Unless your brain is wired to enjoy the details, nobody likes doing grunt work, but it is the foundation of perseverance.

Being persistent in this grunt work will get your foot in the door (for the first time or once again) and produce positive results. It will keep you going no matter what. Staying persistent will establish a solid foundation, a strong work ethic that will carry you throughout your career.

Your Mission, Should You Choose to Accept it...

Whether you're just starting out, have been in the game for a while, or looking to reboot your career, you need to take on and accomplish two specific tasks, two priorities, two *missions* that are vital to your acting career: **Get Representation** and **Get Acting Work.** First up…

MISSION #1: GET REPRESENTATION

What I mean by representation is an agent or manager, a professional in the industry who will help guide you on your career path and get you acting opportunities.

There are many ways to go about getting representation. For some of you, this process will take time, but finding an agent or manager is of the utmost importance. Agents and managers have relationships with casting directors. They know how to market you and get you out on auditions. Good representation will advise you and help you manage your career.

In order to accomplish your mission, you need to put together a Digital Pitch Package. This package will provide agents and managers with a clear idea of your look, personality, acting training, and experience.

3 Essentials for Your Digital Pitch Package:

- Headshots
- Résumé
- Demo Reel

Headshots

The first piece of self-marketing that agents, managers, and even casting directors will see are your **headshots**. These digital headshots are your calling card. They need to capture your look, your personality, and your type (refer to "The Typing Game" in the Bonus Track: Confidence section). Your headshot is meant to establish you as an actor who is open for business and ready to get noticed.

Your pictures need to be taken by a professional headshot photographer. With trends in headshots constantly changing, make sure to research what kind of headshots are popular *now*. As a general note, you can't go wrong with a basic color headshot that clearly shows your face. Most importantly, make sure you get both commercial (smiling) and theatrical (serious) shots. There are several different styles for these pictures, i.e., "close-up" or "three-quarter," which are industry terms for how much of your face and body the headshot shows.

You should not spend a lot of money on your *first round* of headshots. Time and time again, I hear stories of actors who drop the big bucks on their first headshots only to have an agent request that they get new ones once they get signed. Search for an inexpensive yet respectable headshot photographer, then view their headshot portfolio on their website, looking for similar types to you. For those doing their second and third round of headshots, you hopefully know more about yourself, your "look," and the process, so you could invest in a higher end headshot photographer.

After you narrow down your choices of photographers, meet each one and get a feel for them and their style. Then choose the photographer you feel most comfortable with as that is *key* to achieving a successful headshot session. Feeling at ease with your photographer lets them do their magic, their work: bringing out your look and true essence in your headshot.

Once you've chosen a photographer, talk with them about what you want. Make sure you're both on the same page about your *type(s)*, so they know how to light and shoot you. For example, let them know if you're the "cute but quirky best friend," the adorkable type, so you don't get glam lit headshots that portray you as the shimmering ingénue or leading man.

Do research on your wardrobe for the looks you're going for so you can discuss this with your headshot photographer. Watch TV, film, and commercials for character types you might play and how they dress. Check out the hairstyles of the characters and see what styles may fit or suit your type(s) best.

Communication with your headshot photographer is vital to having a successful photo shoot. You must be clear with the photographer about your look, your wardrobe, and your hairstyle. For those who need makeup for your shoot, make sure you hire a professional makeup artist (usually recommended by the photographer) who also needs to understand what type(s) you're going for.

By the end of the session, if you've gotten everything you need and there is a little time on the clock, ask to do some quick *bonus shots*: photos wearing your favorite hat, a funky tee-shirt, edgy hairdo, a quirky expression, or going makeup free, hair disheveled, a grungy, post-apocalyptic look. You never know what might come out of these bonus shots; you might be able to use them for a specific acting opportunity.

Since photographers shoot digitally, they will take hundreds of pictures in your session. You should have no problem finding both a commercial and theatrical headshot you can use. When choosing your headshots, you should seek out feedback from others in the industry. If you have representation, they will ultimately pick the best ones for you. If you don't have representation, take that feedback and then trust your own instincts. You need to have a photo that you're proud of, one that excites you and you feel represents you.

I still think it's important to have *digital postcards* with your commercial and theatrical headshot, as well as all your contact information and your social media handles. Are postcards still effective? Some industry folks say "yes," while others say "meh." But I look at them as another promotional tool for you. You can attach or embed these digital postcards when following up after any industry meeting or audition.

Also, I know it's "old school," but it doesn't hurt to get yourself a standard-size *business card* featuring your headshot and contact info that you can hand out when an opportunity arises (you'll wish you had one). There are many online printing shops that offer super cheap deals on mass quantities of business cards.

Résumé

Along with your headshot, you'll need to have a digital **résumé** that shows the potential agent or manager what you've done and what you are currently doing.

Sometimes, you might need a *hard copy* of your headshot and résumé. You can print your headshot with good 8x10 card stock and attach your printed résumé right on the back, as it looks cleaner and more professional. If you can't print directly on it, simply trim your résumé so it fits the borders of your headshot, and then staple it on the back.

More important is what's *on* your résumé.

You need to have all your contact information, including your cell phone number, email address, and, if you have them, your professional website, IMDB page, and casting profile link (i.e., Actor's Access, Now Casting, etc.). You should list your height, weight, and eye and hair color. However, never list your age as it could limit your roles.

Then, list all acting experience you have, be it theatre (college, community, professional), independent films, commercial work, music videos, web series, industrials, etc. At the top of this experience section should be any professional TV and film credits. Be honest. Don't lie. Don't "pad" your résumé…too much. Let's say you did a staged reading of *A Streetcar Named Desire* in a theater somewhere. Well, that sounds to me like you did *A Streetcar Named Desire* in a theater somewhere. Get what I'm saying?

Make sure you highlight what acting teachers or studios you have studied with or who you are currently studying with. Agents, managers, and casting directors in any Industry City put great value on actors that are studying with well-known, established teachers and studios.

Plus, make sure to include a short list of special skills, whether it be singing, dancing, accents, sports, musical instruments, rock climbing, fencing, juggling, spelunking, animal noises, etc. The more specific, the better. NOTE: Save yourself, your representation, and the casting director a lot of time by being honest and *proficient* in the special skills you list.

And finally, make sure everything listed is up to date, spelled correctly, aligned properly, and there are no grammatical or punctuation errors (typos).

Demo Reel

More and more agents and managers are requesting to see a **demo reel** before they even consider meeting an actor, new or experienced. At its most basic, your demo reel should be a short (and I emphasize *short*) collection of your best work up to that point, giving agents and managers a better sense of who you are, what you look like in action, and what you're capable of as an actor.

More specifically, your demo reel needs to show off your acting range in both comedy and drama, how you physically look and sound on camera, the type of characters you can play, and your marketability.

A demo reel can consist of footage from independent films, self-produced projects, student films, taped auditions, and recorded class work. And, of course, if you got a great co-star role on *NCIS*, be sure to include that at the very beginning of the reel. There are several different schools of thought for how these demo reels should be produced. As a rule, your demo reel should be only two minutes long, involving your best two or three short scenes.

You need to make sure that when you are acting in a project that you always get your footage. But it's important that your demo reel include only *high-quality* footage. Sending in an unprofessional or sloppy demo reel is detrimental to your cause. However, if you have some good footage that shows off your acting chops and is professionally filmed with high quality video, lights, and sound, then it can be a powerful accessory.

Now that you have your Digital Pitch Package, you are ready to do your agent and/or manager emailing.

Your Back Pocket Monologue

Obviously, a **Monologue** isn't something you physically include in your Digital Pitch Package, but it's something you might need to have ready at a moment's notice. There will be times when you will hit it off with an agent in a meeting and they will ask you to do a monologue on the spot and you will need to have one in your back pocket, ready to go. This is a staple, an old school tradition, and you'd be surprised how many agents and managers still ask for it.

I recommend having *two* different kinds of monologues at your disposal: one comedic and one dramatic. These monologues should be no longer than two minutes and they should showcase your best acting strengths and characters that you would most likely play. Find a monologue that suits your age and type, one that you can naturally and organically identify with, a role that you can be cast in.

Feel free to use monologues from TV and film, though I would recommend against performing a famous piece. And if you're a little short on footage for your demo reel, film a portion of your monologue to include in that part of your Digital Pitch Package.

Your 100 Agent/Manager Emailing

Whether you're a first timer looking for an agent and/or manager or an experienced actor looking to find new representation, the best way to get the job done is to throw yourself in and do **Your 100 Agent/Manager Emailing**.

When to do this emailing depends upon your experience and training. Before seeking theatrical representation, you should have at least *a year* of training and intense study behind you. That's the minimum! Remember, if you get an agent, you need to be ready and prepared when audition opportunities present themselves. Once you've been taking classes regularly, graduated from a four-year program, trained in any Industry City, or have professional acting credits, *then* you are ready to do Your 100 Agent/Manager Emailing.

This emailing really serves two purposes: 1) to declare to yourself, the industry, the universe, anyone within earshot, that you are ready and prepared, that the door to your business is open; 2) to land representation (or at least a few meetings).

First, you need to identify who you want to submit to for this emailing. NOTE: this means a hundred *total* agents and managers, not a hundred of each. To find a comprehensive list of legitimate theatrical and commercial agents, go to the SAG-AFTRA website (sagaftra.org) and check out the local SAG-Franchised Agent List. It's a basic list which you can use to start googling and researching those agents. You can also find listings of agents and managers on IMDBPro, which will give you their contact information (email, phone, website, etc.). There are also subscription acting sites that offer opportunities to meet representation and sites where you can upload your Digital Pitch Package for agents and managers to review. Just make sure to vet any of these paid acting sites.

You should, of course, concentrate on agents and managers in your Industry City, but also look at representation in other Industry Cities. With self-tape auditioning and filming in cities other than L.A. and New York becoming more prevalent, this business is now more accessible to "non-local hires," and you might find representation that can help you work in those markets.

Once you have your list, you are ready to do the mailing. To send along with your Digital Pitch Package, you will need to include a simple cover letter introducing yourself and stating that you are seeking representation. There is a format for these letters beyond just keeping them short and professional. For a good example of a *100 Agent/Manager Cover Letter,* check out the Workbook Section in the back of this chapter.

Once you have embedded your cover letter in the body of an email, you will send that with your attached Digital Pitch Package to your hundred agents/managers. Consider this emailing a positive spin on the "throw it out there and see what sticks" philosophy. In my experience, it works.

A student of mine, Taylor (they/them), was reluctant about this idea and thought it might be a waste of time. I said to Taylor, "It doesn't cost you anything to do it except time." They did the emailing and it worked. They got several meetings and eventually signed with a manager. But the biggest thing Taylor got from this emailing were the meetings they went on. Taylor said that they learned so much in every meeting about what agents/manager are looking for, about the industry as a whole, and most importantly, what they need to do to get an agent.

If you email out a hundred Digital Pitch Packages, you should get responses and perhaps a few meetings, if not representation. Even if nothing happens, your future mailings will be easier because now you understand everything involved in the process.

Two weeks after Your 100 Agent/Manager Emailing, follow it up by sending a digital postcard to everyone on your list. As mentioned earlier, there is a question as to whether they're effective, but once again, it doesn't really cost you anything except time, so do it. You already have a headshot you can use for this digital postcard. Or you can use your alternate headshot or even one of your bonus shots. For a good example of a *digital postcard* to send after Your 100 Agent/Manager Emailing, check out the Workbook Section.

Your 50 Agent/Manager Emailing

After Your 100 Agent/Manager Emailing, which is purposely a more general emailing, you should now find yourself getting more educated about your acting career. Over time, you will learn a lot more about the business——be it from other actors in acting class, working on acting projects, research or reading trade websites like *Backstage West, The Hollywood Reporter, Deadline,* and *Variety,* etc.

One of the things you will hear and read a lot about are various agents and managers. You'll learn about the client rosters of agents and managers you're interested in and what "types" they have on their list. You'll learn what representation your friends and classmates have, which agents are currently seeking actors, what types they're looking for, etc. Plus, you will learn more about *yourself*. As you continue your training, you will begin to see what types you can play and how you can market yourself to agents and managers.

Once you have this experience and knowledge under your belt, you are then ready to take the next step. Within a year or so of Your 100 Agent/Manager Emailing, you will then do **Your 50 Agent/Manager Emailing.**

This emailing will be more focused. First, you will prep your new headshots, update your résumé, and edit your demo reel. Also, your cover letter will be a little more specific this time. In this cover letter, you'll give some details about your type, your potential niche, and how you see yourself as an actor. Also, if you can, it's always good to have a "referred by." If you heard about the agent or manager from someone, ask if you can mention their name in your cover letter. For a good example of a *50 Agent/Manager Cover Letter,* check out the Workbook Section.

As for who to send Your 50 Agent/Manager Emailing to, research fifty agents and managers that might be looking for your type and experience. Be sure to look for agencies willing to work with you in building your career and helping you get career opportunities. Too many actors want to jump to major talent agencies when they would be better suited working with a mid-sized firm or even a smaller boutique agency that would make them a priority.

Feel free to follow up at any time with a digital postcard when you have something to report, like you're working on a TV show, film, play, showcase, etc. Make sure you send out these announcements as it will impress upon agents and managers that you are a working actor. For a good example of a *digital postcard* to send after Your 50 Agent/Manager Emailing, check out the Workbook Section.

Since this is your second round and the emailing is more specific, your chances of getting representation should increase.

Sent Postcards and Became a Star

Back in the '80s, when I worked as an agent, I had an actor who mailed me a postcard every month, updating me as to what he was doing, whether it was a showcase, an industrial, or an Off-Off Broadway play. The actor's name was Michael. Because he was so persistent, I met with him. Michael's headshot reflected his look and his personality: an intense, charismatic young actor who knew who he was and what type he played best. He had a New York look with a nice, big Italian nose that he wasn't afraid to show off. Michael embraced his face. I was impressed with his look, personality, training, and his tenacity.

Unfortunately, I had a client just like him so I couldn't sign him. It was a good thing Michael sent postcards to other agents as well, because soon after our meeting, an agent took him on. Then, a few years later, I turned on the TV to watch this new HBO show called *The Sopranos,* and there he was in a perfect role as Tony Soprano's nephew Christopher Moltisanti. The "Michael" who sent me all those postcards is Emmy Award-winning actor Michael Imperioli. I should've signed him; my guy went nowhere.

When you've got an agent or you're at least in the process of getting an agent, you're ready to move on to your next perseverance mission.

Industry Showcases

Showcases are an opportunity for an actor to "showcase" their talent for industry guests, including agents, managers, and casting directors.

These showcases are run by industry professionals and feature actors working on individual scenes or monologues, typically in a theatre space, an acting studio or online via Zoom.

There is usually a charge for participating in a showcase. Before signing up, I suggest getting a recommendation from an actor who's worked with the showcase's producer or director. There are several showcases that do not pull in an industry audience, and you don't want to waste your time or money.

The main point of these showcases is to display your acting abilities (be it comedy or drama) for industry professionals. When I was an agent and casting director, I found many actors from showcases. But be warned, you should only do a showcase when you are *ready* to showcase your acting.

MISSION #2: GET ACTING WORK

Once you get representation, you need to help your representation... represent you. That means getting as much acting work as possible to fill up your résumé and demo reel, so your agent and/or manager can use it to pitch you to casting directors and producers. There is a lot of acting work that you can get on your own to kickstart or reboot your acting career.

Theatre

Joining a theatre company—be it at a nationally recognized playhouse, an improv group, or small theatre troupe—is a great way to keep yourself consistently working at your craft, especially when auditions are slow. Performing with a theatre company keeps your skills sharp. Theatre shows give you a great opportunity to dig into a character, work your techniques and practice your craft nightly.

Theatre also provides a great place for you to be seen, to network, and to meet other producers, directors, and writers as well as to find new friends and build a support system.

Theatre companies epitomize perseverance. Working at a theatre company typically involves a lot more work than simply acting. Actors help put up the shows, whether it's stage managing, building sets, lighting, sound design, marketing, promotion, and even writing, directing, and producing.

Independent Media Projects

Online casting websites like Actor's Access and NowCasting list casting notices for dozens of independent media projects. These listings are looking to cast actors in union and nonunion short films, web series, commercials, student films, etc.

I recommend you submit yourself for as many of these projects as possible. Remember that part of perseverance is constantly putting yourself out there. Think of these auditions as a great opportunity to practice for those higher profile auditions with professional casting directors and directors.

These smaller budget independent media projects are not only a training ground for actors but also for writers and directors, too. Therefore, you don't have to feel intimidated by them or the process. This is a great learning experience on how to audition, book a job, show up on an actual set, and collaborate with directors and writers.

If you submit for these smaller projects, you *will* get called in to audition and you *will* book. Not only is that exciting (and often a much-needed confidence boost), but it can also potentially lead to great footage for your demo reel.

What's great about working these independent media projects is that due to ever-changing technology, there's a lot more access to better video, lighting, and sound quality, so you can now use footage from these ventures on your reel. There are even productions being shot solely on smartphones! As this tech continues to evolve, you'll get even more footage that looks a lot more like bigger budget shoots.

These projects are an excellent way to get your name and face out there (by the way, if you plan to create a stage name, do it before you establish yourself as an actor). They are a great way to make strong contacts as well. If you do good work, you will get recommendations and other opportunities.

I had an actress who did a USC film, and the director liked her talent, personality, and work ethic so much that he recommended her to several other student directors. She ended up doing three more USC films within a couple months. A few years later, one of these directors cast her in his Netflix-produced film.

With a handful of premiere film schools around Hollywood and in other Industry Cities, there are many aspiring filmmakers working on their next project, so there are plenty of acting opportunities. And who knows? Maybe you'll work with the next George Lucas or Steven Spielberg…both USC grads.

Producing Your Own Projects

Why wait to be cast? Produce something yourself. You can star in, write, direct, and/or produce your own project! As I mentioned, with technological advances in digital cameras, smartphones, lighting equipment and sound design, any creative person can create something.

Producing your own projects will keep you working on both your craft and career, while also potentially opening some doors. You can write, act in, and/or direct your own project: a monologue, a scene, a comedic sketch, a short film, a web series, even a feature length film.

Having a good product that you've self-produced and that's posted on a professional website or YouTube channel, or even loaded onto your acting website profiles, gives you a step up from other actors. A high quality, self-produced project can impress agents or managers and possibly get you representation. If you already have representation, it gives them another tool they can use to pitch you.

Plus, with the enormous popularity of apps like Instagram and TikTok, there are now outlets and opportunities for thousands of people to check out your work. Make sure to post on social media about any projects you have produced, especially if your short film gets into a film festival…and wins!

Sometimes these projects can even capture national attention. Think of *Brooklyn Nine-Nine*'s Andy Samberg. That's how he got his start. He self-produced several shorts that attracted the attention of *Saturday Night Live,* which signed him on as a cast member. And the rest, as they say, is history.

If you find other actors, writers, and directors looking to self-produce, you could form your own independent production company. And you should! I'm not talking about a multimillion-dollar studio. I'm suggesting a few bucks, some quality equipment, a handful of creative ideas, and a group of equally ambitious people. Self-producing is a great lesson in perseverance. It's a lot of hard work, time, energy, and even money, but the payoff is worth it.

Becoming Union (SAG-AFTRA)

Being a union actor looks impressive on your résumé and raises your stock value in the eyes of industry professionals.

One of your overall goals will be to eventually join the Screen Actors Guild which merged with the American Federation of Television and Radio Artists to become

SAG-AFTRA, the major union for actors around the country. The rules for joining SAG-AFTRA, as well as the cost involved, seem to be ever-changing. Getting your union card is a vital step for any actor in this business. It's a rite of passage that signifies that you are now part of the same fraternity of professional actors.

Before you join SAG-AFTRA, you should do as much nonunion work as possible, so you can build up your résumé and get experience on set. When you *do* book your first SAG-AFTRA job, you are then SAG-eligible. You can continue to do nonunion work until you book another union job. At that point, you will probably become a "must-join." Once you have joined SAG-AFTRA, you are then essentially barred from doing nonunion work, unless you get specific exemptions. Make sure you only join when you are ready to make that leap!

HELP YOUR REPS HELP YOU

Helping your representation goes beyond just working to fill your résumé and getting your name out there. It's about working together to form a plan that will help navigate you to a successful career.

Many actors think that once they get an agent or manager, they can just sit back and relax, let their reps field offers and wait for the auditions to roll in.

Wrong!

Just because you have representation, your work doesn't stop. You must put yourself in the mind frame that all your agent or manager really is at this point is a letterhead. Yes, having representation is a gateway to opening career opportunities, but you need to be diligent in doing whatever you can to help your representation market you.

When you sign with an agent and/or manager, you not only enter a legally binding contract, you also enter a mutual *partnership*. For your representation, it means they agree to develop, groom, and advise you on your career as well as get you out on auditions. For you, it means listening to their advice, keeping your acting training active, coaching for auditions, continuing to get and produce work on your own, and doing anything and everything that can help your "team" make you a success.

Don't just talk about doing things to help your representation, do them! Have your self-tape home studio set up for use anytime, check your voice mail and email regularly, make sure to confirm appointments immediately. Be prepared for all opportunities, and most importantly, listen to your agent or manager's advice.

You need to inspire your agent and manager and reassure them that you are willing to work with them. Show them that you are a professional, ambitious, collaborative, hard-working actor that's willing to persevere and is worth representing and sending out.

Here are some other specific actions you can take to help your representation get you acting work:

5 Things to Do to Help Your Reps

1) Sign up for acting websites: There are several reputable acting websites that list audition notices and give you a chance to create a profile and post your Digital Pitch Package for directors and casting directors to peruse. You should be signed up with all of them and keep updating them as often as possible. NOTE: Check with your representation to make sure they're okay with you submitting on your own and let them know when you get called in.

2) Create your own acting website: You should set up your own website, a one-stop-shop with your various headshots, résumé, demo reel, and clips from your best acting work (or full videos of short films). You should also include (and update regularly) information on your acting career, as well as links to any projects or shows you're working on. Make sure you link to your agent or manager and clear with them what to post on this site.

3) Do casting director emailings: A variation of Your 100 and Your 50 Agent/Manager Emailing, you are now going to do Your 100 Casting Director Emailing to both commercial and theatrical casting directors with your Digital Pitch Package (now including your agent and/or manager's logo), letting them know you are available for casting.

A few months after this mass emailing, you will do another casting director mailing, this one a little more focused. Find the casting directors that cast TV shows that might use your type. For example, if you're a cop type, look for those casting directors that cast network cop dramas. If you're a comedic actor, focus on sitcom casting directors. You can also target casting directors that are looking for special skills that match your own, like horseback riding, martial arts, or ballet dancing. Remember to keep your representation informed of any auditions you get.

4) Attend casting director workshops: Sometimes your representation will recommend that you take a casting director workshop for you to meet a specific casting director. These workshops typically charge a fee and feature a casting director watching, and perhaps critiquing, scene work from the actors, as well as discussing the business.

When considering these workshops, be smart. Take ones where the casting director is working on a show that frequently casts your type. But don't go into these workshops with the expectation that you're going to get hired or discovered. Instead, use the opportunity to learn about the casting process and to get some face time with casting directors that may one day hire you.

5) Watch TV and film: Watching TV and films—be it on network, cable, streaming, or at the cineplex—will help you gain a general knowledge of what's happening in the industry, what types of films and shows are hot now and what types of roles you'd be cast in. Plus, studying actors on TV shows and films will help you with your auditions.

For a new actor in Hollywood or any Industry City, there are many more TV opportunities than there are in film, and you are more likely to audition for a co-star or guest star on a TV show. Therefore, it's important for you to know the various TV show genres for which you will be auditioning.

You need to know whether the series you're auditioning for is single-camera comedy (*Modern Family*), multi-camera comedy (*Friends*), medical drama (*Grey's Anatomy*), procedural drama (*NCIS*), and so on. You must know the *tone* of the show you're going in for, and you can only learn that by watching the show itself. You don't have to view every episode, but enough for you to get a feeling for the show.

And then, within these TV genres, each individual show has its *own* tone. The tone of *The Office* is very different from *The Big Bang Theory*. The tone of *Law & Order* is very different from *Criminal Minds*. While good acting is good acting, you will need to know the tone of each show and adjust your work and your auditions accordingly.

> *"Success isn't always about 'Greatness,' it's about consistency. Consistent, hard work gains success. Greatness will come. "*
> -Dwayne "The Rock" Johnson

Work Begets Work

You must be willing to find ways to accomplish the mission of getting acting work anywhere and everywhere. Those opportunities are out there and the more work you do on your own, and with your representation, the more professional opportunities will open up for you.

I'm sure you've heard that once you get that ball rolling and start booking a few jobs, your career can snowball quickly. It is true…work begets work. You must utilize the positive energy of booking your last job to propel you to book your next job. You must be diligent in your pursuit of more and more work. You must continue to study, to audition, to market, to work with your representation on your career goals.

Being Consciously Oblivious

While perseverance involves a lot of actual physical work there is also a mental aspect to it as well.

When my book *The Eight Characters of Comedy* was first released back in 2005, I coined a term as a personality trait for the character of the Lovable Loser. I call it being **"Consciously Oblivious."** It describes how this comedic character desperately wants something so badly that they'll *consciously* put blinders on to achieve their Want. It's a positive spin on being in denial.

Being consciously oblivious is also a great tool to apply to your acting career. To be a successful actor, you need to put all your attention on your goals and block out the negative influences around you: competition, family and relationship issues, and the discouraging aspects of the business. You need to set your sights on your goal, invest in your dream, and become consciously oblivious to the challenges and obstacles. You know that they exist, but you choose not to let them deter or stop you.

Think of a thoroughbred racehorse that is fitted with blinders to help keep them focused on the finish line, avoid distractions, and ultimately run faster. Being consciously oblivious helps you overlook and disregard the obvious risks and focus solely on your objective.

Being consciously oblivious also means essentially not letting the frustrations all actors go through affect you as much. It means training yourself to "let go" of all the competition you're facing, those weeks without a call from your agent, or the fact that you're waiting tables to pay the bills.

Instead, it means focusing on how you can prepare for the next audition, what you can do to help your agent get you more auditions, and how you can use the money from your serving job toward your career. It's about turning negative thoughts into a positive perspective.

Work Perseverance with Your CTAG

There will be times when you'll need some help persevering with the "business" side of show business: marketing, promoting, everything you need to do to get your foot in the door. This type of work can be isolating, making you feel alone in your quest, especially when you're not feeling inspired. It can be daunting...and that's a great time to call upon your support group, your CTAG.

Remember, your CTAG is comprised of people with varying levels of experience. There are some actors in your CTAG that will be taking their first steps on the acting path while others have spent years on the journey. These newer actors will be there to take the first steps of this career work with you. Those with more experience will be there for you to draw on for knowledge, advice, and understanding. If you're the most experienced actor in the group, let those newer members give you some fresh perspective and a jolt of energy to inspire you in your perseverance work.

Your CTAG will be there to help you keep your spirits up. Your CTAG will also help you set tasks, accomplish goals, and focus on doing the grunt work involved in persevering. For more specific tasks for you to do with your CTAG, check out the CTAG Career Activities in the Workbook Section.

Your Acting Career is *Your* Business

Any small business owner, like myself, will tell you that owning your own business is hard work. We spend lots of time, money, and energy taking care of our investment. We face numerous obstacles and challenges in getting noticed and recognized. But we do it because we have faith in ourselves, our prospects, and in the "product" that we are selling.

Your acting career is *your* business. You're the owner, operator, treasurer, and CEO. You made a conscious decision to invest in the one person you believed in, who you knew would succeed: you.

Your business is selling an exceptional product: a well-trained, versatile actor. And *you* are the most important asset you can invest in. When you invest in yourself, you are taking complete control of your destiny. Making this investment in yourself is empowering and ultimately will help you keep persevering.

When I opened my acting studio in 1998, I only had ten students, and nobody knew who I was. Friends in the business said I was crazy to try and launch a studio in a town filled to the brim with acting coaches. They weren't wrong, but I knew what I wanted: I wanted to be a successful acting coach. When it came to my career, I put my blinders on and only concentrated on my goal. I chose to be consciously oblivious. That doesn't mean I didn't have a balanced life. It just means that I was willing to invest in myself and work through the career challenges that stood in my way. I believed in myself and in my ability and I had a strong Want. Still do. That's why I have a successful business.

Perseverance = Being A Lifer

A career is a marathon, not a sprint. You must come to Hollywood or any Industry City knowing that you will work hard for many years before you reach the finish line. That's why it's so important to enjoy the process.

It's like any other major career, be it sports, architecture, law, etc. If you want to be the best district attorney in the city, it doesn't happen overnight. You must go to school, compete to get in a good post-grad program, study hard, work internships, and then build up both your career and your reputation as a lawyer over several years. Acting is no different.

If you make the commitment, I promise you it will pay off. I have seen it happen time and time again. Just as I have seen some very talented people get burned out and quit, I have seen the hard workers who persevere eventually get their break. It's almost as if the universe at some point says, "Okay, you've stayed in the game and taken everything I've thrown at you, so here it is…take it, you've earned it, it's yours!"

Dylan Walsh is an actor who epitomizes the idea of being a lifer. I represented Dylan in the mid-1980s when he was just starting out. At the time, I had a very specific program for how to get a newbie like Dylan seen. Being a trained actor, it didn't take long for Dylan to book commercials, co-star roles, and eventually his big break in the '80s sex romp *Loverboy*. That film led Dylan to even more independent films, guest star roles on TV shows, and supporting roles in feature films. But it would take ten more years for this hard-working actor to experience the great commercial success he deserved as Dr. Sean McNamara on the hit FX show *Nip/Tuck*. Dylan Walsh is still a very successful working actor and is a lifer.

You have to want to be a lifer. You have to be in it for the long haul. You have to be willing to be persistent and patient in the pursuit of your purpose...*always!*

On top of that, you have to enjoy your life. Being a lifer in this business doesn't mean that acting is the *only* thing you do in your life. You need to have relationships, experiences, family, and charity. You need to be of service and do community work. You need to expose yourself to different cultures and all forms of art. All of these will make you a more interesting, enriched person and artist.

If you have other things in your life, it will relieve some of the pressure of this business, help you enjoy the process, and keep you positive that all your hard work will pay off. Having a *full life* will make you a better actor. You need to have those life experiences to draw upon. They will enrich your characterizations, your emotional depth, intellect, life perspective, and imagination.

Having a full life will also help opportunities come your way. When they do, you must be grateful. Gratitude is a key to happiness.

You have to say, "Thank you!" to the universe.

Oh, How I Hate Networking!

Though networking is a challenge for many actors, you need to get comfortable with the process. Many opportunities can come from networking events. You will find yourself at parties and industry functions with casting directors, writers, agents, producers, etc. You need to know how to approach them.

Here's a simple approach for you to take at your next industry function if you see a casting director you'd like to meet:

First, take a deep breath and put a self-assured smile on your face. Approach the casting director with confidence and make sure you wait for the right opportunity. Do not interrupt them if they're in the middle of a conversation. When you see your chance, make eye contact and simply say something like the following:

"Hi, I'm Bailey Smith and I just wanted to tell you that I love the casting you did on your last film (or current TV show), and I hope to someday get a chance to audition for you."

Hopefully, that casting director will say "Thank you." That's where you should expect the conversation to end. If the casting director does strike up a conversation with you—asking who you are, where you study, what work you've done—make sure you have a short, prepared answer. You should be friendly, charming, and open, and *not* needy. Having a sense of humor always works, too. Most importantly, be yourself.

When the conversation dies down, say, "It was nice to meet you," and move on. Hopefully you'll walk away with their business card. If they do offer you a card, be sure to hand them one of your business cards in return.

PERSEVERANCE: WORKBOOK SECTION

ACCOMPLISHING GOALS

What have you done for your career this week?

Solo Exercise: **I Persevered When I...**

I want you to think about something of importance that you persevered at in the past, something you willed yourself to do, a specific goal you've accomplished in your life. Keep it away from acting. It can be winning an award or trophy, making a sports team, learning to play an instrument, finishing a writing project, running a marathon, etc.

For example, here's what Jeff, a student of mine, wrote down when he did this exercise in my class.

Jeff's Example: I persevered when I *won my college essay award.*

Your Turn: Whatever it is, I want you to write it down below: "I persevered when I

_____."

I want you to closely examine what you've written down and think of what you did to accomplish that specific goal. What Perseverance Traits (physically, mentally, emotionally, spiritually) did you use in the pursuit of that goal? What exactly did you do, from planning to execution and everything in between?

Jeff's Example: "I persevered when I _won my college essay award_. In order to accomplish my goal, I…"

1) Set daily goals for writing the essay.
2) Wrote at least an hour a day for a month.
3) Spent hours researching what I was writing about.
5) Got lots of critique from friends and professors.
6) Edited my essay five times!
7) Watched less baseball.
8) Sacrificed spending time with friends.
9) Rewarded myself after each accomplishment.
10) Reminded myself to be grateful for doing something I love.

Your Turn: In your Actor's Journal, take a few minutes to write down ten things that you did to achieve that goal. It will probably be easy for you to think of the physical steps you took, but challenge yourself to think of the mental, emotional, and spiritual steps you had to take as well. Write it as follows:

"To accomplish my goal, I_____"

Once you've completed your list, you can see the sacrifices you made and the commitment it took to persevere. Let this list be a reminder that you have the power not only _to set_ a goal, but also to _complete_ that goal.

You'll find that persevering in an acting career is not that different from persevering in anything else you want to accomplish.

Look over your list and check how many of these could apply to your acting career. If you wrote down that you had to set daily goals, you know you must set daily *acting career* goals. If you wrote down that you had to practice a lot, then you know you must practice *acting* a lot. If you wrote down you had to sacrifice hanging out with your friends…yeah, you get where I'm going. As you begin to work on perseverance in your acting career, you must remember that you have persevered before, and you can persevere now.

CTAG CAREER ACTIVITIES

Once again, call your CTAG, find a good location with comfortable chairs, and make sure to have room to write and do some busy work.

For these perseverance-related CTAG gatherings, I suggest setting up a regular meeting time when everyone can get together: once a week, either at the same place or alternating, depending upon your preference. Setting a regular meeting time will help you stay accountable for your own personal work as well as the work you're doing with the group.

These meetings will require a lot of discussion about the business of the business, from headshots to agents, casting directors, auditions, and so on. The main question at these perseverance meetings will be:

"What have you done for your career this week?"

The purpose of these meetings is to work *together* to tackle some of these perseverance tasks and to make them a little less tedious and a lot more fun. It's always easier to pass the time and get through this work when you're doing it with friends.

If you want, each time you meet, you can have a specific topic. The two most important tasks you should be doing in the meeting, however, are Setting Weekly Goals and Information Gathering.

Group Exercise: **Setting Weekly Goals**

Use the first CTAG meeting to discuss each of your goals as specifically as you can. Everyone's overall goal will be to become a successful actor. But each member of your CTAG will be at a different stage, and therefore have different individual goals for their career.

Talk about these individual goals (i.e., getting new headshots, finding material for your demo reel, getting an agent, etc.) and then discuss what work needs to be done for each of you to attain the goals. Then set your weekly goals for yourself and for each other, tasks you can do each week to help you reach those individual goals.

For example, if *your* individual goal is to get new headshots, you should discuss it with the CTAG and get their advice, input, and suggestions. Then you plan, put it on a calendar or write it down in your Actor's Journal. This will hold you responsible for the work. Each week, be sure to talk about what you accomplished as well as next week's individual tasks.

Using our headshots example, your Weekly Goals Setting should look something like this:

Week 1: Research photographers for your type(s).
Week 2: Schedule meetings with photographers.
Week 3: Pick photographer and schedule session.
Week 4: Get your headshots done.
Week 5: Get feedback and choose headshots.

As you can see, ideally, by week five, you'll have shot and picked out new headshots. For many actors, this process takes months, but you can do it in mere weeks (and move on to your next career project). Having a weekly goal, a set schedule, and accountability gives you the necessary stakes to motivate you to get things done. That doesn't mean you should rush the process, as you don't want to put out a sloppy product. It means that setting a schedule will keep you on track and prevent you from being stagnant in your career work.

This perseverance work that you set for yourself each week will be a goal sheet that you can refer to when you need to feel motivated. Use the following meetings to keep track of your week-to-week progress.

Group Exercise: **Information Gathering**

This is where the CTAG can be the most practical, useful, and fun. Have each member of the CTAG do their research and then bring it to the meeting to share.

Research includes everything from watching TV shows to tracking who's casting what, what you read in the industry trades, casting workshops, telling each other about auditioning experiences, etc. You can also have special meetings that are devoted to specific themes.

Here's some tasks you can do at your CTAG meeting:

Headshots: Checking out headshot photographers, comparing stylists and makeup artists, pricing, determining types of shot you should get, choosing the right shots, etc.

Industry Emailings: Gathering info on various agents/managers, checking reps' client rosters, building submission lists, researching casting directors and the shows they cast.

Demo reel footage: Watching each other's demo reels and giving feedback or going through footage to find the best scenes to put on a reel.

Self-producing: Brainstorming sessions to develop projects: a sketch, a short film, web series, whatever. Go through the process of putting together and self-producing a project from start to finish.

AGENT/MANAGER COVER LETTER AND POSTCARD EXAMPLES

#1 Your 100 Agent/Manager Emailing Cover Letter

Dear Agent or Manager,

Hi, my name is Bailey Smith, and I am currently seeking representation. I have been studying with Scott Sedita Acting Studios for the past year, and I am eager to begin auditioning. I have heard wonderful things about your agency and would love the opportunity to meet with you. Attached is my headshot, résumé, and demo reel. Please feel free to call or email me anytime. Thank you for your time and consideration. I hope to hear from you soon.

Sincerely,

Bailey Smith
Phone Number, Email Address, Website, IMDBPro, Actor's Access, and Professional Social Media links

#2 Your 100 Agent/Manager Emailing Digital Postcard

Hello, I just wanted to follow up to make sure you received my materials. I hope to hear from you and have the opportunity to meet with you about possible representation. Thanks, Bailey.

Bailey Smith,
Phone Number, Email Address, Website, IMDBPro, Actor's Access, and Professional Social Media links

#3 Your 50 Agent/Manager Emailing Cover Letter

Dear Agent or Manager,

Hi, my name is Bailey Smith and I am currently seeking representation. I was referred by your client, Jane Doe, who is my classmate at Scott Sedita Acting Studios. I've been studying both drama and comedy, and I am eager to begin auditioning. I am a Lovable Loser type with a Midwestern innocence who has enough depth to tackle a TV drama, and whose strength lies in biting, sometimes sarcastic comedic timing.

I have heard wonderful things about your agency and would love the opportunity to meet with you. Attached is my headshot, résumé, and demo reel. Please feel free to call or email me anytime. I hope to hear from you soon.

Sincerely,

Bailey Smith
Phone Number, Email Address, Website, IMDBPro, Actor's Access, and Professional Social Media links

#4 Your 50 Agent/Manager Emailing Digital Postcard

Hello, I just wanted to let you know I booked a comedy web series and the short film I starred in won a contest. I hope to hear from you and have the opportunity to meet with you about possible representation. Thanks, Bailey

Bailey Smith,
Phone Number, Email Address, Website, IMDBPro, Actor's Access, and Professional Social Media links

BONUS TRACK: PERSEVERANCE

THE LUCK FACTOR

Guess I was just lucky

Many would suggest that all you need to make it in this business is just plain *luck*. That this business is strictly a game of chance: meeting the right people in the right place at the right time. You hear folks, time and time again, say, "They were just *lucky* to get that meeting, that audition, that career-making job."

It seems the word "luck" is often utilized to sum up, justify, or explain how someone became successful. And sometimes you even hear it from those on the receiving end of that luck. I watched an actor I coached on a talk show discussing his well-earned lead role in a film. When the host asked the inevitable, "How did you get this career-making role?" the actor paused, and then, with a shrug, said, "Guess I was just lucky."

Really? That's how you're going to sum up *all* your hard work? You were *lucky*? Why not say, "I worked my ass off for years just to get the opportunity to audition for this career-making role, let alone book it!"

To be clear, I do believe in luck, especially when it comes to our individual lives. We experience luck every day.

Luck is getting that perfect parking spot on a rainy day, avoiding injury in a serious accident, or winning the lottery. Luck is when you're speeding down the highway and pass a cop...who, at that very moment, turns and looks the other way.

Luck is a cosmic blend of fate, karma, and fortune. Luck is forces beyond your control leading you to (or helping you avoid) certain life paths, choices, and events that will ultimately propel you to your destiny.

When it comes to your acting career, however, luck is very different. Luck is something that *you* can help shape. Luck is something you can bring onto yourself by putting out positive energy, which forms positive intentions, which morphs into positive outcomes.

For an actor pursuing an acting career, my motto is a quote attributed to the Roman philosopher Seneca: "Luck is what happens when preparation meets opportunity."

In class, we've shortened it:

"Luck is when preparation meets opportunity."

Write this down in your Actor's Journal. Read it again. In fact, say it out loud. This is a mantra I use and truly believe in. I've seen proof of it over many years. I've seen so many actors create their own luck simply by deciding to work hard.

If you work hard, *luck will come your way*. At some point, you will get an opportunity to meet the right people, audition for the perfect role, and book the job that will launch your career. You owe it to yourself and all the hard work you've done to be ready for the occasion.

As an example, an actor in my class, who I'll call Jerome, has been working diligently at his career for a few years. Jerome told the class a story about a producer who came into his restaurant, where he was waiting tables. He got to talking with the producer about his acting career. The producer liked him, thought he was right for a role on his show, and called him in to audition the next morning.

Jerome went home, got his sides, worked on his material, coached with me early the next morning and went to the audition completely prepared. He ended his story by saying, "I booked the role!" The class gave him a round of applause. Then a classmate said to Jerome, "You were lucky!"

Jerome's booking can't be summed up with a simple "you were lucky." To me, Jerome made sure he was prepared for when the opportunity presented itself and that preparation paid off in the form of an acting job.

*"Saying I was lucky negates the hard work
I put in."*
-Peter Dinklage

Creating Your Own Luck

Luck starts with you putting it out there, stating exactly what you want, what your goal is. You declare it to yourself, your friends, your family, your acting coach, the universe. It can be anything from your overall goals of being a successful actor to more individual goals like getting an agent or landing a good audition. You make that goal your top priority, and you put yourself in the mindset that you *will* accomplish that goal.

Then you work your ass off, you persevere, you prepare yourself to reach that goal. You do so by studying your craft, honing your talent, and building your confidence. The more you prepare—physically, mentally, emotionally, spiritually—the more open you are to the possibility of an opportunity.

Opportunities *will* present themselves. Unfortunately, it's difficult to predict *when*. Timing is the one variant in luck that you can't control. If you work diligently, prepare yourself, and open yourself up to receive opportunities, the less the timing will matter. You will be ready to succeed no matter when your lucky break occurs.

Once you accept the notion that you can create and orchestrate your own luck, it puts your destiny back into your own hands.

If you believe that you can produce your own luck, then I'm happy to report, you'll never be out of luck.

You have the power to be prepared for when opportunity strikes. You have the power to take advantage of all opportunities. You have the power to be lucky.

> *"If you can do what you do best and be happy,*
> *you are further along in life than most people."*
> *-Leonardo Dicaprio*

Acting Career Diet

A Recipe for Success

Talent. Confidence. Perseverance. Those are *your* Three Steps to Success. You can't take one out. You have to activate all three. You need all of them working together in harmony to reach peak efficiency in your career. They are the three ingredients needed for your **Acting Career Diet.**

Think of your acting career as a well-balanced diet which nourishes your mind, body, and spirit to work at full capacity. It's a diet that will maintain your acting career health, improve your performance, and keep you feeling pumped and powered up.

Talent is your Protein. And like every proper diet, you need your daily portion of protein…and lots of it! For your career diet, talent is what feeds, builds, and strengthens your acting muscles. The more you work out your talent, the bigger muscles you'll get and the stronger an actor you'll become.

Confidence is your Carbohydrates. Just like in any diet, there are good carbs and bad carbs. Bad carbs—like cakes, cookies, and chips—make you feel bloated, lethargic, and just plain yucky. Good carbs—like whole grains, legumes, and beans—fuel you with the energy you need. That's what confidence can do for your career: power you up with positive energy.

Perseverance is your Fruits and Vegetables. Perseverance gives your career the vitamins, minerals, and nutrients needed to survive. Just like it's important to "finish your vegetables," or eat "an apple a day," you need to have your recommended daily allowance of perseverance.

This is your recipe for success. You must have all three of these ingredients (talent, confidence, perseverance) working together to nourish, nurture and sustain you on your career path.

SECTION

TWO

CAREER CHALLENGES

Tasks to Do on Your Journey

In my script analysis technique WOFRAIM, the first two letters of the acronym (W, O) represent the basic components (Want, Obstacle) needed to create *conflict* in every scene. As an actor approaching any scene, you must determine your Want: your character's objective. Then you must identify your Obstacles: the person, place, and/or thing standing in the way of getting your Want.

You can apply this technique to your acting career. For every Want, there will be Obstacles. Your overall Want is to be a successful actor. Your Obstacles are the many acting and career *tasks* you need to complete to achieve that Want. And therein lies the conflict: will you or won't you complete your tasks? Will you or won't you get past those Obstacles to achieve your Want to become a successful actor?

These "tasks" I speak of are what I call **Career Challenges**.

Career challenges are positive, productive assignments— big and small, easy and difficult—that *every* actor must complete on their journey to be successful.

Macro career challenges include moving to a new city, getting a survival job, setting up your home studio, landing an agent, putting together a demo reel, joining SAG-AFTRA, getting a major TV credit, etc.

Micro career challenges include smaller, yet equally important, day-to-day tasks like regularly checking audition listings, preparing your weekly class work, self-taping an audition, reading scripts, researching casting directors, meeting with your CTAG, etc.

You need to face and tackle ALL these career challenges. With each challenge accomplished, you'll not only get closer to your overall Want, you will also start feeling better about the overall journey. Working through both big and small career challenges will raise your self-esteem, provide you with a victory, and make you feel positive about your potential. It will stimulate and ignite you to keep moving ahead.

Completing macro or micro career challenges will help you quickly grow as an artist and as an individual.

On the flip side, if you *don't* complete these career challenges, you will not grow as an artist. If you delay or put off your tasks indefinitely, they will take on a whole new form. By avoiding your career challenge, you are creating unnecessary pressure and tension surrounding that particular task. And soon, this unaddressed task becomes so burdensome that it morphs into an obstacle so big that you feel it's impenetrable.

But why would an actor who has such a strong Want even think of avoiding their career challenges?

Well, as an example, let's say you approach the macro career challenge of getting an agent. At first, there may be some uncertainty and trepidation about taking on this task, but it will be offset by a *lighter energy* that comes from your optimism, excitement, and determination to complete that task.

But when the challenge becomes too difficult or time-consuming, or when you start experiencing disappointment and/or rejection, a *darker energy* flows in and takes over. You become consumed with a feeling of hopelessness that you'll never be able to prevail. The idea of trying again feels overwhelming, and so you put the task off. Eventually you might even tell yourself, "I'll never get an agent," and you will give up, feeling frustrated and discouraged.

When you move away from your uncompleted (micro or macro) career challenge, you usually move toward something more comforting, something you can grasp and hold onto that makes you feel at ease, less anxious, and safe. What you're actually doing is stepping off your *career* path and onto the path of **Self-Sabotage.**

At its core, self-sabotage means doing anything to hamper your efforts, undermine yourself, and prevent you from getting what you want. It's a form of subversion that directly applies to your goals. When you are self-sabotaging, you don't properly prepare your acting work, you don't show up to class, you give up trying to get an agent, or you take actions that will cause you to lose your agent, etc. When you are self-sabotaging, you are neglecting and ignoring your career challenges, and you are watching your career goals fade away.

Self-sabotage will cause you to miss the opportunities needed to advance in your career. It will cause you to be unprofessional, unmotivated, and uncertain about yourself and your career. It will sap your talent, cripple your confidence, and impede your perseverance. When you succumb to self-sabotage, it makes it even harder to focus, stay committed, and follow the Three Steps to Success.

So, why do we self-sabotage? Well, it's a little thing called *Fear.*

> *"It takes facing obstacles to grow strong enough to overcome them."*
> -Daniel Dae Kim

FEAR

I'm just lazy

I had a student in my ten-week acting intensive class who was a very good actor. I'll call him Tom. Tom had the talent, confidence, and perseverance it takes to be successful.

At the end of the ninth week, I assigned everyone a monologue from a TV or film script to prepare and perform for the last class. Throughout the course, Tom and the other actors learned specific acting techniques to help them bring scenes and monologues to life. I was excited to see everybody's final work, especially Tom's. He had "arced" several times over the previous weeks, making significant breakthroughs in his acting as well as his ability to bring his own essence to the material.

With his strong build, intense look, and deep emotion, I gave Tom a monologue that was perfect for him. I looked forward to seeing what he would bring to the role of a soldier back from Afghanistan telling his story of what happened over there.

When Tom performed his piece in class, his natural instincts, acting training, and intellectual understanding of the material were clearly showcased. But Tom's monologue never came to life. He brought no backstory, subtext, or real emotional connection to the life of the soldier. It was clear to me that Tom hadn't done enough preparation. When I asked him specific questions about his character, he came back with vague answers. Tom finally admitted that even though he had the piece for a week, he "hadn't really worked on it."

But why?

Tom had said that when he got his monologue, he loved it and instantly related to the character. He wrote down notes of what he wanted to do with the material and was eager to perform it. He was even thinking he would self-tape the piece to show for an upcoming agent meeting.

But during the week, whenever Tom had a chance to work on the monologue, something would inevitably stop him—roommate problems, girlfriend problems, yada, yada, yada. As such, Tom didn't commit to working on his monologue until two hours before class started.

I said to Tom, "But I thought you loved the piece, that you identified with it and were excited about performing it."

He replied sheepishly, "I know, I know." Then Tom smiled, shrugged, and said, "I'm just lazy."

I said, "No, Tom. You're not lazy. You're in your *fear*."

As you can imagine, Tom was caught off guard by my response. As a proud young man, he didn't take it well when I told him that he was afraid. I explained to him (and the class) that there really aren't *lazy* actors, just *fearful* actors. I told them that laziness is just an excuse, a reason, a guise, a cover used to hide what's really going on: **Fear.**

Let's break this down. Tom's micro career challenge was to prepare his monologue. He had a week to do it. He knew taking on this role would be challenging. However, completing it and performing the piece in the way he imagined would be the reward. By not immediately and consistently throwing himself into his work, Tom's feelings of self-doubt started to emerge. He began to think, "What if I'm not good enough to tackle this role?"

So, Tom kept delaying his acting work, using various personal excuses. What Tom did was succumb to his fear and walk away from this career challenge. He not only failed at completing his career challenge, but now he would never experience that reward: the joy of performing the scene like he knew he could. Tom's last hope was that he could muster up a performance without anyone noticing that he didn't do the work. I noticed, and I knew why.

Your fear is the root cause of why you don't address or complete career challenges, which then lays the groundwork for even more fear to set in and take hold. If you let the darker energy of fear override the lighter energy of joy in exploring and completing career tasks, it only leads you to one thing: self-sabotaging your career.

I've seen many actors sabotage their own career. I've seen actors consciously put off studying and honing their acting craft. I've seen actors make excuses for not doing what they came to their Industry City to do. I've seen actors talk themselves out of career opportunities. I've seen actors let their beautiful, innate talent wither and die. I've seen actors quit, never fulfilling their destiny.

This all comes from fear. It is your fear that stands in the way of you achieving your Want of becoming a successful actor. I like to say to my students:

"Don't be afraid to face your fear; it just might save your career."

FEAR is...False Evidence Appearing Real

Fear is a broad topic. There have been hundreds of books, TED Talks, podcasts, and a plethora of *Oprah* episodes tackling the complexities of fear. I'm not a psychiatrist and I don't pretend to be one (though I've spent many years on the couch tackling my own fears). Through many years of working in this industry, I can attest, however, to how fear plays a *very* active role in the life of an actor. The good news is if you feel fear in this business, it is a good indicator that this is your heart's desire.

What is fear? Fear is the anticipation of something terrible. Fear is anxiety and a lack of courage that causes trepidation about everything we do. Fear is also the enemy of ambition. Fear paralyzes us, drives us to inaction, and kills our momentum. Even worse, fear drives us to actions that will be counter-productive to achieving everything we want.

Fear is a lingering feeling that all actors share in some way, shape, or form. Fear permeates both the craft and the career. Actors fear that even if they prepare their acting work, they'll never be good enough. They fear that pursuing a career will be too much of a struggle. They fear that they won't be able to accept the changes an acting career will bring to their lives. And so on.

But here's the deal: you must *experience* your fear to *overcome* your fear. You need to push yourself to take risks, to tackle career challenges, to confront those things that are holding you back and to get past them. If you don't face your fears, they will become amplified in your mind and they will consume you, and you will ultimately fail. It is only when you deal with your fears that you can expect to experience positive outcomes and achieve success.

Think of someone skydiving for the first time. Regardless of how much that person wants to experience the thrill and how much they have prepared for this moment, there will be some fear leading up to the actual jump. In fact, there can be so much fear that they may second guess whether they even want to jump. At that point, they have a big decision to make. If they back out, they won't experience that thrill of jumping or that satisfying feeling of accomplishment. But if they gather their strength and courage and take the leap, they will have a life experience they can be proud of and remember forever.

Now, apply that to your acting career. There will be times when you will have a class assignment that seems difficult, a meeting with an agent or an audition for the perfect role. You will inevitably experience some nerves and fear before these career challenges. You might fear that you won't nail the scene, impress the agent, or that you'll forget your lines in the audition.

Once again, you will find yourself at a crossroads. For some actors, that fear can overwhelm them, and they'll sabotage themselves. They won't do their class work, they'll be late a few minutes for the agent meeting, or they won't properly prepare for their audition. But the real problem is that they are *not* facing what's making them act that way: their fear. To help solve that, here are my...

5 Steps to Overcoming Your Fear

As you move forward in this book, I will help you process and implement each of these *five steps*.

STEP 1: Acknowledge. You first *acknowledge* your fear, recognizing what it is and where it comes from, and accept that it resides in you.

STEP 2: Confront. You choose to *confront* your fear, walk toward it, stare it down, and face it head on.

STEP 3: Experience. You allow yourself to *experience* your fear, to stand in it, and fully embrace and accept the discomfort of it.

STEP 4: Work Through. You *work through* the discomfort of your fear by envisioning a positive result and believing that "I can do it!"

STEP 5: Overcome. You finally step past what's been holding you back. You feel proud, elated, and emboldened that you have *overcome* your fear.

> *"Take chances, make mistakes. That's how you grow. Pain nourishes your courage. You have to fail in order to practice being brave."*
> *-Mary Tyler Moore.*

Fear is Just a Feeling, Not a Fact

Fear is nothing more than an emotion you're experiencing, created by a scenario you're imagining that you believe to be true. Write this phrase down in your Actor's Journal: Fear is just a feeling, not a fact. Once you're able to own your fear and learn to process it, your fear will lose its power to dictate your thoughts, emotions, and actions.

When that happens, you can actually turn your feeling of fear into a positive feeling. You can change your definition of fear to "anticipatory excitement." You can learn to harness your fear and benefit from it, using it as fuel for all your career challenges. And I'll help you.

In the rest of this chapter and in the Workbook Section, we will examine where fear comes from, why you have certain fears, and how to overcome them. I will help you acknowledge and identify your fears, as well as address specific forms of self-sabotage. I will show you how you can use the Three Steps to Success to work past them, rebound from them, learn from them, and/or avoid them altogether.

> *"Try and fail, but never fail to try."*
> -Jared Leto

Where Does Your Fear Come From?

To help you examine your fears, you will need to take the Journey of Looking Inward and do a little self-analysis. It starts with discovering where your fear originates. Like talent, confidence, and perseverance, we are all born with a certain amount of fear. We also develop fears through our upbringing.

Fear is instilled in us throughout our childhood. We learn about fear and *what* we fear from our parents, siblings, teachers, friends, and, most of all, through our individual childhood experiences. The way we are raised and what we learn and experience in the world around us shapes how much fear we have and how willing we are to overcome that fear.

Did you have parents or guardians who encouraged you to take risks, to learn from your mistakes, to overcome your fears? *Or.* Did you have parents or guardians who, because of their own life circumstances, not give you the guidance or support you needed to tackle obstacles. *Or.* Did you have parents or guardians who actively discouraged you from trying new things or confronting challenges? Were there any specific circumstances or events in your upbringing that scarred you, that contributed to your fear?

Let's try and get a handle on how much fear you experienced in your upbringing. Once again, looking back at your childhood, answer the following seven questions with a "Yes," "No," or "Maybe" to get a better sense of where your fear comes from.

7 Questions to Ask Yourself About Fear

1) Were you afraid of what others thought of you? Were you the kid who needed to be liked? Were you afraid to do what you wanted to do out of fear of negative judgment from others? Did you always go along with the crowd to avoid making waves? Did you take it to heart when others criticized you? Were you overly sensitive to feedback from teachers and coaches?

2) Were you afraid that you weren't good enough? Were you hesitant to participate in an activity, project, or task because you were afraid that you wouldn't be able to do the job right? Did your fear of failing stop you from even trying?

3) Were the expectations too high? Did you show signs of being a perfectionist? Did you set excessively high expectations for yourself? Did others have high expectations of you? Did you fear letting others down? Did you fear letting yourself down?

4) Were you afraid of being wrong? Were you afraid to do or say something perceived as being "wrong?" Were you punished if you didn't do the task correctly? Were you put down when you made a mistake? Were you told that you were a disappointment? Were you made to feel that you could never do anything "right?"

5) Were you overly protected? Were you held back from taking risks, discovering things on your own, or learning from your mistakes? Were you sheltered and insulated from the harsh realities of disappointment, rejection, and failure? Did you receive a trophy or medal even though you came in last?

6) Were you discouraged from asserting yourself? Were you ridiculed or told to "be quiet" when expressing your own opinions? Were your thoughts and ideas suppressed as a child? Were you repeatedly told "No?" Were you told "You can't do it" or "Don't ask why" when expressing ambition or curiosity?

7) Did your achievements go unrecognized? Were you not rewarded or even acknowledged for completing projects, accomplishing tasks, reaching goals, or winning? Were you deprived of the reassurance that you did a good job? Were your achievements ignored, or even worse, dismissed? Did you feel invisible?

After you answer these seven questions about fear in your childhood, you need to examine how many of your answers still apply today. Chances are many of them still play a factor in the fear you have as an adult. Do you still worry about what others think of you? Do you still feel like you're "not good enough?" Do you still feel the pressure of expectations from both yourself and from others?

Fear is such a challenge, for it takes root at birth, grows through childhood, and blossoms in adulthood. All people, especially actors, face the challenges that fear brings. And your fears in life will easily translate into fears in your career in some way, shape, or form.

THE TWO TYPES OF FEAR

There are two distinct types of fears that actors face:

The Fear of Failure and **The Fear of Success.**

Both kinds of fear show themselves in many ways. Both emerge more than you would think, and both are equally powerful. Universal to every actor are the constantly dueling fears of "What if I don't make it?" and "What if I *do* make it?" While some actors have more of a Fear of Failure and others have more of a Fear of Success, all actors experience both.

No matter how much talent, confidence, and perseverance you've developed, there will always be an underlying fear of being rejected, humiliated, shamed, and falling flat on your face. Equally, there will always be a fear of the new career challenges and the inevitable change that success will bring. For many actors, it becomes easy to see the possibilities of failure as well as the difficulties of success.

Regardless of how much experience you have in the industry, both Fear of Failure and Fear of Success can dictate how you go about pursuing your acting career.

"You've got to experience failure to understand that you can survive it."
-Tina Fey

THE FEAR OF FAILURE

Don't be afraid to *try* because you're afraid to *fail*.

There's nothing wrong with failure. When you fail, it means you have taken risks and accepted challenges. Only in failure can you learn why your actions (or inactions) were a mistake. Only in failure do you gain the *insight* into how to correct those mistakes. As you read about the Fear of Failure, keep in mind it's about recognizing it in yourself and getting you to turn that fear into something positive for you and your career.

Fear of Failure is a fear that you are going to fail at something you want to achieve. Failure can mean different things to different people. Therefore, you need to figure out what it means for you to fail, why you're afraid to fail, and what lessons can be learned from failing.

Your Fear of Failure can be as varied as your fear of flunking a test to never experiencing true love to not accomplishing your lifelong dream, and so on. Your reasons for fearing failure might be humiliation, embarrassment, abandonment, etc.

Embarking on an acting career is a daunting venture, and you should be aware of that fact as you enter it. Before you set foot in this business, you already may have an inherent Fear of Failure. It's like a soldier going off to war. There are expectations of danger, that they might find themselves in battle or in harm's way. The soldier knows that going in, and they naturally fear that risk. As actors, you know that there are many more actors who fail than those who "make it." So, you fear *that* risk.

There are other ways a Fear of Failure plays into your acting career that go well beyond an overall fear of not realizing your dream. A Fear of Failure also plays into the rejection you face, the pressures of this business, the expectations of your family, and how you perceive yourself. The Fear of Failure is the ever-present feeling that pursuing an acting career was the wrong choice.

I have identified eight different factors that fall under Fear of Failure. These are all crippling fears that, unfortunately, most actors share. The problem is that many of these fears relate to each other. They build off one another, deepening that overall Fear of Failure. Some of you might experience these fears to varying degrees, but it's important to look at each of them closely and see which ones apply to you.

To start, find the one fear that stands out to you, that feels like it impacts you the most. As you know, the first step to overcoming fear is to acknowledge it. I want you to write it down in your Actor's Journal. You may want to pick several fears, but for now, just choose and acknowledge one.

8 Fear Factors of Failure

1) You fear you're not good enough. Every actor has felt this before, even the greats. There is always that lingering feeling that you're not good enough, or not smart enough, not pretty enough, not skinny enough, not talented enough, etc. Most actors who struggle with this in their personal life most certainly bring it into their acting career. You will compare yourself to other actors. You fear that you don't belong or that you're not cut out for show business.

2) You fear you will disappoint your family. It's important for many of us to make our family proud of who we are and what we're doing with our lives. You fear what your family will think you're not successful. You never want to let your family down, especially if they are supportive of you and your career. A family's constant encouragement, high hopes, and even financial investment can put unnecessary pressure on you to succeed as an actor, to show them that their support isn't going to waste.

3) You fear your family will be proved right. Like many actors, you probably didn't choose the career path your parents had planned for you. Instead, you chose to ignore their advice, to go against their wishes and pursue this dream. You came to your Industry City with no emotional or financial support from your family. All you have is a desire to succeed. The fear is, "But what if they're right?" There is a fear that if you fail, you will have to admit defeat, suffer the humiliation, face your family, and prepare to hear the inevitable "I told you so."

4) You fear your own expectations. You set high expectations for yourself in this business. You have a clear vision for your future. You have planned out a career path, and the fear of not reaching your goals can be crushing. You fear disappointing yourself more than anyone. You're afraid that if you fail, you will *really* feel like a failure.

5) You fear you're sacrificing a stable life. Many of us are taught at a young age that life goes as follows: school, college, job, marriage, better job, mortgage, kids, promotion, savings, retirement. An acting career doesn't really follow that pattern (or any pattern for that matter). There is always that fear in the back of your mind that you're letting that "planned" path fall by the wayside. You are sacrificing the lifelong stability that path might have offered you for a career with a lot more risk.

6) You fear you're missing other career opportunities. Chances are there is something else that you excel at, another talent or skill you possess. You fear that you might be giving up other opportunities at success while you pursue this acting dream. Maybe you could have been a writer, an architect, an athlete, a designer, etc. It's a fear that you made the wrong career decision in your life and you hope you never have to look back and say, "What if?"

7) You fear you'll never be a "star." You fear that you won't get your chance in the spotlight. You fear that, for whatever reason, you'll never have your day in the sun. You will always be a co-star, a day player, or at best, a guest star. You fear that you will never really get a chance to shine and show people your full artistic potential.

8) You fear the unknown. You don't know what to expect with an acting career—and there's no security or stability in this everchanging business—so you are afraid to move forward. Lack of predictability and control are contributing factors to the fear of the unknown. It's a discomfort that comes with not knowing or being able to plan and prepare for what's coming next. It is the uncertainty about what will (or won't) happen, and that feeling can be overwhelming.

Once you have acknowledged and written down in your Actor's Journal which of these eight fears most applies to you, it's time to take the next step... Confront it. Reset your mind, take a deep breath, be courageous, and *confront* your fear. Try to visualize your fear, in whatever form, standing in front of you.

Then speak out loud to it...

> *"Hey Fear of Failure...I see you. I feel your dark presence. I feel your control over me. I want you gone. So, starting today, you're in for a fight!"*

Congratulations! You have acknowledged and confronted one of your biggest Fears of Failure and started moving past it. Once you have done that with this fear, go back to the list and see which others you might need to take through the same process.

THE FEAR OF SUCCESS

You might wonder, "Who would fear being a rich, famous, successful actor?" Believe it or not, the Fear of Success can be just as prevalent as the Fear of Failure.

Many actors aren't prepared to deal with the success an acting career could bring and therefore, they fear it. Whether consciously or unconsciously, they prevent themselves from achieving their goals. In each actor, there is a fear of how things would *change* if they did become successful. There are new pressures and new challenges that accompany success. For many actors, this fear starts to emerge after the initial taste of success: getting an agent, booking a job, getting noticed, etc.

If you think back to my student Tom and his story at the beginning of the chapter, he experienced a Fear of Success. He told me that since he had been doing so well over the ten-week class and had received so much good feedback, he didn't think he could live up to the higher expectations and the pressure.

Plus, Tom's plan was to self-tape the piece as something to show for an upcoming agent meeting. After listening to me talk about fear, he realized that he was fearful of that agent meeting…but not of *failing*. Rather, he was afraid the meeting would go well, which would bring him up to the "next level" in his career. Then he would have no excuse not to go forward. He was afraid of his potential for success, and it stopped him from doing the work.

Before we tackle Fear of Success, it's important to first define what *success* means to you. Every actor has a different idea of success. Some actors are content just making enough money to support themselves and their family while others want the fame, acclaim, and the big house in the hills.

What does success mean for you in your acting career? How would having that success change your life? Just like a Fear of Failure, this Fear of Success can take on many different shapes. It comes from pressures and expectations—both internal and external—as well as a preoccupation about the perceptions of others.

Fear of Success also stems from having to change your lifestyle: status, finances, environment, workload, relationships, etc. Change is hard. Many of us fear change, and if success brings change, and lots of it…then we will fear success.

I have identified eight different factors that fall under the Fear of Success. You need to realize that just like the Fear Factors of Failure, these will often build upon each other and add to your overall Fear of Success. Once again, you will experience these fears to varying degrees, but it's important to identify which are the strongest in your life.

Just like you did with Fear of Failure, find the one fear that stands out to you, the one that impacts you the most. I want you to write it down in your Actor's Journal. You may want to pick several fears, but for now, just choose and acknowledge one.

8 Fear Factors of Success

1) You fear your potential. Just like with a Fear of Failure, actors will not give 100 percent because they're afraid of success. When you fear your potential, you fear the emotional and psychological work it would take for you to be your best. You know you can be an amazing actor with a long and successful career, but you fear the internal work involved for you to be as great as you can be.

2) You fear you will forfeit your "bohemian lifestyle." There is a lot of poetry in the life of a struggling artist. There is a fear that if you do anything "commercial," it might ruin the integrity of your art and corrupt your creativity. You fear that success might also set you apart from your "starving artist" friends. You fear the repercussions that this change of status will bring, not only in your own life, but also in how others will perceive you. You fear that your friends might envy your success or be jealous of your career, which would then change your relationships.

3) You fear you will have to work harder. You fear that success might mean longer days, a harried schedule, more commitments, and less time to hang out with your friends and family, watch TV, scroll through social media, play video games, or surf the internet. You feel you will always be stressed and exhausted. Working harder often means leaving your comfort zone and that can be scary.

4) You fear you will lose your privacy. You want to be a successful actor, but you fear that you couldn't handle the scrutiny that goes along with it. You fear you will be living your life in a fishbowl, in the public eye, having your private life out there for all to see, examine, and judge. There is a fear—especially now that everyone has a camera and a social media account—that anything you do or say as a public figure will go "viral" and be broadcast for millions to see. You're afraid that you will lose your anonymity and your ability to live your life as you did before.

5) You fear others' expectations of you. As you succeed, you *will* face higher expectations, and you're afraid that you won't be able to live up to those expectations, whether they are set by your family, friends, representation, or the public. You fear letting people down. You fear that people will expect you to be brilliant *all the time*. They will expect you to always look amazing, put together, charming, or "funny like you are on TV!" It's a fear that you will always have to be "on."

6) You fear your own expectations. As you get a taste of success, you will continue to set higher goals and expectations. You fear that those goals might get to be too high, and you'll no longer be able to reach them. If you do well in acting class one week, you fear you won't be able to top your performance the next week. If you receive great acclaim for your first film role, you fear how you will fare in the next. You fear the more successful you become, the tougher it will be to maintain that success.

7) You fear that you might be a "fraud." You fear you might not be as good as your acting coach, agent, or even your audience believes you to be. You fear that you may have just gotten lucky. You fear that you really don't have the talent and you aren't worthy of all the attention, accolades, and acclaim. You question why this success is happening to you and you wonder if you really deserve it.

8) You fear your family will steal your spotlight. There is a fear that as soon as you start getting successful, your family dynamic will change. You fear your family will want and expect more from you, and not just your immediate family but also your family of friends. You fear that they will try to take over your life, therefore suffocating you and your individuality. The fear is your family will overwhelm you, invading your privacy and putting more pressure on you to sustain your success. You fear that they will try to selfishly benefit from your success by asking for favors or from your celebrity status by spilling your secrets to the media.

Once you have acknowledged and written down in your Actor's Journal which of these eight fears most applies to you, it's time to take the next step... Confront it. Reset your mind, take a deep breath, be courageous, and *confront* your fear. Try to visualize your fear, in whatever form, standing in front of you.

Then speak out loud to it...

> *"Hey Fear of Success...I see you. I feel your dark presence. I feel your control over me. I want you gone. So, starting today, you're in for a fight!"*

Congratulations! You have now acknowledged and confronted one of your biggest Fears of Success and started moving past it. Once you have done that with this fear, go back to the list and see which others you might need to take through the same process.

Don't Be Afraid to Give 100 Percent!

When it comes to your class work, audition prep, and career challenges, many actors aren't willing to invest 100 percent: physically, mentally, spiritually, emotionally. Not giving 100 percent of yourself to your work, your career, has nothing to do with you being lazy or less ambitious; you're just in your fear.

Not putting 100 percent into your work safeguards you from both your conscious and unconscious Fear of Failure or Fear of Success.

You feel that if you put 100 percent of your time, energy, and passion into your class work, auditions, and career, and you *fail*...the fall will be much harder to take. You fear the ramifications of being a failure: humiliation, embarrassment, abandonment. Therefore, you will only put in 50 percent of your time, energy, and passion.

The idea is the less you invest, the less the hurt, pain, or embarrassment you will feel if you fail. You can save face by shrugging it off and saying, "I didn't give it my all."

On the flip side, you feel that if you put 100 percent of your time, energy, and passion into your class work, auditions, and career, and you *succeed*, you'll have to deal with great change. Actors who don't give their all have grown content with their lifestyle, expectations, ideas, and plans...and success would only alter those. So, the less effort you put forward in fulfilling your potential, the less you'll have to worry about change.

Most of you will start with a Fear of Failure because you haven't had that taste of success yet, at least not in your acting career. Some of you might start with a Fear of Success because you've experienced success before in show business or some other aspect of your life.

Whether from a Fear of Failure or Fear of Success, this misguided philosophy is something that runs rampant among many actors in this business who prevent themselves from committing 100 percent to their careers. Once it becomes a regular habit, these actors won't even put in the 50 percent. Their efforts will continue to diminish until they stop trying altogether. At that point, it's time to pick a new career.

You need to give it your all or nothing will happen. No risk, no gain. No pain, no glory. Always remember that you must experience your fear to overcome it. And you can overcome it. You *must* overcome it. A way to achieve that is to do the exercise "Identifying Your Fear" in the Workbook Section.

"Maybe the thing you're most scared of is actually the thing you should do."
-Chris Evans

Fear Manifests into Self-Sabotage

Whether it's the Fear of Success, the Fear of Failure, or both, this fear impacts everything you do in your career, from the choices you make to the actions you take (or fail to take). Both these powerful fears can lead you down a path of self-sabotage, causing you to pass up career opportunities and take on any number of distractions, addictions, and wrong actions.

For the rest of Section Two, I will show you how giving into fear will negatively affect your career, your craft, and your life. I will give you tools, guidelines, and advice on how to avoid the path of self-sabotage altogether. And I will help you correct any past mistakes by showing you the right actions to take.

I have identified the most prevalent ways you let fear sabotage you from fulfilling your dream of becoming a successful actor. I call it…

The Three Ways to Sabotage Your Career.

FEAR: WORKBOOK SECTION

EXPLORING YOUR FEAR

What Do You Fear?

Whether you do the following exercise on your own, in class, or with your CTAG, it will open your eyes and make you consciously aware of what fears stand in your way of being a successful actor. If you're consciously aware of something, then you have a better chance of confronting it, experiencing it, working through it, and ultimately overcoming it.

EXERCISE: **IDENTIFYING YOUR FEAR**

This exercise requires you to look inward, to dig deep inside yourself, and to be completely honest. It's a self-examination of your fears and how they relate to your career.

When it comes to your career, what do you fear? Open your Actor's Journal and on one page, at the top, write this down:

If I fail, I fear...

Then fill up that page with random thoughts about your Fears of Failure. Simply finish this sentence as many times as you can. Don't edit yourself. Write down every possible fear that you have about your career. Write down whatever thoughts come to mind, but don't analyze them. Don't cross off anything or dismiss anything. Just let your thoughts flow on to the page, like a free-flowing stream of consciousness.

When you've exhausted all those fears, turn to a fresh sheet. At the top of that one, write down:

If I succeed, I fear...

Fill up that page with your thoughts about your Fears of Success. Once again, write as much as you can and be as honest as possible. These are your personal thoughts, reflections, your individual fears you have about your career.

I did this exercise in class and afterward, I asked my students if there were any fears on their list they felt comfortable enough to share. Here are some fears that my students shared:

If I *fail*, I fear...

I will disappoint my parents.
I will never get anyone to love me.
I won't be able to afford things that I want.
I'm going to waste a good portion of my life pursuing an acting career.

I'll be humiliated in front of a casting director.
I won't have enough money to even eat.
I'll have to borrow more money from my parents.
I will have to settle for a life as a server.
I will always wonder, "What if?"
I will get high all the time.
I'll never realize my potential.

If I *succeed*, I fear...

I won't be loved for who I really am.
I won't have anyone I can really trust.
I will have more attention than I want.
My agent will expect more from me.
Friends and family will ask me for favors.
I will always have to be great.
I will have to change my lifestyle.
I won't ever have privacy again.
I will be canceled for doing something.
I will have to work much harder than I ever expected.
I'll never be as good of as I'm supposed to be.

One thing you'll probably notice is that you share elements of *both* a Fear of Failure and a Fear of Success. If you look at them closely, you'll see that Fear of Success and Fear of Failure are just two different sides of the same internal struggle. Some may lean more toward a Fear of Failure while others lean more toward a Fear of Success. However, the two are closely connected under the umbrella of fear.

Identifying Your Fear with Your CTAG

You can also do this exercise with your CTAG. If you do, follow the same process as I've instructed with all the other CTAG exercises. You'll need a location, comfortable chairs, and your Actor's Journal.

Each member will participate. On the top of one page of your Actor's Journal, write down, "If I fail, I fear..." and take five minutes to free associate and write down what comes to mind. Then turn the page over and write at the top, "If I succeed, I fear..." and do the same thing.

After those ten minutes, stop writing. Then discuss each other's fears and how they relate to your acting careers. This exercise is meant to give you a deeper understanding of what fears may be blocking you from being a successful actor.

Don't be afraid to keep some of your fears and the negative events that caused those fears private. No CTAG members should judge, critique, or analyze anyone else's fears. This is just a discussion. Also, anything discussed should remain confidential to the group. You will find that many of you share similar career fears and talking about them can be very illuminating and comforting.

THE
THREE WAYS
TO
SABOTAGE
YOUR CAREER

DISTRACTIONS

ADDICTIONS

WRONG ACTIONS

"Your ability to adapt to failure, and navigate your way out of it, absolutely 100 percent makes you who you are. "
-Viola Davis

DISTRACTIONS

Oh, how we love them!

Distractions are the trickiest of the Three Ways to Sabotage Your Career because they are the most elusive, the hardest to recognize.

Distractions are difficult for most actors to detect both in their personal lives and in their acting careers because they often appear comforting and familiar. As such, you don't necessarily see distractions for what they really are: diversions taking you away from tackling your career challenges.

All actors need to take time to reboot and refresh, to practice self-care, relaxation, meditation, and mindfulness. It's important to set aside time to be with friends or family, go on a date, watch a sitcom, play a video game, read a book, work out, play with your pet, and so on. These are all healthy, constructive ways to unwind, recharge, and clear your mind.

But these diversions are only beneficial to you and your career when used in *moderation*. The problem occurs when these occasional positive diversions from life's stresses turn into consistent negative distractions that keep you from doing your acting work. And the kicker is, it's *your* choice. By giving into these distractions, you are making a conscious decision to choose something comforting and familiar over something challenging and rewarding. And that leads to self-sabotage.

Why Do We Get Distracted?

The answer is simple: distractions make us feel *safe*.

Distractions pull us away from the hard work, the hassles of life, and into an environment where we feel we are in control. What makes distractions so enticing is that they are fun, familiar, and pressure-free. Distractions often put us at ease, make us feel calm, and soothe our minds.

Because your career path can be so unpredictable and unstable, it's easy to search for something more solid and tangible to grab onto. But distractions are nothing more than a "security blanket," a way for you to pull the sheets over your head, curl up in a fetal position, and block out all the difficulties of your acting career. And oh, how we love them!

The reason you spend more energy losing yourself in your distractions than doing your acting work is because you are *fearful*. You are fearful of your potential, of the unknown, of the inevitable hard work of your acting career. It is fear that's causing you to distance yourself from your career challenges and lose yourself in distractions.

You don't have the time to let fear lead you to distractions. As you forge forward, you will have to explore so much unchartered territory that you can't be fearful. You must march into those places with strength, desire, and an unshakable will.

You have the power to prevent these distractions from diverting you off your path by always remembering your life's purpose: to impact others with your talent.

However, there are some distractions you will face that will appear to be out of your control. These distractions tend to be the most damaging for actors and come from some unlikely and unexpected sources.

The 3 Most Common Distractions

1) Money
2) Family
3) Romantic Relationships

It's understandable that *Money* would be a common distraction as most of us have, at some point, faced financial struggles. While those with a stable career know that money will be coming in with a steady paycheck, for you actors just starting out, acting gigs are often few and far between. There's no guarantee as to when you'll book your next job and get your next paycheck. Actors, for the most part, are financially handicapped, and that lack of money can distract you from focusing on your career.

But *Family* and *Romantic Relationships* as common distractions?

Your parents, significant others, lovers, and even your friends can all distract you from your career. Now don't jump to conclusions; I'm not going to spend this chapter telling you to sever ties with your loved ones. Family and relationships are vital to having a happy, fulfilling life. However, I will show you how these positive influences can sometimes turn negative—deterring you, pressuring you, and veering you off your career path.

A successful career in Hollywood or any Industry City requires a great deal of focus and energy. You don't have time to be distracted. Let's examine these Most Common Distractions and figure out where they come from, how they affect you, and how you can navigate around them to stay on track.

> *"Your real competition is your distraction."*
> -Author unknown

MONEY DISTRACTIONS

Your dreams and goals, your day-to-day activities, your moods, mindset, and outlook on life are all affected by **Money.** It affects your relationships, *where* you live and *how* you live. Money affects everything, including your acting career.

For actors, money is *the* most common of all the distractions.

There are so many actors that are forced to cut their career short, before it even gets off the ground, because they don't have enough money. A lack of money is the number one reason students "take a break" from acting class. I have seen actors start to progress in their craft, to a point where they're ready to move up to the next level, then suddenly need to leave class—stopping all the momentum they built up—because they run out of money.

If you remember from the Perseverance chapter, I said you need to come to Hollywood or any Industry City with sufficient funds. No matter how much you have in the bank, you will go through it quickly. The cost of living is much greater in most big cities, whether you're talking about housing, transportation, clothes, groceries, or entertainment.

Pursuing an acting career is also a costly venture, especially when you're first getting started. Many actors are unable to cope with the career costs, be it acting class, headshots, demo reels, etc. So, they pack up and leave before they even get started.

Money is the deadliest of the distractions because it can derail you and your career for years. And it can happen in several ways.

I Need to Take a Break

Here are three stories of talented actors from my acting studio in Hollywood who let money distract them from their dreams. You will notice in all three stories that each actor had high hopes and was very ambitious about their career...and then money issues got in the way. Chances are you will identify with one of them. Let their stories be a lesson for you.

Lexi's Money Story

Backstory: Lexi's dream was to be a film actress. Lexi came to Hollywood brimming with talent and with money in the bank. She immediately got into class and progressed in her craft. After six months, however, she came to me and said, "I need to take a break." She hadn't gotten a survival job and her savings had dried up quicker than she thought. She had to leave acting class, find a job, and put her dream on hold.

There are those actors like Lexi who live off their savings when they move to their Industry City. They save up their money before moving so that they don't have to get a job (at least, right away). Rather, they think they can spend all their time focusing on building their acting career. They assume their savings will last them longer than it does.

While actors like Lexi might have it good for a while, their savings will eventually dry up, often quicker than they think. If they haven't found a survival job to help supplement their savings, they'll be in big trouble. For Lexi, her weekly classes, as well as her other acting and career work, came to a sudden halt because she ran out of money and had to find a full-time job.

Many actors don't realize how long it takes and how much it costs to get settled in their Industry City and get their acting career going. They come with an unrealistic belief that they can get their big break in, like, six months. Therefore, they spend money without bringing money in. They might be spending their savings on something positive for their career—class, headshots, demo reel, etc.—but they don't balance it with a survival job. Even as they continue to spend, they *still* don't get a survival job. Eventually it gets to the point where they have nothing left to show for it other than an empty bank account. Then they do get distracted from their acting career because they can't afford to continue their pursuit.

The same problem arises for those actors that are financially supported by their family. You must assume that eventually, at some point, any family funding of your career will run out. If you don't have a survival job backing up that financial support, your career will come to a screeching halt. Plus, with family supporting you, there is always that extra sense of obligation and that pressure to succeed that comes when someone else is holding the checkbook.

Regardless of how much savings you have or how much you are being financially supported, be aware that it *will* run out. This money will help get you started, but you need something to supplement those initial funds. That is why you need to get a survival job as soon as you set foot in your Industry City.

Paul's Money Story

Backstory: Paul's dream was to be a sitcom actor. Paul came to Hollywood and did everything he was supposed to do right away, including getting a survival job and getting into class. He was a smart, funny actor who quickly landed a manager. After eight months, Paul told me, "I need to take a break." He said his survival job wasn't paying enough for him to continue and he had to leave acting class to save money, putting his dream on hold.

There are many actors like Paul who come to their Industry City and get a survival job, but never seem to have enough money to put toward their career. They may be working, but it's still not enough to make ends meet. While I sympathize with Paul and understand his plight, using the excuse that you don't have enough money to pursue your acting career is unacceptable.

You live in a big city and regardless of how many actors are looking for work, there are endless opportunities for jobs. Many famous actors have gone on talk shows and chatted about their "hungry years," their "salad days," where they had to take on multiple odd survival jobs—janitor, nanny, birthday clown, anything to get the money needed to continue pursuing their career. I'm not saying it will necessarily be a glamorous job, but it will pay the bills, and that's what matters.

Not making enough money in your survival job is a legitimate career challenge, but there is a way you can overcome it:

Get *another* survival job.

At the beginning of this book, you signed a contract pledging to do whatever needed to be done to make it happen. You made a commitment to yourself to work hard at achieving your goal of becoming a successful actor. Part of that work includes your survival job(s); earning the money you need to fuel your hopes and dreams, your career.

You can't be afraid to work and work hard. You must be willing to work one, two, or even *three* jobs! If that's what it takes to fulfill your obligation to yourself and your career, then that's what you must do. I know many successful actors who had to work three survival jobs in order to stay in class and keep their dream alive.

Sure, you need to occasionally take some time off for yourself, but if you're sitting around daydreaming, scrolling through social media, or complaining to your friend about how you don't have enough money, you have the time to get another survival job!

Marty's Money Story

Backstory: Marty's dream was to work on a TV crime drama. Marty came to Hollywood with his wife to finally pursue his lifelong dream of being an actor. After fifteen years of working in advertising, Marty was able to get a survival job as a part-time advertising consultant. He got into class, quickly made headway in his acting, and booked a web series. After ten months, Marty told me, "I need to take a break." He explained that his part-time job became full-time with a salary increase, benefits and extra responsibilities. Marty had to once again put his dream on hold.

Actors like Marty will place financial security as their top priority. These are the actors that get wrapped up in their survival job and neglect their acting career. There is an underlying concern or need for financial security and stability, so much so that making money eventually becomes their only priority.

If you're serious about an acting career, your survival job is only there to help you…survive. Your survival job is only meant to fund your life and your acting career necessities, not *become* your life and take you away from pursuing your dream. Don't let yourself get wrapped up in your survival job. While you need to make money, you also need to prioritize and find a job that will be flexible and understanding to your acting needs. Trust me, they exist.

Also, if you have *another* full-time career, it will be more challenging for you to succeed as an actor. Acting requires too much dedication and attention; it's a full-time job. An outside career comes with its own responsibilities, commitments, and pressures. It might bring financial stability to your life, but now you're struggling with time, which is just as valuable. Although I have seen many actors try to balance the two, often it's the acting career that suffers.

If You Don't Have Enough Time, Make Time

I constantly hear actors complain that they don't have enough *time* in the day to balance their career challenges, survival job(s), personal responsibilities, free time, etc. The truth is…yes, you do.

Time management is imperative for an actor pursuing a career. Here is a very simple breakdown of what your daily time schedule should look like. Let's look at an average day during a Monday through Friday work week, divvied up in hourly increments:

Average Weekday = 24 hours

Sleep = *8 hours*
Survival job(s) = *8 hours*
Career challenges = *4 hours*
Friends, Family, Me Time = *4 hours*

If you multiply your daily allowance for career challenges (four hours) by five days (for a normal work week), that means you've got twenty hours to work on your acting career, plus the forty hours for jobs to help you finance your pursuit. That's sixty hours a week that should be spent supporting and maintaining your life as an actor financially and artistically. And that doesn't even include the weekend! That's another forty-eight hours you can split up and use however you need.

If you "don't have enough time," make time.

Fear Leads to Money Distractions

Most actors find themselves facing money distractions at some point in the beginning stages of their acting career. The reason for this form of self-sabotage is fear.

As I mentioned, there is an underlying fear in actors when it comes to taking on both their micro and macro career challenges. It goes back to that idea of having to invest 100 percent in what they're doing. Actors often misguidedly believe that if they invest in their career *completely*, there's a greater risk of failing (Fear of Failure). So, they find excuses to avoid fully investing, and one of the excuses they use most is money.

Actors will blame a lack of money for why they're not taking class, getting headshots, or even auditioning. They'll simply say, "I can't afford it," and that releases them from their obligations, which alleviates their fear.

Or they may fear the opposite...

Actors may fear having *more* money will put them one step closer to their dream and the change of lifestyle that comes with it (Fear of Success). They choose *not* to make more money. The idea is, if they increase their finances, then they have no excuse but to enter that risky, unfamiliar, and often uncomfortable territory of an acting career. In a way, they feel safer not increasing their funds. If they don't have the money, they don't have to face their fear.

Fear of Working Too Hard

Many actors also have the fear of working too hard, and the anxiety that is caused when feeling overwhelmed. It's a common fear in any profession. But when you're pursuing acting, you essentially have to balance both your career and your financial needs, your acting work and your survival job(s). There is a fear for actors that they won't be able to balance the two. They fear that finding time for both will make them feel stressed out or exhausted, which will hamper their pursuit of being an actor.

Think back to the three money stories. Lexi relies solely on her savings while she pursues her career, as she feels a survival job would put too much on her plate, giving her too much to handle. Paul is fearful of working *another* survival job because the long workdays wouldn't leave him enough time to give to his acting work. Marty shares the same fears of being overwhelmed and working too hard, as well as how to balance an acting career with his need for stability and security. These fears also tie in with a fear of the unknown. Lexi, Paul, and Marty truly don't know what trying to balance both would actually entail.

Fear of being overwhelmed, working too hard, not being able to balance your various responsibilities, as well as the fear of the unknown are common fears for many actors. And the only way to find out if that fear is real is to get a survival job(s) and experience it for yourself.

How to Work Through Your Money Distractions

If you're serious about your acting career, there is no reason to let this fear distract you. Remember, fear is a feeling, not a fact. You have the power and the energy to work and work hard. You can learn how to manage and be productive with your time. You can do whatever you need to do to survive and thrive in your acting career.

Trust that you won't be overwhelmed, that you are capable of working a survival job(s) and your acting career at the same time. Have faith that you have the stamina, the strength, and the drive to work a long day. Believe that you're ambitious enough to put in the extra hours, eager enough to learn and experience more, smart enough to organize and prioritize your life, and dedicated enough to make it all happen.

The best way to believe is to *do it!*

Think of this experience of working long days on your career and your survival jobs as preparation for your life as a successful actor. When you become a successful actor, you will work even harder than you do now...whether you have one, two, or three jobs! When you're a successful actor, you will wake up before dawn to work out, appear on a morning talk show, head to the set to film for twelve hours, and have just enough time to dress up and hit the red carpet for a Hollywood premiere. Then you'll hit the sack, ready to do it all over again the next day.

This process of being a hard-working actor will not only rid you of money distractions, but also help you fulfill your dreams and build character, responsibility, discipline, and a strong work ethic.

> *"Do what you have to do until you can do what you want to do."*
> -Oprah Winfrey

FAMILY DISTRACTIONS

As you have seen from reading this book, there is no greater influence on you and your life than your **Family**.

Your family not only shapes your upbringing, personality, goals, and dreams, it also shapes how you handle certain pressures, fears, and responsibilities.

Unless you've come from a destructive, abusive upbringing, I believe your family loves you and tried to do their best in raising you. To begin to resolve any issues with your family, you need to first believe that they tried to give you the best upbringing they could.

That said, sometimes their "best" can still leave you feeling fearful, insecure, and lonely. The effects of your upbringing and the relationship that you have with your family now—good or bad—can also involve a lot of pressure. That pressure your family puts on you, whether consciously or subconsciously, can lead to you self-sabotaging.

While there are many ways that family distraction can manifest itself, I have identified the two most common: **Lack of Support and/or Understanding** and **Being the Family Point Person.** They are both equally detrimental to your career challenges and career goals.

Lack of Support and/or Understanding

"What are you doing with your life?"

That's the question that many actors dread hearing from their mothers, fathers, or any family member.

Chances are, when you first brought up the idea of moving to an Industry City to become a struggling actor, your family didn't understand why you would take on such a risky venture. For some of you, they also may have not supported your decision.

That lack of support from your family and the pressure that comes along with it is a distraction. All it does is build up and reinforce your negative thoughts. You fear that you are destined to fail, that your family will be proved right. You constantly question whether you made the right choice because they constantly remind you that you made the wrong choice. Your family doesn't consider acting a real career and they wonder when this "phase" will pass.

Family expectations and pressure can put an enormous amount of weight on your shoulders. Not only is it a *physical* distraction that keeps you from doing your career work, it's also an *emotional* distraction that eats away at your confidence and self-worth, a *mental* distraction that shifts your focus from what's important to you, and a *spiritual* distraction that takes a heavy toll on the soul.

I have seen actors come into class feeling dejected or demoralized after a simple phone call with a family member. There was a very talented actor named Andy who began to come to class looking defeated and unmotivated. One day after class, I took Andy aside and asked him what was wrong. Andy told me that before class, he had just gotten off his weekly "What are you doing with your life?" call from his father.

He's not alone. Actors hear questions like this from their family all the time:

> "What is it that you do again?"
> "Have you gotten any work?"
> "When will I see you on TV?"
> "Is acting really a good career choice?"
> "Do you *really* want to be an actor?"
> "When are you going to get a real job?"

And of course...

> "What are you doing with your life?"

These questions are not necessarily asked in malice. They might truly be asked out of concern, with the best of intentions. That's where the lack of understanding comes in. Unless you have family members that are artists themselves, they probably don't understand the desire and need to pursue a career in the arts. They don't understand the work and sacrifices you need to make to pursue your dream.

Even if your family does support you, they probably still have many of the same concerns that come from this lack of understanding. They worry that an acting career is not a dependable, respectable, financially stable profession …not nearly as much as a career in law, medicine, marketing, or technology. They worry about the struggle, the rejection, and the fact that you appear to be risking stability and security for a chance to be a working actor. You become so impacted by your family's worries and concerns that it puts enormous pressure on you to succeed.

Family Expectations and Birth Order

When it comes to family expectations about having a stable career and providing for your family, both men and women experience similar pressures. There is an expectation for you to settle down with a life partner, save and invest money, start a family, buy a house, etc. Some may argue that men feel this familial pressure more, as there is still a "male provider" mentality. But I see many actors from all genders, ethnicities, and ages deal with pressure from their family to be the provider.

The amount of pressure your family puts on you for following an acting career path also tends to relate to your *position* in the family.

There are several studies that explore the mysteries of birth order and how the youngest child is treated differently than the oldest child, who's treated differently than the middle child, and so on. I'm not going to delve too deeply into the psychology of birth order, but I can tell you that I have witnessed firsthand some of the results of these studies.

The oldest child in any family tends to get the most amount of pressure to succeed. There is often a lot more attention paid to that child than future siblings and thus, more expectations are put on that child. In most family dynamics, the eldest is often the leader, the most responsible, the one who gets more schooling and usually picks a traditional career that offers financial stability.

On the flip side, the youngest child tends to be the most rebellious. They are often the most creative and the most willing to pursue an artistic career path. In fact, through my years of being an acting coach, I discovered that out of hundreds of actors questioned about their birth order, most were the babies of the family. The youngest child doesn't tend to deal with as much family expectations and pressures. They are often left alone to follow their own path. They are often the social ones, the risk-takers.

The middle child tends to lean either way but never as extreme as the other two. No matter what age, actors that

I've talked to who are middle children often jokingly identify as either a "Jan" (from *The Brady Bunch*) or a "Malcolm" (from *Malcolm in the Middle*). However, they still often forge their own path, not wanting to follow in the footsteps of their older sibling, while also separating themselves from their younger sibling.

As for the only child, they can fall anywhere in this range, taking on the responsibility and leadership qualities of the oldest, or the creative, rebellious nature of the youngest, or somewhere in between. I have also found a number of actors in my classes over the years who are the only child. In fact, they come in a close second to the youngest child.

Regardless of where you fall in your birth order, there will always be a desire to appease or please your family. If appeasing or pleasing your family is a top priority, that will definitely become a distraction.

Family pressure can make you feel defeated, miserable, exhausted, and even sick. You spend enough energy working on building up your own confidence in this profession. Having to continually justify your career choice is draining. It can deplete you of the energy needed to endure, to persevere.

Helping Your Family Support and Understand

While it's not easy to make your family support or understand your desire to be an actor, the best thing you can do to relieve some of the pressure is to *communicate* with them. Tell them about why you *need* to be an actor as well as the complexities of the craft and the business of acting. Then, show them your progress.

For many of you, your family will only have limited knowledge of what pursuing an acting career involves. As such, they'll only look at your career in black and white. Your family may only see it as "you're a working actor" or "you're *not* a working actor." They don't understand that there's also a *grey* area. The grey area is the process of taking classes, getting your reel, finding representation, self-taping auditions, etc.

You need to share with them what you do, enlighten them on the process. By doing this, you are also overcoming your fear of tackling these career challenges and you're holding yourself accountable for getting them done.

7 Simple Ways to Educate Your Family

1) Tell your family your Want. Let them know exactly *why* you want to be an actor. Explain to them your desire, your innate ability, and how your purpose is to act, entertain, and move others. Be as open and honest with them as you can. Show them why this is the career choice for you and that you believe with hard work and perseverance, you can "make it."

2) Let your family know that acting is a craft. Like any other craft, acting requires time, patience, and hard work. In order to be skilled at your craft, you need to be taking weekly acting classes. Explain the importance of consistent acting class to help you build up your acting muscles, hone your skills, and prep you for auditions, which will eventually lead to work.

3) Talk to your family about your career work. Explain how your Digital Pitch Package (headshots, résumé, demo reel) is your calling card in this business and thus necessary expenses. Inform them on what agents and managers do and how they are vital to opening doors and getting you opportunities to succeed. Explain the importance of casting director workshops for networking and making industry contacts. Let them know about the various career challenges you accomplish each week, and how you're holding yourself accountable.

4) Walk your family through the audition process. Many parents think it's simply about coming out to your Industry City and being discovered. Let them know that it's more complicated than what they've seen in the movies. Introduce them to the audition process from start to finish. Tell them about casting notices, agent submissions, callbacks, and producer sessions. Share with them some of your best self-tapes and talk with them about some of the feedback you receive. It will help them understand what you mean when you use words like "SAG-AFTRA," "pinned," "co-star," or "on avail."

5) Show your family your career plan. Tell them your overall goals and your plan for achieving those goals. This should not just be your overall Want, but your daily career challenges. This will show them that it's not just a dream, but something tangible that you're serious about, and exactly what steps you're taking to get there. Plus, once again, by giving them a clear career plan, it also will make you more responsible and accountable for your own actions. Once you tell your family your plan, you need to follow through; you have to practice what you preach.

6) Tell your family about your accomplishments. If you get an agent, an audition, a callback, or an acting job (no matter how small), tell them about it. Show your family that you are on a successful path, that you are doing more than merely saying, "I'm an actor." Let them know that you *are* an actor.

7) Control the message. There are many ways to maintain communication with your family about your career. One alternative is a brief, informative email or private message on social media. In this kind of message, you have more control; it allows you to put a more positive spin on whatever you want to tell them. It also minimizes the possibility of being trapped in a conversation you don't want to have.

Here's an example of a mock email:

> Hi Mom. Hope everything is going well. I'm thinking of you all. I did a scene in class last night that went really well, and my acting coach loved it! He says I'm progressing. I also met with a potential agent this week. Wish me luck. FYI: I have an audition for a short film this weekend so I'm keeping busy. Well, I gotta run. I'll FaceTime with you soon! Love, Bailey

Keep it short, succinct, and most of all...*positive*. That's not to say you can't share your struggles or feelings with your family. However, when it comes to your career, putting positive energy out to your family will help relieve the pressure that comes from their concern and worry.

Surviving the Holiday Season

There's no getting around it; family holidays can be stressful for you actors, especially those of you who aren't currently working. That's when you get a barrage of questions from your parents, aunts, uncles, grandparents, and cousins about your acting career.

It's even more painful when you have those discussions about when you're going to settle down and get a real job, when you're going to give your mother grandkids, why you won't go into business with your brother, and so on. Sure, it's done out of love, concern, or maybe even well-intentioned humor, but it's still grating to have to constantly explain yourself.

You also may face these "What are you doing with your life?" questions from your hometown friends who you haven't seen in a while. It can be frustrating not only to explain what you're doing, but also to deal with the constant ribbing ("Oh, it's the big L.A. movie star!").

The solution is...have a plan! Have an idea, a script, if you will, of what you're going to say to your family and friends, so you're not caught off guard when the questions arise. Have a list of what you're going to tell them (projects you've been working on, your career challenges, accomplishments, etc.). Keep it short, keep it honest, and keep it positive. It'll give you the freedom to have the happiest of holidays

Being the Family Point Person

Are you the family point person? If there's a problem at home, are you the one they call? Do you have to settle the arguments between your siblings? Do you have to help your mother get out of a bad mood? Do you have to listen to your father complain about your mother's bad mood?

There is usually one point person that everyone in the family relies on to take care of family issues…and yes, sometimes that point person can be one of the children, i.e., *you!* And if you are the point person, that can be extremely distracting to your career.

I had a student named Maria who missed an audition because she was on the phone that morning refereeing multiple calls between her mother and brother. Maria was so emotionally drained and mentally exhausted that she couldn't focus on her sides. She was too wiped out to do her self-tape. All she could do was go back to bed.

She made up an excuse to her agent, saying she was sick. Maria felt terrible for lying to her agent, but she at least found solace in the fact that she solved the problem for her mother and brother.

Next week, Maria got the same phone calls. She asked me for my advice. I asked her what would happen if she let the calls go to voicemail. Maria said that if she didn't answer the phone and intervene, her mother and brother would either continue to argue or they would have to resolve the issue themselves. Maria said she didn't really know because she always comes to the rescue. Regardless, they would be back at it again the next week.

I asked, "Then who are you really helping?"
Maria said, "I guess, nobody."
I continued, "And who are you hurting?"
Thinking back to her skipped self-tape, Maria replied, "Me."

The Burden of the Point Person

Being the point person isn't easy. I was the point person in my family. I was the one my family called if they had a problem, if they needed someone to settle a disagreement, if they were looking for advice, or if they were down and needed a quick pick me up.

What's worse, they would call me at work. As a young agent in the '80s, this was horribly distracting. I would get calls at my office at all hours of the day, which would deter me from my work. It was mentally and emotionally draining, and my work began to suffer.

I finally reached a point where I couldn't do it anymore. With help from my therapist, I had to sit my family down and tell them that they had to solve their own problems with each other; I would no longer be the designated mediator.

For a while, I had to endure the guilt trip they bestowed on me ("All you care about now is work. Don't you love your family anymore?"). But once I got my family out of the habit of calling me for everything, I was able to maintain a relationship with them without the pressures or distraction of being the point person.

The point person is often the most responsible one in the family. Your family will always look to that person who is good at helping. The problem is, the more you help, the more everyone leans on you for help, and the more you end up helping. It's a helping merry-go-round that never ends. And if you're an actor who is also the responsible one in the family, they will inevitably assume you are the one to call on. They think that, as an actor, you have loads of free time. You don't work a "normal" schedule, so you're available to deal with these issues, to help whenever they need, like an on-call 24-7 family counselor.

Taking on the burden of your family issues is nothing more than extra weight. Not only are you enabling your family, but you are also sacrificing your own dreams and career goals.

Being the Point Person is a Choice

Family issues are too much of a distraction, and unfortunately, they're hard to put aside. Many of you were brought up to "always put family first." That's not a bad philosophy. You do need to be there for your family when they need you most, just like they would hopefully be there for you. However, that doesn't mean you must absorb *all* of the family drama.

Every family has a caretaker and if you want an acting career, that can't be *you!* Being the point person is a choice. Do you choose to be an actor or the family therapist?

There's a sense of comfort and satisfaction the point person receives from solving issues and taking care of others…and that's a distraction derived from fear. The more you focus on your family, the less you need to focus on the uncertainties of your career.

It's easy to get wrapped up in the role of the family caretaker, especially if that is part of your nature. Being the family point person is more familiar and comfortable, especially if you've been doing it your whole life. The longer it continues, the more you will be accustomed to this role and the harder it'll be to extract yourself.

How to Set Boundaries with Your Family

If you are the point person, then you must be willing to step up and tell your family "No" from time to time. You must summon the strength to tell them that sometimes you're not available, sometimes you're too busy, and sometimes they just need to resolve their own problems. Be honest, kind, compassionate, and stay positive, but be firm.

Trust me, from my own personal experience, I know that's not easy—especially if you've been the point person your whole life—but you need to set boundaries.

Eventually, they'll understand. They are adults, after all, and part of being an adult is being responsible for one's own self.

You are allowed the freedom to focus on your own life and career…and you need to be willing to take it. To set boundaries with your family, you must become a little selfish, especially with your time. After all, you need that time, energy, and focus to put into your acting. Here are some pointers for the point person:

5 Easy Ways to Set Boundaries with Your Family

1. Don't answer it. You need to remember that you don't *always* have to answer that phone call from Mom or Dad. You also don't have to immediately return that text message from your brother or DM back your sister. You have the right to turn your phone off, let it go to voicemail, and reply on your time.

2. Set scheduled times to chat. Find time in your scheduled work week that is convenient for you to set weekly phone calls (or FaceTime) with your family. Make sure to put it on your schedule and stick to it. This will help you be more accountable and responsible with both your family and your career challenges. Schedule your family chat aside from your daily acting work so it doesn't become a distraction. That way you can avoid being interrupted and give your family your full attention when you do chat.

3. Take advantage of email, text, and DMs. They're shorter, sweeter, and you can get to the point quicker. If you're in the middle of doing a career challenge and they call, you can text "Hi, I'm working now, call you later." If you have a family that needs daily updates, take advantage of email, text, or direct message via social media.

4. Show them that you're busy. The best way to let your family know you're too busy to be the point person is to show them how busy you are in the pursuit of your career. Show your family what you're doing. Show them your new headshots, the scripts you're working on, the demo reel you're editing. With self-taping now so prominent, it's also easy to send them a prepared class assignment and/or self-taped audition. This shows your family that you have little spare time as you are keeping busy, being productive, and improving in your craft.

5. Tell them you can't be the point person. Let your family know that while they're important to you, you simply can't be there to solve every single issue. Let them know that you want to help, and you will do your share, but you can't be the family mediator, counselor, or planner. Your family might be upset with you at first, but if they love you (and I'm sure they do), they will ultimately understand that you need time and space for your career. In fact, over time, they will grow to respect you for taking charge of your life and doing what you need to do to become successful.

Being Your Friends' Point Person

Being the point person isn't limited to just your immediate family; it also translates to your family of friends.

Each family of friends has its own point person, the one friend that is the catalyst holding everyone together, the one who's a good shoulder to cry on, the one that plans the group's next big outing, the one that sounds a lot like the TV character Monica Geller from *Friends*.

Like Monica, this is typically the most responsible, practical, and organized person in the group. If this is you, the problem is that you might start out simply as a helping hand, giving good advice or solving a group problem. Next thing you know, you're the point person; you're the Monica.

The issue is you *like* being the point person. You excel at it. And you feel needed and comfortable in the role. But it's just not conducive to having a successful career. I'll put it to you this way, I believe if Monica Geller had made the choice to *not* be her friends' point person, she would have realized her dream of becoming a top chef, if not the next Rachael Ray.

Whether it is with your friends or your family, being the one who is expected to always "be there" for everyone can be an unnecessary distraction. It's best to nip it in the bud sooner rather than later.

ROMANTIC RELATIONSHIP DISTRACTIONS

Starting, building, and maintaining a **Romantic Relationship** is always a challenge…especially if you're an actor whose priority is their career.

There are many successful actors who are involved in long-term, healthy relationships. A relationship with the right person can bring a lot of excitement, joy, growth, and, most of all, comfort to your life. There is nothing better than sharing your journey with someone who loves you as much as you love them.

However, the nature of a career in this industry offers many obstacles to a romantic relationship, especially when it comes to such vital necessities as time, energy, and dedication.

An acting career can put a strain on any kind of relationship, especially if your partner isn't an actor (or in the arts) and doesn't understand the work involved. Being an artist means constant hard work, inconsistent pay, and unrelenting devotion, and that requires a tremendous amount of patience from your partner. When you don't have that in a relationship, it can become a major distraction to your career.

Are You in an Unhealthy Relationship?

I believe a healthy relationship is a mutual exploration to understand and help fulfill each other's needs and desires.

That mutual exploration takes a certain amount of work that each partner needs to *equally* participate in.

In an unhealthy relationship, the work becomes unbalanced and one-sided, as one partner's needs (and issues) take top priority. When a relationship becomes unbalanced, one person finds themselves giving in, forgoing their own set boundaries, and sacrificing their own individual needs and desires. They relent to the pressures of the relationship and the expectations of their partner, distracting themselves from what they really want to do.

I have seen many actors struggle with relationship problems, but when these problems persist, they become a distraction to your career. Because your significant others are so important, these problems are tough to shake or simply ignore. They fester in your mind and heart, and they distract you from your career challenges. You love that person, and you want to fix the problem within the relationship, so that's where you put *all* your focus.

Romantic relationships are like family in that way. Your partner will have a tremendous influence over anything and everything that you do. They will impact you and your decisions daily. They may put certain pressures or restraints on you—consciously or unconsciously—if they feel your career is becoming more of a priority than the relationship.

It can become more problematic when your partner isn't involved in an artistic field. Just like your family, they might not understand why you chose such a "risky" profession. If they have a steady job, they won't understand when money is tight or why you might have to work at all hours. They don't understand your true desire and need to pursue this career. Or they do understand it, but don't really accept it. They might *say* that they support you, but their actions say otherwise.

This unhealthy relationship will affect you, going beyond just the discussions and arguments over your career and your priorities. When you don't have someone who understands or supports your dreams, your self-esteem plummets, making you question yourself and your choices. It keeps you from putting your energy toward your craft and career. You love and respect this person so much and to have them not support you is upsetting and depressing. It trickles down into everything that you do.

It's even more difficult when you're married or if your partner has moved out to your Industry City with you. Suddenly there is that extra pressure on you to produce. If you're married, you may need to provide for your spouse and possibly children. That can be tough with any career, especially when you're just starting out. If you had a romantic partner move out with you, there will be a feeling of responsibility toward them. You will feel like you need to show them why it was the right move to make, which only adds to your stress.

They Just Don't Understand…

The most common distraction I've seen in romantic relationships is the metaphorical tug of war with the actor and their career. More often than not, the partner expects their relationship to be the sole top priority. If an acting career is important to you though, then that career must also be a top priority.

Your significant other will want your time, energy, and focus; it's only natural. But if they don't understand why you can't always give them that time, energy, and focus, then problems will arise.

I've seen actors come to class moody, distant, and agitated, sometimes with tears in their eyes because they just had a fight with their mate. It's almost always about their acting career taking priority over their relationship. The most common statement I hear is:

"They just don't understand…

…why I can't skip class to go out to dinner with their family on a moment's notice."

…why I can't go out with our friends because I have a self-tape the next morning."

…why I can't just spontaneously go out of town for the weekend during pilot season."

To avoid confrontation, many actors will prioritize and become the *good* partner. They do whatever they can to appease their mate, including forfeiting everything they came out to their Industry City to accomplish. They play the role of the obedient girlfriend or boyfriend or spouse, slowly but surely losing themselves in the relationship.

Or they become the point person in the relationship: the responsible, practical, organized one who must take care of all their partner's needs. Once again, all their efforts go into the relationship and there is nothing left to put toward a career. Then suddenly, months and even years have gone by, and they have nothing in their own career to show for it.

Sometimes these distractions are hard to spot. I've seen many romantic relationship distractions from actors who say they have partners who "totally understand them and support them." But when push comes to shove...they don't.

I Should've Gotten on That Plane

There was a beautiful, young actress I represented in New York City back in the '80s. I'll call her Jenny. She had a flourishing career with commercials, co-stars, guest stars, and film roles. As her star continued to rise, I got Jenny an audition for a series regular on a hit TV show that filmed in Los Angeles. It also happened to be her favorite show.

Jenny was excited, but I was concerned. I got to know Jenny quite well. She had an out-of-work boyfriend named Bobby who was insecure and jealous of her career. He constantly seemed to try and talk her out of opportunities, sabotaging her career at every turn. Plus, he was very controlling. Needless to say, Bobby and I did not get along. Jenny loved him, though, and assured me that he *was* supportive of her career.

I knew better.

Jenny went on the audition and the next day I got a call from casting. They wanted to fly her to L.A. for a screen test. The casting director told me that Jenny was perfect for the role, and she was the only one being considered. This was Jenny's big moment. She was eager, ready, and prepared to take advantage of this opportunity.

As I expected, she told me Bobby didn't want her to go. He gave Jenny reasons why she shouldn't screen test: She could find just as many acting jobs in New York, this is where their family and friends were, New York was their home. They argued and Jenny almost backed out, until she realized the significance of this career-defining opportunity.

The next day, I personally put Jenny in a cab and off she went to JFK International Airport. An hour later, I got a phone call from Jenny saying that she decided not to get on the plane. She told me that I should cancel her screen test because she wasn't going to move to Los Angeles. I was stunned and asked her why.

Here's roughly what Jenny said:

> "Oh my God, Scott, it was like a movie. Just as I was about to step on the plane, I heard someone yelling out my name. I turned around and see Bobby running down the terminal with flowers in his hand. It was the sweetest thing. He got on one knee and in front of everyone, Bobby proposed to me. Scott... I'm getting married!"

Oy.

Jenny never got on that plane. She never screen-tested. She never appeared on her favorite show. She *did* end up marrying Bobby...and after two rocky, tumultuous years playing the role of "depressed wife" and not doing anything toward her career, she divorced him.

Lucky for her, Jenny was able to jump back in the game and ultimately rebound. A few years after her divorce, Jenny got a role as a series regular on a hit series...that shot in Los Angeles. Jenny relocated to L.A. and continues to be a successful working actress.

I bumped into Jenny at an awards dinner. After we chatted for a while about our lives in L.A., she said, "I should've gotten on that plane." I knew what she meant. I gave her a hug and as I was leaving, she called out, "Tell your students to 'get on that plane!' Tell them my cautionary tale...just change my name!"

Distractions don't always smack you in the face. They're not always noticeable right away. But if you're in an unhealthy relationship, they *will* at some point rear their ugly head.

As easy as it would be to put the blame on your significant other for distracting you from your career, you can't. Just like with family, it comes down to you and your personal choice.

Whether it's blatant or more subtle, your romantic relationship can only be a distraction if you choose to let it be. After all, you have the power to work on your relationship, to set boundaries, find balance, and have a healthy, loving partnership.

However, many actors choose to let an unhealthy relationship become a distraction to their career. The main reason, as always, is fear.

Understanding Your Role in the Relationship

Working toward a relationship, even an unhealthy one, is often more familiar, and thus more comfortable, than navigating the unknown territory of an actor's life. Because of that fear of the unknown, you turn your attention to your partner and their needs which feels safer. It's what you know.

Many of us play a similar role in our romantic relationships that we do in our family dynamic. If you are the point person in your family, you are probably the caretaker in your relationship. If you are more dependent on your family, you probably need more from your partner. We can identify with these roles, and we seek solace in their predictability.

When we take on these roles in relationships, they can feel very reassuring and familiar. Having a relationship is a good thing and can provide a wonderful escape from your busy acting career. Whether it's going out to dinner, cuddling on the couch, making love, talking, and yes, even working on your relationship, it's a welcome reprieve from your career. But you can't do it all the time. If acting is important to you, then your career must be a priority. You need to find a balance. It can be done.

I truly believe...

When two people love each other, they want to help fulfill each other's destiny.

6 Tips to a Better Relationship

Here are six tips to help you maintain balance in your relationship and to ensure that your relationship doesn't become a distraction to your career.

1. Be upfront about what you want in your career.
Know what your priorities are and share them with your partner. Say "I want you to know how passionate I am about my acting career. This is what I want to do with my

life." This way you're not presenting any false impressions of yourself to prospective (or current) relationships. Tell them how focused, determined, and passionate you are about being an actor. Then you also need to acknowledge, respect, and embrace *your partner's* dreams and ambitions.

2. Explain your life as an actor. Talk with your partner about the time, commitment, and sacrifices that an acting career requires. Let them know that auditions may come in last minute, and when they do, you will have to prepare. And sometimes that might mean you will have to miss a previously scheduled event. Equally important, let your mate explain and share *their* goals and passions.

3. Choose someone who's supportive. It's vital that you have a relationship with someone compatible, who "gets" you and what you're doing. Make sure you are with someone who is loving, compassionate, understanding, and for God's sake, not someone who is needy! Your acting career is needy enough. Remember though, once again, that support is a two-way street. If you want your partner to encourage you in your pursuit, then you must encourage them.

4. Set boundaries. Be aware how easy it is for you to get lost in the comfort of your relationship. Make sure that while you make time for your partner, you also make time for your acting career. You need to let them know that you will need time and space—both physical and emotional—to put toward your career. You must also respect that they will need time and space to give to their own career. Sit down with your partner and discuss each other's career needs, schedules, and routines. Make agreements and rules and stick by them (except for sudden opportunities that arise in both of your careers).

5. Get them involved. The more your partner knows about what you are trying to do, the more they'll understand the importance. Talk to them about a role you're preparing and researching. Get their feedback on your new headshots or demo reel. If you get a last-minute self-tape, ask them to run camera or be your reader. But make sure to be fully prepared and ready to record when you bring them in. Your partner has their own time commitments and priorities, and you must respect that. Also, your partner's perspective should be considered (and appreciated), but it is not the final word; that goes to industry professionals. Bottom line: get them involved...but not *too* involved.

6. Be a good listener. To be a good actor, you need to be a good listener. It's also important for a healthy relationship. There is a big difference between "hearing" and "listening." Hearing is the passive action of sound or dialogue entering your ear. Listening is the active action that requires you to process the information you are hearing. In relationships (and in acting) you must be, or learn to be, a good listener.

As with most things, romantic relationships come down to communication and commitment. Find the person that brings out the best in you, not the worst. Find someone who loves you for who you really are. Be open and honest in your relationship and help each other grow as individuals, free of distractions.

"It was a million tiny things that, when you added them all up, they meant we were supposed to be together... and I knew it."
– Tom Hanks

The Over-Extended Actor

There are those actors that *do* find a balance when it comes to their survival job(s), family, and relationships. They have the support, understanding, and, most of all, time to tackle their goals, both in their career and their personal life. But they struggle with a different kind of balancing act: juggling *too many* goals. They try taking on too much, and that can be a major distraction for **The Over-Extended Actor.**

The Over-Extended Actor has high hopes, stars in their eyes, and they think they can do it all. When it comes to the industry, they want to be a jack-of-all-trades: acting, writing, directing, producing, editing, sound design, you name it.

Then there are those who over-extend when it comes to their hobbies, community work, or other skills: teaching, design, building websites, decorating, planning, massage, etc.

The Over-Extended Actor has *way* too many things on their plate, and they struggle to multitask and get everything done at once. I believe in working hard. I believe that dedicated, diligent individuals can accomplish multiple tasks. I believe you can do all that you want…but not all at the same time.

Please, feel free to write a screenplay in your spare time, especially if it can be another steppingstone that helps you get closer to fulfilling your acting dream. But first, you need to focus on completing your many *acting* career challenges before committing to any *other* career challenges. Once you become a successful actor, then you can become the painter, writer, director, or rock star you always wanted to be.

ADDICTIONS

I can stop at any time

Addictions?!

Yikes! Who wants to read about that?

I know, but don't be afraid to read this chapter as it will help you understand and feel compassion for *why* people take on addictions. It will also help you feel compassion for yourself and why you do the things you do. And it will help you identify and avoid the things you *shouldn't* be doing.

Being enlightened about addictions serves as another opportunity for you to look inward…and it comes with a trifecta of benefits. First, it'll keep you on your career path by helping you make clear life decisions and positive choices. Second, it will make you a better actor if you understand why someone becomes addicted, and then you can infuse that into your characterizations. Lastly, and most important, it could SAVE YOUR LIFE! So, read on…

Actors + Party Scene + Bad Habits = Trouble

Addictions are the most dangerous of the Three Ways to Sabotage Your Career because they will not only harm your career, but also your health and potentially your life.

As you hit roadblocks on your journey to becoming a successful actor, you will often find yourself looking to emotionally, physically, and mentally escape. It's not surprising how many actors turn to alcohol, drugs, pills, food, and sex for that ultimate distraction. And these distractions can quickly turn into an addiction, and those addictions can turn deadly. How many actors and performers have died of "accidental overdoses" in your lifetime?

An addiction is the desire to continually partake in an activity despite knowing that there will be harmful consequences. It's doing something you know you shouldn't be doing. Addictions are mood-altering activities a person engages in to help them escape. An addict justifies their actions (their addiction) with the thought that it will help them deal with a problem or an emotion like anger, anxiety, depression...and fear.

Drinking, eating, smoking pot, and even consuming caffeine; they are all ways we deal with stress. None of them are necessarily bad if you limit your intake. It's when you become *dependent* on those influences, or you take on harmful influences like harder drugs, that they become a big problem.

Every generation in Hollywood has had its "party scene." It's part of the allure of being in any Industry City. It's a communal scene where actors meet new people, try different things, celebrate their artistry, express their freedom, and share their hopes and dreams.

As inviting as the party scene can be, it often opens the door to temptation. That presents a challenge to actors who will inevitably look for ways to relieve their frustrations, fears, and anxieties in both their career and their life. Whether it's drinking or drug use, it can start as an experiment, then turn into recreational use, then become a habit that you tell yourself you can "stop at any time." Next thing you know...it's an addiction.

That addiction becomes a major obstacle, slowly chipping away at your talent, self-worth, and purpose.

WHERE DO YOUR ADDICTIONS COME FROM?

The topic of addictions is a complex one, so I'll give you the basics. Most experts agree that addiction is a brain disease of sorts, a result of chemicals and neurotransmitters in the brain being out of balance. It's a mix up in the brain that tells a person that even though they recognize that doing this activity is wrong, they still need to do it.

As far as what exactly triggers addictions, that gets a little more complicated. Many specialists say that stress (caused by negative events, traumas, fears, etc.) is the number one cause of addiction. When you experience stress, the brain and the body constantly search for ways to relieve that tension. Many say that hormones play a role, as well as hereditary genes. If you have a history of addiction in your family, there is a strong probability that you will be more susceptible. Still others associate addictions with societal pressures and environmental influences, as well.

I am not an expert on addiction. My intent is not to solve any addiction problem you might have. You will need a twelve-step program, rehab, and/or treatment for that. Rather, I want to help you identify the types of addictions that I've seen many actors experience. I want to shed some light on how these addictions originate from fear, how they can hurt you (and your career), and how you can seek help and get past them.

Why Do You Face Addictions?

Life as an actor can be an emotional roller coaster. There will be some incredible highs and a ton of lows. It's those lows that lead you to look for something to make you feel better. Whether it's a coping mechanism, comforting crutch, or just the need to get *high*, actors will turn to negative outside influences.

Many of these negative influences—like using drugs and drinking alcohol—come directly from fear. Addictions emerge from the struggles you face in your career or the struggles you don't *want* to face. As an actor, you'll sometimes feel disappointed, rejected, unappreciated, etc. You will sometimes question your dream, your purpose, your future. Your self-esteem can plummet, and you will ask, "Why am I doing this to myself?!" Or worse, "Was my family, right?"

Creative people are inherently more sensitive and emotional. Actors are specifically trained to be vulnerable, to draw from their emotions, and to be open to *experience* whatever is happening in the moment. Combine that sensitivity with a volatile career like acting, and it becomes a breeding ground for fear. Actors turn to substances to avoid that fear, to numb themselves from their feelings and experiences.

That applies to both the Fear of Failure and the Fear of Success.

Making a habit out of drinking, doing drugs, overeating, or not eating enough are all ways an actor deals with their Fear of Failure. They take on these addictive influences because they feel like they're not good enough, they're letting themselves down, letting others down, and/or sacrificing other opportunities.

Actors with a Fear of Success also turn to addictive influences when they start to experience their lives *changing*. They find vices when they have to venture out of their comfort zone, when they deal with the limelight, higher expectations, and the new pressures of having success.

I'm not naïve. I know that many of you will drink, smoke pot, or do other drugs at some point. For those of you who occasionally partake in these activities, it doesn't mean you have an addiction or that you'll ever be addicted. However, you do need to look at your own life and figure out how often you turn to these negative influences and more importantly...*why*.

I will help you identify the most prevalent addictions that actors face, and the most frequent ways that these addictions can self-sabotage an actor's career.

ALCOHOL

Many people drink or at least try **alcohol** at some point in their lives. In the life of an actor, it might seem almost unavoidable. Whether it's at parties, industry functions, hanging out with other actors after class, a show, a shoot...the "Let's go grab a drink" mentality has always been part of the acting scene.

Sometimes that's okay. We all need to unwind, decompress, or celebrate an accomplishment, but from these social occasions, alcoholism *can* creep in.

Alcoholism is a disease that you can willingly trigger and enable. At its core, alcoholism is continuing to drink even when your drinking causes problems, be it health, behavioral, social, or career. Many people that are addicted to alcohol are often aware of their addiction, but they still can't stop. Or worse, they are in full denial of their drinking problem.

Alcohol is a depressant, and in an industry fraught with rejection, you need to watch your intake of any depressants. I've seen how alcoholism derails careers. As you work hard for that one big opportunity, you don't want an alcohol addiction to get in the way.

She Was Supposed to Be a Star!

I had a student who I'll call Lucy. She already had some acting training before we met. She was twenty-one years old and everyone who met her and saw her act knew that she would be a star.

She was not "model beautiful," but she had something extraordinary about her: big blue eyes, coquettish smile, and an infectious personality. She was charming, funny, and endearing with just enough "quirk" that everybody wanted to be her friend.

I introduced her to an agent, and he signed her. Soon she was auditioning and booking commercials and co-star roles on TV shows. For a survival job, Lucy worked as a hostess in a restaurant, a perfect job for her extroverted personality. Lucy was popular and made great tips, which she invested into her career.

Every night after work, Lucy would sit at the bar for "just one drink," and entertain everyone. Soon, her one drink became a few drinks, and then it became *too many* drinks. Each morning, she would get up for her auditions feeling foggy and unfocused. No matter how much Visine she used, her eyes were still bloodshot, and her pocket strips of Listerine couldn't hide the smell of last night's alcohol on her breath.

After a producer session for a TV show, her agent received a call from the casting director saying that Lucy came in "obviously hungover." They wanted to hire her, but they were fearful that she had a drinking problem, so they "passed." A former addict himself, Lucy's agent confronted her on her problem and, at first, she denied it.

However, after she saw how it was affecting her career, she agreed to seek help and join a twelve-step program. Lucy is now many years sober. She says her addiction took years off her acting career, but she is still a working actress and grateful to live a sober life.

> "Life is very interesting...in the end, some of your greatest pains become your greatest strengths."
> -Drew Barrymore

To Drink or Not to Drink?

To make drinking a part of your life is an individual choice. With that comes a responsibility and accountability to yourself and to others. But there are times you should *never* drink; more specifically, when it could interfere with your acting work. You should never drink before a class, an audition, or a job. You should never drink the *night* before a class, an audition, or a job. You should never, EVER drink and drive.

A former student of mine, who I'll call Willie, was a series regular on a TV show in his early twenties. Everything was going great for Willie except for the fact that he was dependent on alcohol. His agent, friends, and family all tried to make him aware of his issue, but Willie was in denial. Then, one night he was pulled over for swerving on the road and given a DUI.

That DUI turned Willie's life around. He not only finally acknowledged that he had a problem, he knew he had hit rock bottom that night, which led him to Alcoholics Anonymous. When Willie first told me about the DUI, he said everyone asked him why he didn't just take a cab, an Uber, or hire a car (he *was* on a TV series). Willie told me, "Your addiction talks to you, fools you into believing you can do anything, especially get behind the wheel of a car."

Willie said his rock bottom wasn't so much getting the DUI, but the horrible thought that he could have killed someone that night. Fortunately for Willie, he was able to get sober and he continues to be a successful actor.

If you choose to drink, you will have to monitor yourself and the reasons *why* you are drinking. Drinking to cope with pain, frustration, depression, anger, or any other negative emotion is detrimental to your well-being. Having a beer to celebrate booking a commercial is great. Having a six pack of beer the night before you shoot that commercial is a "red flag!"

There are several red flags for someone who has a drinking problem and the potential for an addiction. These are the warning signs that you can watch out for in both yourself as well as friends and family.

NOTE: Part of your work as an actor might, at some point, require you to have an understanding about a character who suffers from addiction. While it is most important to identify these red flags and the reasons behind an addiction for the sake of your life, it's also important to know them for your career work, when delving into a character that is inflicted or suffering from an addiction like alcoholism and/or drug use.

Alcohol Red Flags

Impaired conditions: Slurred speech, stumbling, disorientation, or a lack of coordination; displaying "drunken behavior" regularly.

Erratic behavior: Shifting from happiness and giddiness to depression, impatience, and even anger at the drop of a hat.

Self-neglect: Not caring about appearance and health; poor hygiene, unkempt, and disheveled. Red inflamed eyes, a swollen or blotchy face.

Hangover syndrome: Dehydrated, groggy, sluggish, nauseous, smelling of alcohol.

DRUGS

A drug addiction is one of the easiest (and most damaging) addictions to fall into.

Drugs can give you a high, a sense of power, a feeling of invincibility and omnipotence. They create a false sense of hope, security, and confidence that you can do anything or be anyone. They can make you believe that you have "superpowers."

Drugs are also used to numb the pain. People turn to drugs as a buffer between their feelings and the world around them. They numb the user to the point that they fall out of touch with their feelings and feel nothing but the effects of the drug.

Not every actor who comes to Hollywood (or any Industry City) does drugs, but each one of them will at some point in their career face the temptation. Each generation has its illegal substances to go along with its wild, spontaneous, care-free, "nothing matters but this moment" lifestyle; whether it's the 1920s Prohibition Era, the Reefer Madness of the '30s, the Psychedelic Drugs of the '60s, the Coked-Out '80s, Ecstasy (Molly) of the '90s, Meth (Methamphetamine) of the 2000s, or the more recent abuse with Opiates.

I'm Going to Be the Next Brad Pitt

Years ago, I received an email from an eighteen-year-old boy from Missouri—I'll call him Cal—who had seen me on my reality TV show *Fight for Fame*. Cal wanted to move to Los Angeles, study with me, and pursue an acting career. He wrote that he was going to get his finances together and he would be out in Hollywood in six months.

Six months later, Cal showed up at my studio ready to begin. He was a handsome, well-built, blond-haired, blue-eyed, determined young man. He had some acting experience in his hometown, but he was here to train and focus on his Hollywood dreams. Cal said with great self-assurance, "I'm going to be the next Brad Pitt." I believed him. He got into class right away and studied intensely. He was eager to learn, a hard worker with a positive outlook.

As opportunity would have it, one day a photographer stopped him outside my acting studio and told him, "You have a great look." He called him in for a big print job and Cal booked it. That gave Cal even more motivation to work harder and, as such, he progressed quickly. The print job led to booking a national commercial, which then led to booking a co-star role on a TV show. Cal was on his way!

However, a few months later, Cal began to show up late to class and unprepared for his assignments. He also came in looking drawn, run down, and tired. I pulled him aside and asked him what was going on.

Cal said he had been out "partying at the clubs" with all his new friends. I could tell from talking with him that while he was enjoying the attention, he was also overwhelmed by the scene. I discovered that Cal was using cocaine…and his cocaine use had become a huge problem.

Cal started to miss class altogether. He wouldn't return my calls or emails. I found out later that Cal was arrested outside a Sunset Strip club doing coke. After only being in Los Angeles for a year, everything he worked for started to unravel. As most drug users eventually do, he hit rock bottom. His parents came to bring Cal back home to Missouri to get him help.

A year later, I received an email from Cal saying he was now drug-free and hoping to return to Hollywood…still with dreams of being the next Brad Pitt. I lost touch with Cal, but then one day, years later, I turned on my TV, and who did I see? Cal, ten years older, looking terrific and starring in a series. In an article I found online, he talked about getting sober and living his life one day at a time.

Many actors will experiment with a drug of some kind or another in their lifetime. I can tell you not to do it, but I know better. Instead, I'll tell you to BE CAREFUL. As you can see from Cal's story, drug use is a slippery slope with horrible consequences.

Drug Red Flags

Extreme behavior: Cocaine, meth, and other stimulants make the user excitable, hyper, restless, anxious, unable to focus; can become excessively manic, jumpy, or "twitchy." Opioid abusers display sluggish behavior, paranoia, or unusual giddiness.

Mental effects: Regular drug users often get confused easily, are more apt to be forgetful, or they have completely illogical thinking.

Looking tired: Pot addicts generally have a drawn look with red, inflamed eyes. Harder drugs like cocaine and meth lead to wide eyes, dilated pupils, as well as inflamed nostrils. Sleep deprivation, dehydration, and constant "highs" and "lows" damage the body and mind.

Talkative: Cocaine and meth addicts, tend to talk excessively; they are overly intent on the subject at hand and more likely to say inappropriate things.

Alcohol and Drug Treatment

If you have a drinking or drug problem, you need professional help. You *can't* kick it on your own. You need a place to detox, a twelve-step treatment program, counselors, and a support group that will help you get past your substance abuse. On top of that, there are some things you can do individually to help you stay clean after you've kicked the habit.

Keep up with your twelve-step program. It's always good to be surrounded by others who are trying to kick their own addictions and can understand what you are going through. Not only will you get to "share" your struggles and stories with the group, but you will gain insight from listening to others share their stories. In twelve-step programs, you will also get help, and support on how to cope. And you will learn to *be of service* to others.

Be open and honest with friends and family. When you're seeking treatment, don't be afraid or ashamed to tell your close friends and family about your alcohol or drug problem. They can be there for you to lean on. Be open with your friends so they know why you're not drinking or partying.

Avoid functions where drugs and alcohol are involved. Addicts who have gotten sober say the temptation is always present in their lives. Until you have a few years of sobriety under your belt, it's best to avoid that temptation at all costs.

Find other positive outlets. Find substitutions that can replace that high you get from drugs or alcohol. Running, lifting weights, yoga, meditation, gardening, cooking, golf, tennis...find something that will keep you occupied and satisfied with your life. Focusing your energy and working on your career will not only keep you from drinking and doing drugs but will also lead you to a positive outcome: success!

> *"The longer space you put between yourself and the addiction, the easier it gets."*
> -Jane Fonda

EATING DISORDERS

There are many actors who deal with **eating disorders**. The three most common are Bulimia, Anorexia, and Binge Eating.

Bulimia and anorexia stem almost exclusively from image and control issues, while binge eating is more of an anxiety-related addiction, an escape from the pressures of life, much like drugs and alcohol.

Eating disorders are just as deadly as any other kind of addiction. They come from several places: family history, genes, upbringing, societal expectations, low self-esteem, industry pressure, and, worst of all, fear.

Hollywood Beauty?

The TV and film business will have certain physical expectations for actors, and you need to come to terms with that. It will be up to you to monitor yourself, to ensure that the desire to drop or gain a few pounds doesn't become a problem. Sometimes that can be tough in an image-conscious, weight-obsessed industry where you will be bombarded by what Hollywood considers "beauty."

If you're leading man material, for the most part, you must be in good physical shape. There are many talented actors out there, including several who fit the leading man type. Often, casting will come down to appearance, who fits the "look" of what's currently trending on TV or film. I'm not saying that it's right; I'm just telling you that's how it is.

If you're a leading lady, an ingénue, the historical struggle comes with the need to be thin. The good news is times have changed and you don't need to be a size zero anymore. But still, the industry ideal of beauty is often defined by models and young starlets that are much thinner than the average woman. Often, actresses playing leading ladies or ingénues feel the need to lose weight at any cost just to keep up.

It can affect men as well, especially in terms of finding their particular brand. I've seen many leading men *not* get certain roles because casting said they were "a little too heavy," they're "full in the face," or they have a "beer gut." Yet that look, or perhaps even heavier, might be perfect for more character actor roles.

You need to know your type and be comfortable with your type…as long as it doesn't jeopardize your health. For example, if you want to be an ingénue and you think you would be better served by losing a few pounds, order that salad. If you're a character actor and a couple of extra pounds will help you get work, find a healthy way to maintain that weight.

As I've said throughout this book, your best chance at getting work is for you to feel confident in who you are, and that includes your appearance. When it comes to your health, though, especially your own eating habits, you need to watch yourself closely.

You Looked a Little Heavy on Camera

I had an actress in my class who I'll call Amanda. She was a young, attractive, gal next door type, who was very talented and hard-working. On the surface, she appeared to have a lot of confidence. She quickly got representation, started booking small jobs, and got a nice break as a guest star on a hit show as the lead character's girlfriend.

After Amanda appeared on the show, her agent said to her, "You looked a little heavy on camera." He suggested that she lose a little weight and tone up, especially around the lower half of her body.

Amanda smiled and told her agent, "No problem." When she got back home, she broke down crying. She was upset by what her agent said, but she knew that eating was always a problem for her. She was very sensitive about her weight, especially through her hips and legs. When the agent offered his suggestion, Amanda knew he was right, and she didn't want to jeopardize the possibility of losing work (there was talk of her role becoming a recurring guest star). Because of her love of eating, Amanda didn't know how she would lose the weight.

A couple days later, she was at a birthday party, still feeling down about her weight. Even though she vowed she wouldn't eat any birthday cake, she gave into her temptation and had a slice…and then another. Amanda felt so sick to her stomach from the sugar that she went into the bathroom and forced herself to throw up, something she had never done before.

Amanda told me later that the minute she threw up, she felt "a euphoric sense of satisfaction and relief." It was at that moment that she realized how she was going to control her weight. Amanda secretly began binging and purging. She would eat and eat, mostly sweets, and then force herself to throw up multiple times a day.

Friends started to notice that she wasn't looking well, but nobody would have guessed the cause. The irony, she said, was that she did this to have control over her weight, but it was the bulimia that had control over her. Amanda finally sought help. She still struggles, but she's now managing her bulimia and continuing her career as a working actress.

> *"Weight is still a struggle. Every video I'm in, Every magazine cover, they stretch you–they make you perfect. It's not real life."*
> -Lady Gaga

Bulimia and Anorexia

Bulimia and anorexia are two distinct eating disorders, but they both share one important trait: they both come from an uncontrollable desire to lose weight and to keep losing weight beyond healthy limits.

Bulimia is a disorder that includes eating large quantities of food, often several times a day, and then immediately purging the food, mainly through vomiting. Again, this comes down to "control" as well as feelings of guilt or shame. Bulimics like Amanda will often eat unhealthy foods, feel guilty, and then purge, making them feel empty once again. So, they eat again, and this unhealthy cycle continues.

Anorexia is defined as having abnormally low weight with the fear of gaining weight. It's a deadly disease because people who are anorexic often willingly omit the essential vitamins and nutrients that food provides, making them sick.

According to the American Psychiatric Association, anorexics, as well as bulimics, are often perfectionists, people who are very driven and like to be in control. When their lives start to spiral out of control, they turn to their weight or diet as that is something they *can* control. It becomes an obsession and an addiction.

Bulimia and Anorexia Red Flags

Weight loss: A problem occurs when weight loss is happening at a rapid pace, to the point where the person begins to look unhealthy and continues to lose weight.

Talking about body image: An obsession with image. Weight becomes their main topic of conversation, whether its calorie intake, diets, or different techniques to keep weight off.

Not ordering food: This can range from ordering only small portions to not eating at all. Anorexics will often make excuses for not eating, such as "Oh, I ate earlier." On the flip side, bulimics will often order a huge portion of food when dining out but will almost always visit the bathroom immediately after eating, often multiple times.

Taking other steps to stop weight gain: Working out excessively, taking supplements or weight loss pills, using laxatives, enemas, or simply fasting.

Binge Eating

This affliction is a bit tougher to recognize. The problem with **Binge Eating** is that we all have to eat. And if we're being honest, we all binge from time to time. We all stuff ourselves, especially if we're having a bad day or if we just want to indulge…or if it's Thanksgiving. The difference is that someone with a binge eating disorder will do it *all the time*, often to deal with feelings of stress, sadness, anger, and depression.

They will eat large amounts of food very quickly in the hopes that it will fill that void and make them feel better. They will often binge in private, ashamed of their habits, trying to hide them.

Tearing Into a Bunch of Cheeseburgers

I introduced one of my students, who I'll call Eddie, to a sitcom casting director. He was a funny, pudgy character actor with an endearing, "teddy bear" charm.

The casting director loved Eddie and she brought him in for her show. Although he didn't land the part, she kept his headshot on file and was determined to find him the "perfect role." A few months later, that role came up. This time, she called Eddie back in to meet directly with the show's producer.

When the casting director saw Eddie again, she was surprised. He had gained quite a bit of weight. He was no longer pudgy; he was now *heavy*...too heavy to cast him in that particular role. Later, she told me that she was disappointed because she wanted to work with him. After that conversation, I thought it was important to talk to Eddie about his weight gain.

He said that he had been through a lot lately with family and work problems. He told me that when he felt stressed out or fearful, he would deal with it by "tearing into a bunch of cheeseburgers." Most people with a binge eating disorder have a "trigger food," a favorite food that they most often turn to when they feel the compulsion. Eddie's trigger food was cheeseburgers, which unfortunately put on the pounds quickly.

We chatted a bit and the conversation went well. I felt sympathetic for him; you could tell he was ashamed and embarrassed. I recommended he get help and he said he would. Therapy led him to Overeaters Anonymous, and though Eddie still struggles with his weight, he works hard to keep it in check. A few months later, the casting director called him in again and he was back to his pudgy, endearing teddy bear self…and he booked the job. Eddie continues to be a successful character actor.

Binge Eating Red Flags

Noticeable weight gain: A sudden increase in weight, going up a few sizes over a short period of time (weeks, months).

Appearing depressed: Depression often leads to binge eating. The two work hand in hand. If someone is depressed, frustrated, or embarrassed, those afflicted will eat to comfort themselves.

Unkempt appearance: Tend to look slovenly and unkempt, from hair to hygiene to clothes. They usually wear the same clothes because that's what fits.

Eating unhealthy foods: Fast food, salty snacks, sweets, and sugary drinks are all part of a binge eater's diet. There is often a trigger food, one that makes them feel good and is usually the worst for them.

Eating Disorder Treatment

As with any addiction, if you have an eating disorder, you need to immediately seek therapy, counseling, and a treatment program. Here are some other tips that can help you confront this specific addiction.

Monitor your diet. Watch what you eat. Practice portion control. Make sure you're eating enough healthy foods. There is plenty of information available online about healthy eating. Don't ever be afraid to ask friends for help.

Watch out for triggers. Acknowledge your trigger food—what you eat when you're feeling depressed, rejected, frustrated, etc.—and try to avoid it.

Work out regularly. This will help you keep your weight at a manageable level. If you're fighting anorexia or bulimia, working out regularly (but not excessively) can give you a sense of accomplishment and a good feeling about your body image.

I suggest you hire a trainer and/or a nutritionist to help you get started and give you guidance. There are several in any Industry City who are struggling like you to jumpstart their careers, and they are often willing to offer discounts to attract new clients.

Other Addictions…

Alcohol, drugs, eating disorders…these are by no means all the addictions that actors face. An addiction can be any kind of activity that becomes an obsession, causes harm, and disrupts a person's career and life.

The most common addiction among actors is, well, right in your hand. No, not smoking. That bad habit has dropped off. Thank goodness, as the smell of an actor returning to class after a smoke break is gross. I'm talking about your smartphones. More specifically, your addiction with picking up your smartphone and scrolling through your various social media sites. I do realize the soothing repetitive aspect of scrolling on your device for a few moments. But, unless you're a social media influencer doing research, I'm sure you have a career challenge to complete.

Then there are those more recreational addictions, like playing video games, gambling, or shopping, which is even easier and more enticing in the age of Amazon. Sure, it's nice to have an occasional diversion, and to treat yourself, but it's sometimes too easy to get lost in these activities, spending too many hours on them instead of working on your career.

There is also sex addiction, which many actors lose themselves in to compensate for the feelings of loneliness, lack of self-worth, etc. Besides the health risks—especially if you have sex with multiple partners––there is an emotional toll that a sex addiction can take.

Then, of course, there are the addictions like sugar and caffeine. They can't necessarily derail your career, but they can affect your health, so you need to watch and limit your intake or stop altogether.

You must remind yourself that all addictions are distractions—unhealthy substitutes, roadblocks and obstacles keeping you from doing what you came to Hollywood or your Industry City to accomplish.

RESOURCES

Alcoholics Anonymous aa.org
Al-Anon (888) 425-2666 al-anon.org
Cocaine Anonymous (310) 559-5833 ca.org
Narcotics Anonymous (818) 773-9999 na.org
National Eating Disorders Association
(800) 931-2237 nationaleatingdisorders.org
Overeaters Anonymous oa.org
**Substance Abuse and Mental Health Services
Administration** (800) 662-4357 samhsa.gov
The Actors Fund (800) 221-7303 (N.Y.) (888) 825-0911
(L.A.) actorsfund.org

*"I don't drink these days. I'm allergic to alcohol
and narcotics. I break out in handcuffs."*
-Robert Downey Jr.

WRONG ACTIONS

And the Right Actions to Take!

Of the Three Ways to Sabotage Your Career, **Wrong Actions** will have the most immediate and profound effect. Choosing to take wrong actions is the quickest way to sidetrack you from your career, if not derail it permanently. Choosing to take **Right Actions** will keep you on track, guide you to wonderful opportunities, and lead you to your destination.

On your path to becoming a successful actor, you will face daily choices that will impact your entire career. The various inner thoughts you have as you make your daily decisions might sound something like:

"Do I *need* to put 100 percent into my class work?"
"Do I *need* do an agent mailing?
"Do I *need* to research the show I'm trying out for?"
"Do I *need* to memorize my sides?"
"Do I *need* to be on time?"

And so on. How you respond to your inner thoughts—and the actions you choose to take—will determine your fate as an actor.

Wrong actions can hurt you, your reputation, and your career. What's worse is that they can sneak up on you without you even realizing it. Over time, they can accumulate. And, unless you quickly learn from your mistakes and take the right actions, a negative trend will develop.

For actors, work begets work. You start to build a *positive* momentum with the work you put out, the art you bring to life. That work leads to more work, which leads to achieving small victories, which then adds to your momentum, and soon your small victories become bigger and bigger victories.

The same is true with wrong actions. When you take wrong actions, a *negative* flow starts to take over your positive momentum. Then those wrong actions beget other wrong actions and manifest into bigger wrong actions, which will have a negative impact on your career.

For example, if you repeatedly show up late to acting class, you could develop a reputation as irresponsible and uncommitted. If you are unprepared for an audition, you could hurt your chance at a role and future audition opportunities. If you procrastinate from doing your daily/weekly career challenges, you *will* delay your journey to becoming a successful actor.

It will be up to you to recognize your wrong actions and either avoid them or quickly learn from them and pivot into taking right actions. You will always create more opportunities by taking right actions.

Why Do I Choose to Take Wrong Actions?

Wrong actions come from, you guessed it, *fear*. Actors take wrong actions because of both the Fear of Success and the Fear of Failure.

In the Fear chapter, I talked about a student, Tom, who didn't properly prepare for his final acting scene. He told me he was being "lazy," and I told him he was being *fearful*. Tom chose to take the wrong action of putting off his work till the last minute because it was easier. He was faced with a choice, and he chose *not* to work on his scene, not to fully prepare...and he did so out of fear.

You consciously, or unconsciously, take wrong actions which will then lead you off your career path. Remember, the further you remove yourself from your path, the less you must face your Fear of Failure or Fear of Success. You feel more comfortable, less at risk, more in control. It also means a lot less work that you have to put toward your career.

For example, you are fearful of the ramifications of pursuing an acting career and thus you take wrong actions to avoid it. More specifically, you may fear that you're *not good enough* to be an actor, so you show up unprepared for class. This often starts the chain reaction of one wrong action leading to several more; you're not prepared for class one week, then show up late the following, and then be a "no-show, no-call" the next week.

Sometimes, these wrong actions can be influenced by several other factors, including addictions and distractions. If you think about it, your addictions and distractions can cause you to procrastinate, show up late, act unprofessionally, avoid opportunities…take wrong actions. Here's a chart to demonstrate:

Turning Wrong Actions into Right Actions

Taking wrong actions is something you choose to do. If you do choose to take such actions, for whatever reason, you must then learn from those mistakes and choose to take the right actions to fix them. When you do, those right actions will empower you as an actor.

*"Mistakes are always forgivable,
if one has the courage to admit them."*
-Bruce Lee

I'm going to lay out the most common wrong actions that actors take, be it in their career challenges, acting class, agent and/or manager relationships, self-tape auditions, casting rooms, on set, etc. These wrong actions are also a list of what industry professionals may refer to as their "pet peeves." These are by no means all the wrong actions an actor can take, but they are the most prominent.

I will also identify the *right actions* for you to take to help you both avoid and correct any wrong actions. Remember, if you do engage in negative actions, you must learn from them, and correct them by turning them into *positive* actions. It's about failure, correction, then, if needed, re-correction. You fail and you correct, but you might make the same mistake again, so you must keep re-correcting until you get it right.

So, without further ado, here are my…

Top 10
Wrong Actions to Avoid

and

The Right Actions to Take

#1

CONSCIOUSLY CHOOSING FEAR

I should be practicing, but…

Number one on my Top Ten Wrong Actions to Avoid is **Consciously Choosing Fear**. After reading this book, you have already begun Looking Inward and identifying and understanding your fears. For the most part, you have become more conscious of when fear arises. When you're about to take that wrong action, you must acknowledge you are *consciously choosing* to give into your fear.

I realize that's a bitter pill to swallow, but it's the truth. The quicker you start acknowledging that you're self-sabotaging, the quicker you'll be able to confront, experience, and work through your fear.

One of my former students, who is currently a series regular on a TV show, came to class one night completely unprepared and in a gloomy mood. On break, I went up to him and I asked what was going on. He said, "Just like your book says, Scott, I'm self-sabotaging." Having the awareness of that is one step closer to getting past it.

The more you consciously choose to give in to your fear (and take wrong actions), the more fearful you'll become. The more you give into fear, the more you *normalize* that fear, and the more that fear will eat away at your desire to be an actor. Choosing to give into your fear instead of working on your career challenges will make you feel anxious and frustrated and cause you to doubt your abilities. And it will slowly pull you away from what you love.

For example, let's say you have a class assignment due in five days. You feel excited to dive into the scene, but in the back of your mind you feel a bit anxious it might not go well. Unless you dig into the scene right away and commit to dig in a little every day throughout the week, that little bit of anxiety snowballs into fear that will overshadow your excitement. By class time, your fear will have taken over and you either haven't prepared properly or you just don't show up for class.

Write this down in your journal…

Succumbing to your fear leads to inaction in your career.

Giving into Fear in the Audition Process

You cannot be fearful of opportunities. You cannot be intimidated by people in positions of power. You cannot fear your acting coach, agent, or manager and their expectations of you; they are working to help you succeed.

Most importantly, you cannot fear the casting director or the audition process in general. You must embrace the fact that the casting director *wants* you to do well at the audition (it makes their job that much easier).

It's easy to think that casting directors have the power to make or break your career, but don't allow yourself to look at them that way. You can't give anyone, even a casting director, that kind of power. It's only one audition, and you'll have many more. There is never one last chance for you in this business.

You can't be fearful of the "audition process" itself because there are so many factors that are beyond your control. If you don't get the part, it doesn't mean you did something wrong in the audition or that you're a bad actor. It could be you're just not right for the role, either because you're too tall, too short, too good-looking, not good looking enough, or they decided to use the producer's cousin instead. All you can do is fully prepare, give your self-tapes and live auditions your very best, and be ready to move on if you don't get the part.

Even if you worked hard to prepare but felt like you *didn't* give the best audition, perhaps because you flubbed a line, don't worry about it. I can't tell you how many times actors flub something in the audition only to get a callback.

What's funny is that sometimes that unintentional flub (and I stress *unintentional*) will relax you, alleviating some of your nerves. Suddenly, you become more focused, more alive. The pressure's off and you give a stronger audition and finish well. Don't be afraid of making a mistake; casting directors are human, too.

You need to breathe, release your fear, go into that audition prepared and professional, and realize that if you don't get this one, there will always be another one. Always push yourself to do the best you can, whether it's class, meetings, or auditions, but don't burden yourself with unnecessary pressure and fear.

THE RIGHT ACTIONS TO TAKE

1. Learn from your mistakes and move forward.

2. Practice the 5 Steps to Overcoming Fear: Acknowledge, Confront, Experience, Work Through, Overcome.

3. Talk about your fears to family, friends, other actors, or even a therapist.

4. Treat every career challenge with importance without putting high expectations and unnecessary pressure on them.

5. Accept that your acting coach, representation, and casting directors want you to win!

6. Take pride in all your individual efforts.

7. Try your best at each opportunity and then accept that there will be other opportunities.

8. Know that acting is a process and that with time, energy, and skill, you will be successful.

9. Tackle your career challenges as soon as you get them. Work on them a little every day throughout the week, making them part of your routine.

10. No matter the activity, relax, breathe, and have fun.

#2

STAYING UNINFORMED

I gotta do research?

"Don't be a Joey!"

That's what I say to my actors who are **Staying Uninformed,** who don't do the necessary *research* for their acting projects and career work. "Joey" is the beloved Dumb One character Joey Tribbiani from the sitcom *Friends.* Beyond being dim-witted, Joey's biggest disadvantage as a struggling actor of the 1990s was...he didn't have the internet, Google, YouTube, actor apps, and Actor's Access at his disposal!

YOU DO. You literally have everything you need in the palm of your hand, at the touch of your fingertips. Your smartphones allow you to do your career research in mere seconds; all you have to do is "Google it!" But the problem is, you *don't.*

Knowledge is the vital key to success. Without knowledge, you will remain an uninformed actor. I have seen that many actors are unwilling to do their actor research. Their rationale—or what they tell themselves––is either they're lazy or they don't know how. Neither one of them is true.

When you're not doing your research, you are consciously choosing to remain uninformed.

I understand that actors have an artist mentality. You don't want to spend hours and hours in front of a computer or in a lab, which is why you didn't go into academia. You didn't desire a career of intellectual research, writing, homework. And studying might not be something you like to do or are very adept at. But in the field of acting, the answer to the question, "I gotta do research?" is YES. Acting is not just an emotional pursuit; it is also an intellectual pursuit.

Also, you need to acknowledge that the reason you're not doing your research...is fear. Once again, you're letting fear step in and dictate your choices for your career. You are giving into that negative voice in your head that says, "Research is too hard; I don't want to do it." Or "It'll get me too much in my head." By succumbing to fear, you are once again empowering that negative voice in your head, stopping you from growing and moving forward.

Your fear of doing research—that dreaded "R" word— manifests when you do your class assignments, auditions, and career work.

The Dreaded "R" Word in Your Acting Work

You will always need to do a certain amount of research for your acting projects: class assignments, audition sides, and shooting scripts. When working on a scene from a TV show, it means researching the genre (drama, comedy, procedural, etc.), the style (pacing, tone, single-camera, multi-camera, etc.) and the platform the TV show appears on (network, cable, or streaming service).

It also means you are responsible for all your *character* work research, circumstantial or created, to learn all you can about your character and the world they live in. You need to incorporate each of what I call:

The 5 Points of Character Research

1. Know your character's background: education, profession, religious and political beliefs, etc. as well as any inflictions, impairments, or conditions.

2. Understand the world in which your character exists: their specific time, place, and period in history.

3. Get comfortable with vocabulary, pronunciation, foreign words, specific terminology, etc.

4. Learn how to speak like your character, considering their education level, social status, use of slang, etc. If your character has a certain regional dialect (Boston, New York, Chicago) or accent (British, Russian, Spanish), you need to train with a speech coach or watch tutorials on YouTube.

5. Familiarize yourself with the other characters that affect your character in the story. Research any references the other characters make (i.e., political, religious beliefs, physical and mental conditions, etc.) as well as any specific medical, legal, or technological terminology they may use in the scene.

I Don't Know That Show

Character research is important and if you don't do it, it will clearly show in your work. As an example, in my Audition Technique class, I sent out sides for a new character: a young E.R. doctor from the long-running ABC medical drama *Grey's Anatomy*. A week later, my students came in and auditioned. Afterward, we all talked about the *Grey's Anatomy* sides. One student, who I'll call Karly, gave an honest performance, but seemed lost when it came to understanding the genre, the world of a hospital, and medical terminology she spoke and heard in the scene. It was as if she never watched an episode of *Grey's Anatomy*. She hadn't. Karly admitted in class, "I don't know that show."

Grey's Anatomy has been on TV since 2005 (and is always streaming), and it is a roadmap for acting, writing, and directing for all medical dramas. Karly needed to be familiar with the show. At the very least, she should have watched an episode or two on online. She needed to know the genre, the world of the medical drama, as well as the style of the series. And since the breakdown was specific, she also needed to research and know what an E.R. doctor does and the proper pronunciation of the medical terminology she was using.

Staying Informed for Your Auditions

As an auditioning actor, doing research is your job, and you must put your focus on completing that specific task. It has nothing to do with your acting talent; it has to do with understanding the *story*. Doing your research helps you place yourself in the universe of the character and the story that the writer is telling.

Reading the full breakdown, including the other character descriptions, will also help you understand the story. You will learn a lot by looking up the writer and director of the project, specific information about the production itself or the production company, the casting director, shoot dates, etc.

Plus, you must be informed of any *audition rules*, specifically when it comes to self-taping instructions. It can be a note from casting on how they want the scene played. It can be technical information, anything from how casting wants the framing (medium shot, long body shot, close-up, etc.) to how they want the video delivered (WeTransfer, Vimeo, etc.) to slating, be it what they want in the slate (name, current location, passport status, etc.), if the slate should be upfront or at the end of the tape, etc.

The Dreaded "R" Word in Your Career Work

Working at an acting career is like any other profession. You must be educated and knowledgeable about your industry. You must be, that's right, *informed*.

There are plenty of resources to help you gather information for your career. You can research acting studios online in the various industry trades and blogs, "Google" specific agents and managers, and use IMDB to get info on casting directors, producers, and your favorite shows. You can even browse industry-related websites to find out what's "hot" in television, what films are being made, and who's casting what.

Beyond that, there are many actors who are more than willing to share their experience. There are acting coaches, seminars, classes, books, videos, the industry trades, you name it...they are all there as a resource for you to utilize to learn more.

Plus, there's always my favorite way to do research, for both acting and career work: watching film and television. You can watch just about anything you need to see on Hulu, Amazon Prime, Netflix, Disney +, HBO Max, Apple TV, and more. And if you can't find it on the streaming service, you can for sure at least find a clip or two on YouTube.

Doing research is a constant process. You need to keep yourself up to date about the industry and your career. Learning about the business is equally as important as learning about your craft. Whether it's your acting work or career work, the dreaded "R" word is a necessity. You need to do the research and learn all the information you can to be a successful actor.

THE RIGHT ACTIONS TO TAKE

1. Learn from your mistakes and move forward.

2. Research the show you're auditioning for, not just the genre, but also the specific style. Find out who wrote it and what they have written before.

3. Use the 5 Points of Character Research to learn about your character and the world they live in.

4. Read the full breakdown and follow all casting notes and self-tape and audition instructions.

5. Educate yourself. Talk to folks with experience, people you trust who have knowledge of this industry.

6. Subscribe to the top acting and trade sites and check them every single day.

7. Research who's casting the top shows and films.

8. Read acting books, watch instructional videos, attend seminars...build your career knowledge.

9. Don't let fear stop you from doing your necessary research.

10. Don't be a Joey!

#3

BEING UNPREPARED

I'll just wing it

When it comes to your acting craft, there is no excuse for **Being Unprepared.**

For acting class assignments and auditions, I tell my students that to properly prepare for a three-page set of sides, you can expect to work on them for a minimum of six hours. You need to have your lines memorized, have written pages of backstory, and worked on your relationships. You need to have done all your character history and other research, as well as worked out the physicality of any activity that your character does in the scene. This is how an actor prepares; anything *less* than this means you're not giving it the time, attention, and work it deserves. It means you are being unprepared. And that is a wrong action.

I coached an actor (I'll call him Phil) who was making progress in his acting work and appeared ready to get representation and auditions. I set up an appointment for him to meet with a reputable manager. Phil was very excited. The manager emailed him two different scenes——one dramatic and one comedic—and gave him a week to prepare.

The day of his manager meeting, I got a call from Phil saying he wanted to schedule a last-minute private coaching session to work on the material. I thought it was a smart move to have me tweak and refine his audition. But when Phil showed up for his coaching, it was apparent that his scenes would need a lot more than tweaking and refining. Phil hadn't prepared.

He had no backstory, wasn't off book, and he had no "character." And his meeting was in an hour! Whether it was his naivete or his fear, Phil honestly thought that he could just "wing it." He thought his acting instincts, along with a little polishing and a sprinkle of "Sedita stardust," could pull him through. Not having much to work with, I coached him as best as I could and sent him on his way.

The manager called me and said he wasn't interested in representing Phil. He said that although Phil had a great look and a wonderful personality, he didn't have a grasp of the material and he wasn't ready for representation. I talked to Phil about his lack of preparation. He apologized, saying there were no excuses and that he had learned his lesson: winging it wasn't the way to go.

It never is.

There's no way around it, you must always be fully prepared when it comes to your acting work. Otherwise, you will not grow as an actor. And when it comes to acting, nobody is good enough to just wing it.

As an acting coach, I will often give my students material to take home, scripts to work on either alone or with a partner. After weeks of lectures on the importance of preparation and working on their material outside of class, I trust that they will do the work. Inevitably, there are always students who, when it comes time to perform, are ill prepared…and they always have a poor excuse.

Being Unprepared in Your Auditions

Being unprepared for a self-tape or live audition is also the number one pet peeve of agents and managers as well as casting directors. As an agent, when I worked hard to get an actor an audition, I hated getting the call from casting that the actor didn't prepare properly. This is the gravest of acting sins. Not only does this wrong action affect the actor, but it can also hurt their agent's reputation, which in turn will hurt your relationship. Even if you only have a few hours between hearing about the audition and self-taping it, you need to use that time and do your best to *prepare*.

As I mentioned, there was a major shift in the business a few years back that introduced the self-tape into the casting process. That advancement in technology enabled agents and managers to peek inside their clients' auditions, something they never had access to before. Previously, they only had the casting director's feedback (if they could get it) to see how their clients' did on their auditions. But now, agents and managers can see for themselves! They are watching your self-tapes, so you better be prepared.

Do I Really Need to Memorize My Sides?

Yes! Being prepared means memorizing all your lines, or what's called "being off book." Casting directors are telling me that some actors (who were given ample time to prepare) are turning in their self-tapes without being off book. Instead, they have scripts in their hand, searching for lines on the page or even off their computer screen.

When you are not fully memorized in your audition, the casting director can see you thinking "What's my next line?" That takes you (and the viewer) out of the scene. Even worse, it also makes your character seem hesitant and unsure. Plus, watching an actor's eyes dart back and forth to grab a line of dialogue is very distracting, especially on a self-tape.

Not being memorized also hurts the scene you're performing. If you're not off book, you are more apt to change the story by paraphrasing, improvising, altering words, or not recognizing the punctuation: all big no-no's, especially in comedy. TV and film scripts have a specific tone, pace, and rhythm, and if you're not memorized and speak the words as written, you will for sure miss that rhythm.

I realize that memorization is one of the most challenging and time-consuming tasks for you. But it is a basic necessity for the craft of acting. There's no way of getting around it. You must learn the skill of memorization. Whether it's class work or an audition, your dialogue needs to be fully memorized for you to be present and in the moment. The less you're thinking about your next line, the more you're in the story and the life of the character.

There are many different methods to help with memorization; find the one that works best for you. If you work your sides long enough, you will inevitably memorize them. And the more you practice memorizing, the faster you will be at memorizing.

Unprepared actors are also guilty of not defining a strong "Want," not incorporating the 5 Points of Character Research, not writing a full backstory, or establishing a dynamic relationship in the audition scene. Being unprepared makes for bad acting. It is a wrong action that will frustrate your acting coach, upset your agent or manager, and keep the casting director from hiring you. But it's an action that you can easily correct right away.

THE RIGHT ACTIONS TO TAKE

1. Learn from your mistakes and move forward.

2. Prepare, prepare, prepare.

3. Memorize your lines and always be off book.

4. Do your homework. Set aside a specific time each day to work on your class assignments and audition scripts. Repetition. Repetition. Repetition.

5. For your auditions and self-tapes, read all the material given to you, including your character (and other characters) breakdown, the "For Your Information" (FYI) marked scenes, and any extra lines on the page (even if they're crossed out). If the entire script is available, read it.

6. Look for information, clues, and hints in your audition sides to help give you a better understanding of the story and the characters.

7. WOFRAIM it! (check out Bonus Track: Talent).

8. If there is something you don't understand about the script, ask your representation or acting coach before going on or taping your audition.

9. Be sure your self-tape setup is working properly; camera, lights, sound, Wi-Fi, delivery method, etc.

10. Enlist the help of a private acting coach if you need guidance tackling a role or preparing for an audition. A coach can help you focus on the nuances of the character and find an approach to the text that can aid you in booking the job.

#4

PROCRASTINATING

I'll do it tomorrow

Actors of all experience levels always say they need to get back in class, get new headshots, do an agent mailing, etc. They have the hope and good intentions to accomplish these tasks, and yet…they don't.

Sure, they have their reasons (which I'll get to soon enough), but the truth is they are **Procrastinating.**

Procrastination occurs when you lose sight of the immediate task in front of you and use any excuse not to do the work. You do this for one of two reasons. One is because the task itself is so overwhelming that you put other priorities ahead of it. The other is because there is simply something else you'd rather be doing. Both, once again, come from fear.

Don't get me wrong. I get it. Procrastinating is a wrong action we *all* share. It's easy to look at some daunting work and say, "I'll do it tomorrow. I'm going to play Fortnite." Then you keep procrastinating until the very last possible moment. You say, "What's the big deal if I still get it done?" But do you? Get it done? The way you're *capable* of getting it done?

Procrastination *is* a big deal, especially when it comes to those weekly career challenges and tasks. Even though you might feel that procrastinating gives you more time, ironically, that time is usually filled with fear, worry, and guilt about how you're *not* working on your task.

It is easy to procrastinate, especially in beautiful, sunny, laidback Los Angeles. Monday easily merges into Tuesday which merges into Thursday, and suddenly it's the weekend and you wonder where the week has gone. If you're not careful, those days merge into weeks, then into months, and then suddenly it's three years later and you wonder, "What the hell have I done with my career?"

There is an anonymous quote that I share with my students, and I think it says it all:

"Procrastination is the grave in which opportunity gets buried."

The more you procrastinate from doing your work, the more you will sacrifice potential opportunities, and the less those opportunities will come your way. In essence, the more you procrastinate, the deeper you bury your chance of being a successful actor.

It's easier to put off any of your career challenges, be it joining an acting class, doing an agent mailing, getting the new headshots your manager requested, etc. But the longer you procrastinate each of these challenges, the longer it will take for you to move on to the next one.

That means the longer it will take you to grow in your career and achieve success.

Since acting class is a miniature version of an actor's career, I find that what actors put into class they tend to put into their career. If you procrastinate doing your class work, chances are you'll procrastinate doing your career work.

This is wasted potential. You are not taking advantage of the financial, physical, and emotional investment you've made in an acting class, and both your craft and career suffer. Putting off your acting means putting off your career. You need to fight through the fear, fight through procrastination, and stop that habit before the habit stops you from achieving success.

Think of all the things you could have accomplished if you had just started when you said you would. You still can, so start right now!

THE RIGHT ACTIONS TO TAKE

1. Learn from your mistakes and move forward.

2. Do what you came here to do. Get into class, get new headshots, edit your demo reel, do your industry mailings, etc.

3. Reward yourself when you accomplish a challenge.

4. Designate times each day for your career work. A regular schedule will keep you disciplined and accountable.

5. Set yourself a deadline for getting work done and stick to it. Use the calendar app on your smartphone.

6. Make a list of daily, weekly, and monthly goals and place it by your computer.

7. Your acting career is a priority, treat it as such.

8. When you feel like you want to procrastinate, say out loud to yourself, "Procrastination is the grave in which opportunity gets buried."

9. Remind yourself that the sooner you get it done, the sooner you can carry on.

10. Think of all the things you can accomplish. Begin today. It's never too late to start!

#5

SHOWING UP LATE

I know, I know, I'm late…

Perhaps the rudest of the wrong actions, the one that can really rub people the wrong way, is **Showing Up Late**.

Here is a great mantra I practice that you should always adhere to when going to class or auditions, logging into Zoom meetings, showing up on set, or even turning in your self-tape assignments.

> *"Early is on time.*
> *On time is late.*
> *Late is unacceptable."*

Successful folks in the entertainment industry are always busy, on a tight schedule, moving quickly from one project to another. Therefore, coaches, agents, managers, casting directors, and producers don't have the time to wait for you, nor do they have the patience to hear your reasons why you're messing up their schedule.

Nobody appreciates someone who is late. Showing up late is disrespectful. Worse yet, it gives you a reputation as someone who can't be relied upon. It mars people's perception of your professionalism. In casting, they say, "If they can't show up on time for an audition, then…"

Unfortunately, many actors are guilty of this.

Tardiness often begins in acting class and, unless it's corrected immediately, this habit will spread into other areas of the industry. A former student of mine, who I'll call Mitchell, was almost always late to class. I had a long talk with him and told him that I felt he was being disrespectful to me and his classmates. He apologized, but the following week, he showed up late again, interrupting the class as he walked across the room to take the last remaining seat.

Finally, I had to dismiss Mitchell from class. Sometimes there are lessons that can only be taught through tough love, and this was one of them. I knew that I had lost an actor with potential, but I hoped it would serve as a wake-up call to Mitchell.

Since the first writing of this book, Mitchell went on to become a popular series regular on a TV show. I saw Mitchell on a morning show where he told the interviewer that he's always punctual because as a young actor, he was "kicked out of acting class for always being late."

Time Is(n't) on My Side

Being tardy can come back to haunt you. Repeatedly coming to acting class late may eventually get you kicked out. Not calling with a good excuse or being a "no-show, no-call" actor will get you kicked out faster. An acting coach would rather open a spot for someone who will be dedicated to learning and growing in their craft. Plus, acting coaches can't let this behavior become the norm in their classrooms; if one student is permitted to always be late, they'd have to allow others as well.

If you do come into class late, be respectful and as quiet as possible. I had a student named Tasha who was always ten minutes late for class. Tasha would scurry into the classroom in the middle of a lecture, carrying a huge bag that had bells attached. She would drop her bag on to the floor with a big loud clang, plop into her chair, sigh loudly (making everyone aware of her bad day), and then apologize with, "I know, I know, I'm late…"

I've always wondered why some actors are always late. Is it that they don't want to get to class too early because they're uncomfortable talking to the other students? Is it their sense of entitlement that they think they can show up whenever they want? Is it a power trip, thinking they're better than the class? Or is it because they don't know how to manage their time properly? Whatever it is, being late only places negative attention on you.

This applies to your meetings with your agent or manager as well. If you're late at all, it not only throws off your appointment, but *their* entire day. This wrong action is also destructive when it comes to your auditions. Being tardy will strain your relationship with your representation and hurt future opportunities with casting directors.

When it comes to your self-tape auditions, never send your tapes in late. It doesn't matter if a casting director has given you a couple days or a couple hours, get your self-tape in on time. Better yet, get them in early, before the deadline. You should only ask your reps to request an extension on your self-tape deadline as a last measure. Also, if your representation is submitting it for you, that's another good reason to get your self-tapes to them earlier, so they have time to possibly review it.

I'm Late! I'm Late! For a Very Important Date!

Don't be the White Rabbit. You should never be late for an in-person live audition. You need to show up at auditions early enough to give yourself time to prepare. You need to make sure that you're ready when the casting director calls your name. If you get there at the last second, you won't have time to prep. If they call your name and you're not there, they'll simply move on to the next actor. So, if you have an audition at 2 p.m., show up no later than 1:45 p.m.

If for any reason you are running late to an audition (or acting class) call or text your representation (or acting studio) *immediately*. Be as succinct as possible and let them know when you can be expected. Such as "I'm sorry. The freeway is backed up, please let them know I'll be ten minutes late." They'll understand if you're late once or twice. After all, traffic in an Industry City can be difficult. Once tardiness becomes habitual, however, then you have a problem.

Showing up late (or not showing up at all) is not only inconsiderate and disrespectful, but also a quick way to sabotage your career. When you are late to a class, meeting, or audition, you are blocking yourself from going forward in your acting career.

Don't become "that person" who's always late, late, late for a very important date!

THE RIGHT ACTIONS TO TAKE

1. Learn from your mistakes and move forward.

2. Remember, "Early is on time. On time is late. Late is unacceptable."

3. Set date notifications on your smartphone to ensure you don't miss class, auditions, or appointments, and set alarms to make sure you're on time for them.

4. Assume classes and appointments always start at least fifteen minutes earlier than scheduled to ensure you're on time.

5. Examine why you're always running late and how it could affect your future opportunities.

6. Manage your time, plan out your day, and be organized; that will help you avoid being late.

7. Leave earlier. Plan your route in advance and even plan an alternate route. Use your GPS for the quickest routes and to help avoid traffic.

8. Be respectful of other people's time.

9. Make sure to text or call if you're running late. Apologize succinctly and sincerely. Assure them it won't happen again.

10. BE ON TIME!

#6

MAKING EXCUSES

My dog ate my sides

Actors have always had the most creative explanations for blowing off class, not preparing, neglecting their research, or being late. They are (in)famous for the time, effort, and energy they put into **Making Excuses**. With great sincerity, actors will weave elaborate excuses which include stories of danger, disaster, tales of bewitchery and mystic cosmic circumstances beyond their control.

I believe all the excuses I hear are legitimate. I'll take you at your word, even if your grandmother *has* died seven times. But if excuses are your way to absolve yourself for not doing the work you love, then making these excuses becomes a wrong action.

Making excuses links closely to the wrong actions of Staying Uninformed, Being Unprepared, Procrastinating, and Showing Up Late. Excuses are the vehicle driving those harmful wrong actions. If you continue to make excuses and don't learn from your mistakes, they can pile up easily and divert you off your career track.

Why Do You Make Excuses?

You make excuses to either *gain sympathy* or *to be exonerated*. When you're looking to gain sympathy from someone, you are trying to elicit an emotional, compassionate response from them ("I feel so bad for you."). When you're looking to be exonerated, or let off the hook for your mistakes, you're targeting an intellectual response ("It's okay, I get it.").

Whatever reaction you're trying to get, excuses are really a way of justifying your wrong actions because making excuses is *easier* than taking the right actions.

The truth is...

The reason we make excuses is to
protect ourselves from blaming ourselves.

Saying you are late because of traffic, or uninformed because you didn't read the breakdown, or unprepared for class because, "My dog ate my sides" is placing the blame on some other person, place, or thing. Not taking blame or responsibility for your actions makes you feel better about the bad decision you made. Rather than attempting to seek a solution for being late, ill-prepared, uninformed, or procrastinating, you give into your fear and go the easy route by making an excuse for your wrong action.

I've Had a Bad Day

Over my many years of teaching, the most popular, widely used, mega-excuse to fall from the lips of actors is, "I've had a bad day." The belief is that by simply muttering these five words, it will automatically grant pardons and give exemptions for any infractions that actors can possibly make. It's as if it's a secret password that swiftly removes accountability for any craft and career responsibilities.

As your teacher, I am not quite sure what you want me to do because you've "had a bad day." Do you want me to give you a sympathetic look, a gentle hand on the shoulder and say to you, "I understand?" Or do you want me to excuse you from your class assignments, commitments, and obligations? Or do you want both?

In fact, I *have* said and done both because everyone deserves one "I've had a bad day." But when you return to the next class with the same excuse or a brand new one, then there's an issue that needs to be addressed. It means you're not taking your craft and career seriously. You're using excuses to rationalize putting off your work.

What you're *really* saying is your art is your lowest priority. It should be your highest.

Excuse Me?

When you make excuses, you are affecting two significant aspects of your career.

First, making excuses can hurt your **reputation**. Industry professionals don't care about *why* you didn't do what was expected of you. They just want it done. And on time! They're not interested in your excuses (fabricated, real, or a mix of both), nor do they have the time or bandwidth to listen to them. If making excuses becomes a trend, it will raise a red flag for all industry professionals and start to reflect poorly on you and your reputation.

When I first opened my acting studio in 1998, I implemented a "No Excuses Rule" which meant not wasting class time with anyone's excuses. I even hung a big, framed sign on the front of my classroom door which read, "NO EXCUSES." If a student came into class late and tried to make an excuse, I'd simply nod toward the big sign on the door and wait for them to acknowledge the rule and take their seat. It worked.

Second, making excuses can hurt your **motivation**. Excuses are a byproduct of fear, a mask you wear to hide the fear you feel inside. If you're making excuses for not doing what you truly love, it means you're not confronting your fear, you're not being honest with yourself. And you're not fueling what motivates you: acting.

Whether it's the Fear of Success or the Fear of Failure, making excuses is your way of *releasing* yourself from doing work that asks you to be disciplined, focused, and determined. And that can kill your motivation, your mojo.

Making an excuse for not doing your work is a form of cheating. You cheat yourself, your potential, and your craft when you make excuses.

If you do not examine your excuses, and why you make them, you will not be able to make progress in your career. If you are making excuses, then this is the time you need to look inward and analyze your reasoning.

Answer this question:

"Besides getting some short-term relief, where does making excuses ultimately get you in your career?"

Acknowledging and having awareness of why you're making excuses is a step in the right direction. So is owning it and not cheating yourself. By agreeing to the No Excuses Rule, you'll have to be honest with yourself about why you're taking wrong actions.

THE RIGHT ACTIONS TO TAKE

1. Learn from your mistakes and move forward.

2. Remind yourself that excuses only hurt your reputation and motivation.

3. Know why you're making excuses; analyze and be honest.

4. Accept that "I've had a bad day" can only be used once. Maybe.

5. Acknowledge that all excuses stem from fear. Face that fear.

6. Identify and correct the habits that cause you to make excuses. Practice the No Excuses Rule.

7. Don't cheat yourself. Learn to say, "I have no excuse."

8. Seek sympathy from family and friends, *not* industry professionals.

9. Don't try to get anyone to let you off the hook, not even yourself.

10. Don't make excuses. Own it. Do your work.

#7

GETTING STUCK IN NEGATIVITY

This business sucks!

We all sometimes experience negativity about this business. It's normal. Hopefully, these negative feelings are fleeting, and they soon pass, whether by talking it over with family and friends or tackling career challenges. The wrong action is **Getting Stuck in Negativity**. Once again, this derives from fear, and you must get past it.

Nobody in this business has time for negativity, yet industry professionals experience it with actors all the time. The tricky part is that sometimes you might not realize you're being negative and/or putting out negative energy. It's important that you identify and recognize your negativity, as it can not only affect you but everyone around you.

To help you, I have identified three different types of actors who get stuck in the cycle of negativity. Although these are archetypes, you will be able to recognize characteristics you can identify with as an actor in this business. Introducing...

The Three Negative Actors: *Defeated, Needy, and Disgruntled.*

The Defeated Actor laments to the world, "This business sucks...I'll never make it." They are the Charlie Browns, the dreamers, the Lovable Losers who had great optimism about the industry but now just feel beaten down. And they are always willing to tell you about it. The Defeated Actor feels not good enough or worthy enough, even when they are or could be. They question why they should even bother working on their class assignments, self-tapes, or looking for "yet, another agent who won't send me out." They stand with one foot in the business and the other foot in a deep, dark, defeatist hole.

The Defeated Actor can also let their negative attitude affect their acting work. Unless it's called for, this mopey, wounded demeanor does not fare well in characters that are strong, confident, and bold.

The Needy Actor whines to the world, "This business sucks...why haven't I made it yet?" They want everyone to like them, but they feel like nobody does. They exude a desperate energy, try to hide their insecurities behind their self-deprecating humor, and play the "poor me" victim to get attention. They'll ask a question they already know the answer to just to feel heard or seen. They are constantly searching for reassurance, approval and validation ("I wasn't very good, was I?").

The Needy Actor's self-doubt and need for sympathy can sometimes seep into their acting, even when it's not called for in a character. Warning: casting directors can sniff out desperation and neediness in an actor in seconds.

The Disgruntled Actor snarls to the world, "This business sucks...I was supposed to make it by now!" They are often cynical and bitter at what they perceive as their many unfair defeats. They had a clear-cut vision for how their career track was supposed to go and they're frustrated by the lack of progress or the numerous roadblocks they've encountered. They are shut down emotionally, letting their negativity take over in everything they do. They weaponize their cynicism by taking a caustic, sarcastic tone to express their many frustrations about the business. As eternal pessimists, they have a chip on their shoulder and a grudge against the industry.

The Disgruntled Actor's personal anger issues often bleed into their acting work. And, unless they're playing a character who is cynical, sarcastic, and embittered, it doesn't work.

Three Negative Actors Walk Into a...

When it comes to auditioning, our three negative actors mainly present themselves at two separate times: entering the audition and exiting the audition.

When *entering the audition,* the Defeated Actor, before they even open their mouth, sends the wrong message to the casting director. Their body language, attitude, and thought bubble say, "I know, I'm not good enough."

The Needy Actor enters an audition fueled by an underlying desperation that cries out, "Like me, please, please like me!"

The Disgruntled Actor enters distant with an attitude of "Why do I have to audition for a part I won't get? Again!"

When *exiting the audition*, the Defeated Actor, even before the casting director can say anything, assumes the worst and judges their performance. They exit with their shoulders rolled down, face drawn, thinking, "I suck." Or they will use humor to hide their pain by saying something sad sack-ish like, "Hope that wasn't a waste of your time."

As the Needy Actor exits, their insecurities come pouring out. They ask the casting director, "Did that work for you? Because if it didn't, I can do it again with a totally different take."

The Disgruntled Actor exits with head tilted, eyes rolled up, a scowl on their face, grumbling an obligatory "Thanks," then sarcastically whispering to themselves, "Love this business."

Professional casting directors will pick up on all your negativity, and that *will* affect their overall impression of you. Casting directors do not have the time or patience for negativity. They want to see a cordial, prepared, focused, positive actor who's ready to work and who would be easy to work with on set.

Nobody Wants to Carry Your Baggage

Every acting class has that one actor who walks into the room with their shoulders slumped, head down, and a cloud of doom hanging over them. They seem to be unhappy, anxious, or just plain grim. They often sit in the corner restless, and sulk or brood, intentionally or unintentionally sapping the energy from the entire room. And at times, without you even realizing it, that actor might be you.

This negativity is often caused by a troublesome event in your life that hasn't been resolved or frustration with your current situation. It permeates everything you do. Many times, you may not even realize that you are doing it.

What's worse is when you choose to share your negativity in a professional setting. In acting class, that negativity can show itself at any time, even in the middle of your scene work. When you grumble or whine "I'm tired" or "I had so much to do today" or "It's been a rough week," it disrupts the teacher from giving you an adjustment and always brings an uncomfortable hush over the classroom. When you vent about your personal problems in a professional setting, that negativity becomes "baggage." And nobody wants to carry your baggage. Apparently, neither do you, as you keep trying to give it away.

I realize this may be your way of expressing the pain you feel inside. It's okay to experience feelings of anger, sadness, or frustration and even bring those feelings to your acting work…if the circumstances call for it. But when your drama, your emotional baggage becomes disruptive to your work, as well as the work of others, then it's a wrong action.

It's even *more* detrimental when you bring this baggage to your representation. Your agent or manager probably represents many actors, and they don't have time to deal with anyone's negativity. Even if they only represent a few actors, time spent dealing with your defeatist, needy, or disgruntled attitude is time better spent finding you work. The more negative you are, the less they will want to work *with* you or work *for* you.

This is downright *disastrous* when it comes to auditioning. Bringing your negative energy into an audition will suck the positive energy out of the casting room, leaving the casting director drained and uninterested in you.

How's it Going?

When I was a casting director, there was an actor (I'll call him Manny) who came in for a producer's session. When Manny entered the room, I greeted him with the requisite, "How's it going?" Well, Manny launched into a diatribe on how his girlfriend was mad at him, how he was getting kicked out of his apartment, and how his dog had worms.

Neither I, nor the three producers in the room, knew how to respond. He was great for the part and had the right look, but his negative energy was off-putting and made us feel uncomfortable. Even though we all felt bad about his situation, the producers felt nervous about casting him. One producer said, "This kid's got *a lot* of drama," while another said, "We have someone we like just as much who isn't a downer."

When you answer the question "How's it going?" with a reply like Manny's, you are revealing that you are in your fear. You're either trying to vent, to release some stress or anxiety so you can relax and perform better, or you're complaining to garner sympathy, to soften the criticism you feel is coming because you feel like you're not good enough or talented enough to get the part. Neither is a good reason.

When your coach, agent, or casting director asks you, "How's it going?" before class, a meeting, or an audition, it's a *rhetorical* question. Your response should only be a short, positive one ("Great! Thank you!"). This is *not* your opportunity to vent or complain about your life. It's inappropriate and it never works in your favor. Industry professionals don't want to hear about your bad day. They're probably having one themselves.

You must remember that this is a business, and as such, bringing in your personal negativity is a wrong action. You need to think of each class, meeting, and audition as a career opportunity and treat it as such.

THE RIGHT ACTIONS TO TAKE

1. Learn from your mistakes and move forward.

2. Identify your negativity and where it originates. Learn to do this before negativity becomes a habit, consciously or unconsciously.

3. Don't be the Defeated, Needy, or Disgruntled Actor.

4. Leave your drama at home and your baggage at the door.

5. Before walking into any professional setting, take a deep breath, exhale negativity and inhale gratitude.

6. Learn to change your negative thoughts into positive thoughts. Say your affirmations like "I choose to be positive" out loud every day.

7. No matter what, always be positive, polite, professional, and prepared.

8. Remain optimistic about your audition—before, during, and after—no matter what happens in the casting room.

9.When meeting an industry professional, always have a short, positive response for when they ask you, "How's it going?"

10. Be cordial and focused, interested, and *interesting*. Most of all, make your acting work enjoyable.

#8

NOT BEING A TEAM PLAYER

Why am I not being sent out?!

There are some basic wrong actions actors engage in when it comes to working relationships with their representation. **Not Being a Team Player** is perhaps the most serious. If you're not communicating with your agent and/or manager, doing what they need you to do, or treating the relationship respectfully, that will negatively impact your relationship and your career.

Not being a team player often starts with not being aligned with your reps. You have to make sure that you and your representation are both on the same page when it comes to your career. It is essential for you to discuss with your agent and/or manager your career goals, your "type," how to market you as an actor, and a plan for building your career together as a team.

Your agent and/or manager are there to help you succeed. If you currently have representation, then you must have done your due diligence—either off a recommendation or a Google Search—then submitted your Digital Pitch Package, had a sit-down meeting, and then signed with them to represent you. You signed with them for a reason: you trust them. Having trust is the basis for a good relationship with your rep.

Being a team player means *knowing* what to expect of each other, *talking* about your goals, and *listening* to their ideas, counsel, wisdom, and vision for you.

You want to come in with ideas of your own, but you must always be receptive to taking your representation's advice. That advice can be on anything from what acting classes to take, what headshot photographers to use, how to best put together a reel, to overall career strategy, etc. Then you need to act on that advice and be proactive about their input and suggestions.

If you are not listening to your representation or doing what they need you to do, then you're not being a team player. If you don't trust their judgment or opinions, then they really can't do anything for you.

How to Properly Communicate with Your Reps

There are several dos and don'ts when it comes to the means of communication with your agent or manager, be it email, text, or phone calls. But most important is to keep any communication with your representation clear, focused, positive, and to the point.

If your agent or manager texts you, text them back immediately. If they call you, answer the phone. If you can't, call them back ASAP. Also, your voicemail greeting should be professional and brief. There is nothing more annoying than quickly trying to reach an actor to give them a last-minute audition only to get a goofy cartoon voice, a standup routine, a jingle, or a rap interlude before being able to leave a message. It might be funny once, but that's all.

Most reps use email to relay audition information to their clients, so make sure to respond back to any emails quickly as well. A simple "Got it! I'll be there. Thank you!" will suffice. Get a separate email address for your acting career to keep your auditions and acting business organized, archived, and separated from all the other junk that can fill up your personal email inbox. You should be checking that actor email account *several* times a day. You never know when you're going to get an audition.

Your agent or manager should also know your social media handles, as well as any actor website or pages you set up. Speaking of your social media presence, be careful with what you post. Agents, managers, casting directors, and producers all can see what you post publicly, and if you post anything that might be considered inappropriate, you could shoot yourself in the foot.

On that note, never ever post any audition or production materials to your social media. This is confidential information and should never be shared. Doing so could get you let go from an audition or even a booked project.

If you email, text, or call your representation, make sure that you are organized, prepared, and clear about what you want to ask, say or discuss. Do not waste their time with unnecessary questions or chitchat. Be personable, upbeat, and concise. And, if it comes naturally, a sense of humor always helps.

If you want your reps to respect you as an artist and a business partner, you must respect them and their time. You are one of many actors they represent. Many agents and managers complain that their actors expect them to drop everything when they email, text, or call. True, your representation is there to help, but you need to prioritize when reaching out to them.

Why Am I Not Being Sent Out?!

Many actors don't know how to appropriately communicate with their representation when they feel they're not getting sent out on auditions. That's when actors are most likely to stop being team players. That's also a time when the Three Negative Actors tend to re-emerge, especially during a sit-down meeting with their representation.

The Needy Actor enters their agent or managers office, smelling of desperation, plops down in the chair, and dramatically whines, "Whyyyy am I not being sent oooout?"

The Disgruntled Actor enters with a sour face, annoyed, and gripes, "Why am I not being *sent out?!*"

And, of course, the Defeated Actor comes in all mopey, talking to their shoes, "Why...umm...am I not...umm being...umm...sent out?"

This kind of behavior will get you nowhere. It will only make your agent or manager feel cornered, defensive, irritated, and exhausted. It may also get you dropped. They may forgive, but they won't forget.

Instead of asking, "Why am I not being sent out?" your best approach, the right action to take, is to ask your agent or manager *this* question:

"What can I do to help you in representing me?"

Simply asking your representation that question shows them you take your career seriously, you hold yourself accountable, you're willing to do whatever it takes, and, most importantly, you're a team player.

Understanding Your Business Relationship

You may spend quite a bit of time with your agent and/or manager as you continue your career path. Sometimes it can be unclear as far as what you should expect of each other, how to conduct yourself, and what kind of relationship is *appropriate*.

First and foremost, you must remember that this is a *business* relationship, and you must always treat it as such. Sure, as time goes on, you might form a personal relationship with your agent or manager, but it should always start and develop as a business relationship. It will be up to you to understand and be respectful of the boundaries of that relationship.

I've seen many actors get too close to their agent or manager...and that's not always healthy for the actor (or the representation). Sure, it's fine to go out for coffee, drinks, industry functions, or the occasional party together. It's even okay to form a friendship with your agent or manager. But when the *personal* side supersedes or interferes with the *business* side, things can get messy rather quickly. You must remember that it takes a strong, respectful bond in the relationship to balance both.

THE RIGHT ACTIONS TO TAKE

1. Learn from your mistakes and move forward.

2. Respect your agent and manager. Respect their time and the opportunity you have working with them.

3. Build a strong, friendly, healthy business relationship with your reps. Set boundaries.

4. Listen to and take your representation's advice.

5. Follow through on tasks and strategies you and your representation discuss. And let them know you followed through.

6. Keep your reps current with what you're doing for your career. Send them the occasional email informing them of career developments.

7. If you do need to chat with your representation, set up an appointment to discuss your career.

8. If you're not getting sent out on auditions, instead of whining or pulling attitude with your reps, be positive and proactive. Ask them, "What I can do to help you in representing me?"

9. Show gratitude to your representation. Thank them for the work they do (an occasional Starbucks gift card is a nice way to show your appreciation).

10. Be a team player!

#9

ACTING UNPROFESSIONALLY

My shit don't stink

When it comes to **Acting Unprofessionally**, there are several wrong actions you can take while "in the room," be it in the classroom, an agent and/or manager's office, the casting room, or at an industry function.

In the Classroom

Even though acting class is a professional setting, there are those actors who don't treat it as such. You can identify the actors right away who will act unprofessionally and "pull focus" during class.

First up...

The Talker. The Talker can't stop talking ...and it usually *isn't* about class. They are always whispering to anyone who sits next to them. It's usually in the middle of a lecture or worse, as a scene is being performed. This "side-talking" is unprofessional, impolite, and shifts attention away from the class onto them. Don't make your coach "Shhh" you in class; it's uncomfortable for everyone.

The Texter can't stop, well, texting. But it goes beyond that; they are always checking their messages, social media, email, and then *responding* to all of them...IN CLASS! When they do this, they're not being present, not fully taking advantage of the investment they made to help them in their craft.

Whether it's an "important" DM from your friend or just plain FOMO, texting and scrolling during class is rude, disrespectful, and distracting to your classmates and teacher. Turn off your phone (or switch it to airplane mode) and put it away until a class break.

The Disagreer, you got it, disagrees with every adjustment, suggestion, and direction they're given. An actor should always be able to have a good, healthy discussion about a scene or a role with their coach. But instead of taking the note and seeing how it plays, the Disagreer will challenge it, and say, "Well, I disagree with your note." This forms an untrusting, combative relationship with their acting coach, which makes the class feel uneasy, and stops the actor from growing in their work. If you have a problem with a coach, speak up, but do it in a private conversation after class.

I always say...

What you do in the classroom is a microcosm of what you do in the industry.

In the Agent/Manager Office

I've heard stories about actors answering their cell phones or checking their text messages in the middle of a meeting, being negative and argumentative with their representation, or trying to get too personal.

Remember you're in *their* office, their professional workspace, so be respectful. Don't put your bag, knapsack, dog carrier, or shoes up on their desk. Don't bring any uninvited family, friends, or pets into a meeting. Don't charge up your mobile devices in their socket unless asking first. Don't come in for an office meeting buzzed or high. On that note, don't *ever* write, text, or call your representation if you've been drinking or smoking pot. That's not the time to share with them your new grandiose, multi-tiered vision for your acting career.

Come into your agent and/or manager meetings ready to listen, talk, take notes, ask questions, and be a team player.

In the Casting Room

If there is ever a place where actors need to be professional, it's in the casting room at an in-person audition. You'd be surprised how many actors not only show up late or unprepared, but also act unprofessionally.

They'll try too hard to impress the casting director by talking about their current project, the showcase they're in, or the last job they booked. Unless the casting director asks you specifically about what you've been doing in your career, this is unwanted information they'll see as an intrusion on their time. They have a lot of actors to audition, and they want to keep on schedule.

And remember, when they ask, "How's it going?" or "How are you?" it's a rhetorical question. Don't talk too much; there's a greater chance you'll put your foot in your mouth and talk yourself out of a job.

Asking casting directors *unnecessary* questions about the project is also considered acting unprofessionally. When the casting director says, "Begin when you're ready," that means you can take a moment, not a minute, to "prepare." The biggest no-no of all is questioning the casting director's adjustment, if you receive one. There's no room in the casting room for a disagreeable attitude. Only a professional, positive, agreeable attitude is welcome.

Some casting director pet peeves are more about common courtesy.

Don't wear perfume or strong fragrances in the casting room as some people may be allergic. Don't come in carrying multiple bags, backpacks, clothes on hangers, etc. Don't come in smelling of cigarettes, alcohol, or pot. Don't bring a "plus one" to your audition, especially if that plus one is your pet. Also, don't offer your hand for a handshake; let them extend the courtesy first, if at all.

At an Industry Function

Finally, when attending a professional industry function, make sure you limit your alcohol intake. And, for the love of Meryl Streep, it's no place to pop an edible. You need to be focused, alert and articulate for any conversations you might have as they could lead to career opportunities. Better yet, stay sober for the event. You really don't want to be known as the tipsy actor who spilled a drink on a manager, knocked over a tray of hors d'oeuvres onto an agent or tried to seduce a casting director.

Don't Be a "Diva" or a "Dick"

Lastly, and most important, when you do become successful (and you *will* if you follow this book) maintain a high level of professionalism, always. Those actors who achieve success and are arrogant, disparaging, and disrespectful to others in the industry are acting unprofessionally, and it will affect them over time.

Whether you think the industry was difficult for you on your way up, that you had to work harder than others, that you faced setback after setback, whatever …it doesn't give you the right to bestow that negative energy onto others. Even if you think you are more talented and deserving of your accolades and achievements, that doesn't mean you can look down on others with a "my shit don't stink" attitude.

Throughout my long career, I have seen actors who get a big taste of success and suddenly turn into Divas or Dicks. They try to mask their insecurity and self-doubt with a sense of superiority, judgement, and entitlement that carries into their behavior. They don't value anyone else's time or effort, and they think the world revolves around *them*.

If it's not caught early, the "my shit don't stink" attitude can develop in class, meetings, and auditions and blossom fully on the set. If that happens, trust me, no matter how talented you are, nobody will want to work with you.

You can't forget about your journey and what really got you there. You need to stay humble, professional, and appreciative of your opportunities and successes.

THE RIGHT ACTIONS TO TAKE

1. Learn from your mistakes and move forward.

2. In any room, always be considerate of people's time and energy. Spend more time listening than talking.

3. Don't be The Talker, The Texter or The Disagreer.

4. When you talk to industry professionals, be courteous and concise.

5. Respect the professional spaces you're invited into.

6. Stay focused on the class, meeting, audition, or function. Shut off your phone and shut out distractions.

7. Take the note, suggestion, or adjustment from the acting coach, agent, manager or casting director.

8. After your audition, you can sometimes ask (if it feels right), "Is there anything else you'd like to see?" If the answer is no, you say, "Thank you" and leave with a smile.

9. Be helpful, ready to work and eager to participate. Stay positive and upbeat and people will remember you and want to see you again.

10. Stay humble, professional, and appreciative when it comes to success in your career.

#10

DOING NOTHING

I wannabe an actor!

The best way to fail is not to try. The best way not to try is by **Doing Nothing**. Unfortunately, the act of doing nothing is very easy for many artists because their work is an unstructured and self-motivating solo venture.

When you choose to do nothing, you remain stagnant; there is no change, no momentum, no progress, and that is harmful to you, your career, and your dreams.

Doing nothing is the most dangerous wrong action you can take because not only will it sabotage your acting career, but it will kill it *slowly*. Unfortunately, I've seen this all too often. I refer to those actors who are doing nothing for their art or career as "Wannabe Actors."

Don't Be a Wannabe Actor

When it comes to your acting career, you're either in or you're out. If you're *in*, then you must be *all* in. You can't just say "I wannabe an actor!" Anyone can declare that (and they do!). You must do the *work* to be an actor.

The Wannabe Actor is someone who aspires to be an actor yet does zilch to become one. They want an acting career, yet they do nothing to launch or maintain it. They identify and introduce themselves as an actor, yet they rarely study, rehearse, or exercise their craft. Or worse, they don't do it at all.

At one time, the Wannabe Actor might have had a blossoming career, along with classes, an agent, auditions, and maybe even an acting job or two. But they slowly started dialing back their career, for whatever reason, until one day it just stopped. Now they are stalled, waiting, standing idle, while their career wilts. The Wannabe Actor lets their career, their craft, and their talent fade with *inaction*.

An Actor Acts

To call yourself an artist, you must create art. If a writer writes, a singer sings and a painter paints, then an actor *must* act.

Every actor must *always* be doing something for their craft. If you are not engaging your talent—if you don't consistently study, practice, take classes, ACT—then you're letting your talent, your gift, wither and die. You can't deprive your talent of the work and fine-tuning it needs to survive and thrive. You cannot be an actor without acting, just like you cannot have an acting career unless you are actively pursuing one.

You can't be an "all talk and no action" actor.

When asked about your acting career, you should, at the very least, be able to rattle off something like, "I'm in a class that's challenging me, I'm submitting myself for auditions, working on my demo reel, trying to find an agent. Oh, and I just filmed a great short."

That's what *doing something* looks like. To be an actor, you need to activate your talent. To be a working actor you need to activate your talent constantly!

Be a "Will-Do" Actor

If you think you might be the Wannabe Actor, you have three choices:

1) Continue doing nothing.

2) Stop pursuing acting and place your energy in a different career that better suits you.

3) Learn from your mistakes, reboot your career, go all in, and move forward with your talent, confidence, and perseverance working in harmony.

If you're choosing number three, be reassured it's never too late to start again. Now you know *exactly* what you must do (and what *not* to do).

To make it in Hollywood (and New York, Atlanta, Vancouver, Chicago, and any other Industry City), you must always be working your talent, raising your confidence, and doing your perseverance work.

You must want to be an actor so badly that you are willing to do everything in your power to make it happen. And now you know how.

So…MAKE IT HAPPEN!

THE RIGHT ACTIONS TO TAKE

1. Learn from your mistakes and move forward.

2. Don't be a Wannabe Actor. Be a Will-Do Actor.

3. Know what you Want: To be a successful actor.

4. Always work your Talent.

5. Consistently build your Confidence.

6. Persevere always and forever.

7. Recognize when you're Self-Sabotaging.

8. Acknowledge, Confront, Experience, Work Through, and Overcome your Fear.

9. Avoid the pitfalls of Distractions, Addictions, and Wrong Actions. Take the Right Actions.

10. Most importantly, enjoy the acting process, stay positive, and have fun!

SECTION

THREE

BELIEVE

You Can Fulfill Your Destiny

There is one more thing you need to know to make it in this business.

You need to *believe*. You need to believe in *you*.

You need to believe that you *will* become a successful actor.

If you follow the Three Steps to Success and avoid the Three Ways to Sabotage Your Career, you have a shot, a really good shot, to get what you want. You can live your dream; you can fulfill your destiny.

Just have faith, stay focused, be determined, and get ready to work harder than you have worked at anything in your life. Take advantage of all opportunities, learn from your mistakes, and create your own luck. Always be grateful for the experience, enjoy the journey, and believe in what you're doing.

Celebrate your decision to pursue this profession, embrace your life as an artist, be proud of it, and give it the drive, dedication, and work ethic that it deserves…that you deserve.

HOLLYWOOD SUCCESS STORIES

Knew them when…

I want to end this book the same way I end my motivational seminars: with success stories of some actors you most certainly know. There is nothing more inspiring than hearing the stories of other struggling actors who have gone on to achieve great success.

In my years in the industry, I have worked with countless actors and actresses who have had wonderful careers. But I chose these five actors because they embody everything I've discussed throughout this book. They each have talent, confidence, and perseverance. While they each took their own path, they refused to let anything stand in their way. Most importantly, they all had a Want to be a successful actor. I knew them when.

I hope you learn from their stories and feel inspired by their success. But most of all, I truly hope each of you creates your own success story.

Remember to spread love, compassion, patience, gratefulness, and positive, fun, creative energy into the world. That energy will reflect back on you.

THAT'S WHAT IT TAKES TO BE AN ACTOR

When I was a freshman in the acting program at Boston University, I lived across the hall from a short, stocky, funny kid from New Jersey. We became fast friends, as well as an "Odd Couple" of sorts. He was the slightly disheveled, wise-cracking Oscar to my high-strung, fussy Felix. His name was Jay Greenspan.

Truth be told, he was not the best-looking guy in acting school, but he was charming and very talented...and incredibly self-confident. To some of us who envied his confidence, he could seem arrogant. In actuality, at the age of eighteen, what he had was a great sense of self-worth. He knew who he was and what he wanted, and he had the confidence to get it. Jay understood his purpose.

Jay was the first person I met on the first day of college. My mother was helping me move into my dorm room, which was right next to the student lounge. As we were carrying boxes, I heard singing coming from the lounge. I opened the door and there was Jay, sitting at the piano singing "Corner of the Sky" from the musical *Pippin* with his parents standing behind him. I went over to introduce myself, my mother in tow.

I remember Jay's mother saying, "My Jay is so talented. He writes, he acts, he sings..." Although Jay was a bit embarrassed by his mother's adulation, it seemed like it wasn't the first time he had heard this. Of course, my mother instantly retorted with an equal attempt at praise on my behalf. But I immediately saw a difference between my mother's belief in me and the adoration that was coming from Jay's mother. As much as my mother loved me, she had just recently accepted my desire to be an actor ("Oh my God, *not an actor!*"). It was clear that Jay's parents had been encouraging him and his creative aspirations his whole life.

You could see how those eighteen years of belief, faith, and support had instilled that confidence in him. Jay knew what he wanted to do, was focused, and he had the talent to back it up. Jay walked around as if he was already a successful actor.

Although Jay's work in acting class was always good and had a natural progression, there was one specific time where his talent (and his self-confidence) came into question. Ultimately, it was his belief in himself and his unflinching perseverance that pushed him through.

One day in acting class, Jay performed a monologue. It didn't go well. Whether it was an odd choice or that he didn't go deep enough into the work, the professor was highly critical of Jay and ripped into him in front of the class (as only a college professor can). Jay had never received such harsh criticism in class before. You could see the look of disappointment on his face.

Later that afternoon, I walked over to Jay's dorm room to console him. I recommended that the best thing to do when feeling sad or rejected is to have a pity party (just like I would). But Jay had other ideas. He told me to go ahead and have a pity party without him. So, I did!

When I came back a few hours (and a few beers) later, I walked by Jay's room. The door was closed, but I heard him shouting. It was passionate, spirited, full of emotion. As I slowly cracked opened the door, I immediately felt heat emanating from the room. Every light was on. I could smell sweat, as if he had been working out for hours.

I peeked my head in and I saw Jay pacing with an intense look on his face. He was in the acting zone. He was working on his monologue from class that day. He was so immersed in his work that he never even saw me standing there. I quietly closed the door and walked across the hall to my room. As I opened my door, I felt a very different vibe. My room was dark, cool, and untouched; no work had been done there.

The next day in class, Jay asked the professor if he could perform his monologue again and the professor said no, telling him he needed more time to work on it. Jay persisted and the professor relented. Jay took the stage, paused for a moment, and then did his piece. After he finished, there was silence in the classroom, followed by a round of applause. He nailed it. I mean, he was terrific. Even the professor thought so.

It was at that moment, sitting in class, I whispered to myself in awe…

"That's what it takes to be an actor."

I realized how much an actor needs to want it, how much they have to believe in themselves, and how they need to fight through rejection and disappointment. I realized that you can't sit back and feel sorry for yourself. Instead, you have to rebound, you have to jump back in. You have to sweat so much that you smell up your room with your passion, your drive, and your talent.

What Jay did in that *class* is what an actor always needs to do in their *career.* You need to take the feedback—no matter how good or bad—go back home, work on improving, and then fight to present it.

My story about Jay is a microcosm in time, but that moment defines a career. Jay Greenspan later became known as multi award-winning star of stage, screen, and *Seinfeld,* Jason Alexander.

YOU REALLY DON'T WANT TO SEE ME DANCE

When I was an agent in New York, I represented a nineteen-year-old actress who was brand new to the business and had little training. But she did have a great look: she was a beautiful southern tomboy with short-cropped, dark hair, sparkling blue eyes and a Colgate smile. She had a positive disposition and a great, self-deprecating sense of humor, which counteracted her insecurities as a new actor.

Her name was Courteney Cox.

I sent Courteney out on auditions, and it didn't take long for casting directors to take notice. While she began booking commercials and building her reputation in the business, we never expected what was about to happen next.

It was the early '80s and music videos were emerging as a mainstream form of entertainment, all due to the birth of MTV. As this new exciting medium grew, music videos became a great opportunity for new actors (and dancers) to get work that paid well. Actors appeared in music videos usually as the singer's "main squeeze," or their "object of desire." As there was no dialogue, and lots of close-ups, actors in music videos learned to express their feelings of joy, sorrow, or seduction behind their eyes.

It proved to be a great training ground for actors. Even famous directors wanted to direct music videos. Because I handled many young actors, I was busy booking my clients in a number of music videos for top '80s artists (many of them now classics).

I got a call from a casting director requesting an actress to appear in a music video for Bruce Springsteen's new single, *Dancing in the Dark*. The casting director wanted a teenage girl with lots of personality and big hair (it was the '80s after all), who could dance. I instantly thought of Courteney. Even though she had short hair and no dance training, I knew her infectious personality would get her noticed.

But Courteney didn't want to go on the audition. She was nervous, didn't think she could dance, especially in front of other people. In fact, she was petrified at the thought. I assured her there was no choreography involved, that she just had to be herself and...dance!

After the audition, she came back to my office, tears in her eyes, very upset with me. She said, "Scott, that was the worst audition I have ever been on. I was totally wrong for the part. All the girls were dancers...and they all had big hair!"

I felt horrible. My outside-the-box thinking backfired big time...and left my client feeling embarrassed and humiliated. Bad agent.

Then the phone rang. It was the casting director. They loved Courteney and wanted to bring her in for a callback. Good agent?

Courteney didn't want to go. I had to sit her down and convince her to go on the callback. I reassured her that the casting director loved her and that this could be a terrific career opportunity. It was not only a chance to be seen, but also to work with one of the '80s most prominent directors, Brian DePalma. (As a newbie, Courteney didn't know who Brian DePalma was until she saw the poster of *Carrie* in his office.)

Courteney agreed and went on the callback. After her meeting, she returned to my office...beaming! She told me that she and Brian talked for a while and got along great. Then he put on some music and asked Courteney to dance. Using her self-deprecating sense of humor to diffuse her anxiety, she told DePalma...

"Believe me, you really don't want to see me dance; it will ruin your day."

Brian laughed! Courteney danced. Good agent.

A few days later, Courteney was on a plane to St. Paul, Minnesota to shoot the video at a live Bruce Springsteen concert. You can only imagine how she felt dancing in front of thousands of people!

When the *Dancing in the Dark* video premiered on MTV, it became an overnight sensation for Springsteen as well as the unknown girl from Alabama. When Springsteen sang out "Hey, baby..!" tossed his mic over his shoulder, and reached for Courteney's hand, she not only jumped on stage to dance with The Boss, but she also jumped into the limelight. Her slightly embarrassed, wonderous expression of "Oh my God, he picked me!" won over the hearts of viewers as well as an industry.

The next day, my phone didn't stop ringing. Everybody asked, "Who's that girl?"

From the moment the video debuted, Courteney got opportunities to audition, and she took advantage of all of them. She became a CoverGirl on a Noxzema campaign. She appeared in many national commercials, including one for Tampax, where she was the first actor on a network commercial to utter the word "period." She appeared on Johnny Carson's *The Tonight Show* and eventually booked a series regular role on the short-lived TV show *Misfits of Science*. Her most recognizable role at the time, however, was Alex P. Keaton's girlfriend Lauren on the show *Family Ties*.

Courteney had the talent and the confidence, but it was going to be her ability to stay in the game, her perseverance, that was now going to be tested.

After *Family Ties,* Courteney continued to work, appearing in some films and TV shows, but for the next few years, she essentially fell off the Hollywood radar.

But, with her contagious personality, charm, sense of humor, and work ethic, Courteney didn't give up. She kept working and it paid off...again! After a few years, Courteney Cox got her next big break by booking a little show called *Friends.*

NOW THEY'RE GONNA PULL MY SKI MASK OFF

In the mid '80s, when I was an agent in New York, I met a young actress I was interested in representing and asked her to prepare a scene with a partner. She did all the right things an actor should do when performing a scene for an agent. She found a scene that had depth and emotion and one that was driven by her character. She also picked a scene opposite a male character; agents like to see the male/female dynamic.

The young actress came prepared and showed talent, but it was her scene partner who interested me the most. That actor was Christopher Meloni.

Even though his part was minimal, Chris fascinated me. His listening, his reacting, his stillness made me want to watch him. It was obvious he was a well-trained actor. But mostly it was his confidence in himself that kept me captivated. At the end of the scene, I told the actress that I'd be in touch. She thanked me, and as she left, I whispered to Chris, "You, I want to represent."

A few days later, I met with Chris. He told me that after graduating from an acting program, he came out to New York, continued to train, and tried to get representation...for four years! He was often told by agents that he was talented, but "too old." The sad thing was Chris was only twenty-six.

I believed in him, so I signed him. As an agent. I was very successful at representing a niche market; actors in their late teens to early twenties. Chris would be my oldest client (and also my age).

Although he had no professional credits on his résumé, Chris had talent and a belief in his talent. I found Chris to be very focused. He took all the right actions: going to class, auditioning for student films, doing anything and everything he could to get noticed…even helping a friend perform a scene for an agent.

Chris had a wise-cracking, glib personality, but he was also intense and showed signs of great vulnerability behind his "guy's guy" exterior. He understood who he was and that gave Chris a great deal of confidence. I knew that once I got Chris out there auditioning for the right roles, he would book.

Because of his age and my reputation of only working with young adults, I had to really work hard to pitch him to casting directors. I remember talking to Lynn Kressel—one of New York's top casting directors at the time—about bringing Chris in for a show she was working on: *The Equalizer* (the original). I had a good relationship with Lynn, but she was cautious about seeing Chris because of his lack of credits.

I told her that she could "either see Chris now or beg to see him in a year when he's with William Morris and too busy." We both laughed at the reality of that possibility. She brought Chris in to read for a co-star role of Terrorist #1. He booked it.

Chris was so thrilled he finally got his "big break" that he invited some people over to his apartment to watch his TV debut live. We were supposed to keep an eye out for the terrorist in a ski mask (Chris), and the moment when "The Equalizer" pulled the mask off to reveal him. Finally, we got to Chris' scene, and there he was in his ski mask. He spoke his one line of "threatening" dialogue and we all applauded. Though I did think to myself, "Gee, Chris changed his voice. What a great actor!"

Then it was time for the big reveal. Chris quieted everyone down and said..

"Now they're gonna pull my ski mask off!"

Unfortunately for Chris, his big reveal got left on the cutting room floor. We never saw his face. Not only that, but Chris also told me his character's voice wasn't his. For whatever reason, they dubbed over his line with another actor.

After almost five years of waiting for his big break, they didn't feature his face or even his voice. Nevertheless, Chris didn't allow what happened to deter him. He still considered his first TV appearance a victory, and he was determined to experience and celebrate many more victories. He knew the best way to do that was to find more work.

His determination paid off and Chris continued to book jobs. He appeared in several national commercials where he could showcase both his funny, easy-going persona and his "macho guy in peril" attitude.

I booked him as a series regular on the HBO show *1st & Ten*, which lead him to star in the short-lived sitcom, *The Fanelli Boys*. Chris went on to do several pilots, made-for-TV movies, and feature films. This eventually led Chris to great success, starring simultaneously as a series regular on two hit TV shows: *Oz* and *Law & Order: SVU*. He's continued his success, starring in hit shows like *Happy,!* and the *Law & Order* spinoff *Organized Crime*.

Chris told me that his early years of struggle gave him a strong work ethic and an appreciation for what he has now.

FOR THE FIRST TIME, I FEEL LIKE AN ACTOR

Josh Duhamel came to my acting studio in 1999. He had never studied acting before. He was handsome, charming, and affable. I liked him immediately, mainly because he had a great sense of humor about himself.

At our initial meeting, Josh told me that he wasn't sure if he was an actor or, for that matter, if acting was something he wanted to pursue. He did say, though, that he had a desire to test the waters, to explore the craft. So, I put him in my acting class.

Once I saw Josh's work, I immediately knew he had the Acting Gene. He had the potential to be a good actor. However, I wasn't sure yet if he had the commitment it takes to have a career.

In my acting class, Josh found a safe place where he could explore his creativity. Like many young actors, at first he struggled with being honest in his work. I would often yell out at him, "I don't believe you!" Josh was not to be deterred. He had the courage and conviction to dig deep inside himself and find the truth in his acting. And the more he found that truth, the more he embraced being an actor.

As I gave Josh techniques to access his emotions and open up his imagination, he learned how to tap into his talent. Josh was a sponge and within months, he began to show progress in his work. He started to get more and more excited about not only the prospect of becoming an actor, but also having a career.

Josh got an agent and started to go out on auditions. The more we worked together on his auditions, the more he became committed to the craft. But it wasn't until he got an audition for an independent film *The Picture of Dorian Gray* that I really saw how committed he could be. Josh wanted the role of Dorian Gray and worked intensely to prepare himself for the audition. He carried around the script, talked about both the screenplay and the character, and immersed himself—mind, body, and soul. He *became* Dorian Gray.

Josh said to me…

"For the first time, I feel like an actor."

He booked the role. And, after completing the film, Josh made an appointment to coach with me for an upcoming audition for the soap *All My Children*. Since he was filming on location, I hadn't seen Josh in a while. When he walked into my studio, I was looking at a very different Josh Duhamel. He was focused, committed, confident, driven, and passionate. He was a professional actor.

After coaching him on his audition, I knew Josh would get the role. He flew out to New York, screen-tested, and booked the job. He went on to win the Daytime Emmy for his role as Leo du Pres on *All My Children.*

Three years after his soap contract ended, Josh went on to star in other hit TV shows like *Las Vegas,* as well as many films like the *Transformers* film franchise.

Josh Duhamel is a perfect example of an actor who had the talent, chose to embrace it, and brought an intense commitment to his craft, which led him to have a very successful career.

ONE DAY, I'M GOING TO BE THE NEXT MERYL STREEP

It was the winter of my final year of film school at Boston University.

One of the first things they taught us student directors at film school was that actors were called "talent." It was recommended that we use non-actors for our initial films because the concentration should be on "getting the shot" (lighting, camera angle, everything that's vital to becoming a filmmaker). Because we were encouraged to use non-actors, we aspiring directors were never taught how to direct, connect, or even *talk* with actors. I hear things have changed…slightly.

Considering I had come from acting school with the purpose of directing actors on film, the thought of working with non-actors was unacceptable. From the first day I set foot in film school and began shooting my projects, I would only use trained actors. And I knew lots of them. They were my friends from the theater department. I knew they were hungry to explore the film side of acting. By my senior year, I was the first film student to lobby for and get theater school actors credit for appearing in a Boston University Film School project.

The friend I cast the most was a young actress by the name of Julie Smith. There was something captivating about Julie. She was down-to-earth but always the optimist. She was focused yet spontaneous. She had a great sense of humor about herself and about life. Julie had red hair, porcelain skin, and a vibrant smile. She also had talent...and lots of it.

By the time I graduated, I had directed Julie in a half a dozen student films and TV projects. She was fun to work with, incredibly hard-working, and eager to learn. She was always willing to act, which was perfect for this aspiring filmmaker who would call on a moment's notice when feeling inspired.

One of those "inspired" moments was a morning after a major snowstorm in Boston. I was in the midst of working on a short film about a Lovable Loser who fantasized about being with his secret love...Julie. In his fantasy, I was going to shoot the lovers' "walk-on-the-beach" scene often seen in romantic movies. After the snowstorm hit, I thought instead, I'll shoot the playful "snow fight" scene where the star-crossed lovers make snow angels, throw snowballs at each other, roll in the snow, and ultimately end up kissing.

At 8 a.m. on a Sunday morning, I called Julie and the film's leading man and had them meet me at the Boston Common, a well-known public park in the city. It was a beautiful day. The park was empty. All the storm clouds had passed, leaving a clear blue sky above. The grounds of the Common were blanketed white with fresh snow...and it was cold!

As the male actor complained about the freezing temperature and danced around trying to stay warm, Julie stayed calm and collected. She kept herself warm with the excitement and anticipation of the shoot. She was doing what she loved to do.

After an hour of filming, we took a break. I went over to Julie. In her wool cap, with her red hair draping down over her parka, she looked absolutely beautiful. I said, "You know Julie, one day, you're going to be a star." She looked up at me, smiled, and with a humble self-assurance, Julie said...

"One day, I'm going to be the next Meryl Streep."

Julie Smith became Julianne Moore.

Years later, sitting at home watching the Oscars, I watched Julie walk down the red carpet with Meryl Streep. I felt a great sense of awe for that actress who had such faith in herself, knew what her destiny was, and had the talent, confidence, and perseverance to make her dreams come true.

And I watched and rejoiced when Julie won the Academy Award for Best Actress for her performance in *Still Alice*.

About the Author

Scott Sedita is an award-winning, highly in-demand Acting Coach and Motivational Speaker. He is the owner of Scott Sedita Acting Studios in Los Angeles where he works with actors from all over the world.

Scott is the author of the internationally bestselling book, *The Eight Characters of Comedy: A Guide to Sitcom Acting & Writing* which has been translated into different languages. Scott has travelled the world teaching his comedic technique "The Sedita Method." Scott is also the first acting coach to develop an acting-based app, called *Actor Audition App*.

Scott has starred in the E! reality series *Fight For Fame*, VH1's *New York Goes to Hollywood*, and MTV's *Adventures In Hollyhood*. He was also seen on Showtime's *La La Land*, as well as MTV's *My Perfect Life*, USA Network's *Character Fantasy*, Fox Sports Network's *Helmets Off*, and Bravo's *Faking It*.

A graduate of Boston University, Scott has more than forty years of experience in the entertainment industry. He began his career in New York as a talent agent, where he helped to launch the careers of many top actors, including Courteney Cox, Matt LeBlanc, Christopher Meloni, Teri Polo, Dylan Walsh, Jerry O'Connell, and Vincent D'Onofrio, to name a few.

In 1990, Scott relocated to Los Angeles where he worked as a sitcom writer for Howie Mandel, Bobcat Goldthwait, and many others. In the mid-90s, Scott worked as a casting director for Danny Goldman Casting until launching his Scott Sedita Acting Studios in 1998.

Scott has worked with many of today's stars, including Holly Taylor, Parker Young, Lana Condor, Michael Weatherly, Brandon Routh, Meagan Tandy, Ross Butler, Joseph David-Jones, Haley Bennett, Charles Melton, Nelly, Josh Duhamel, 50 Cent, Chace Crawford, Paula Abdul, Kevin Alejandro, Sydney Sweeney, JT Neal, Jason Thompson, and many more.

Scott has appeared on numerous TV talk shows. He's been the featured story in such publications as *The Hollywood Reporter, Inside TV,* and *Backstage,* among numerous others. He has also appeared on CNN and programs like *On the Red Carpet, Entertainment Tonight, Extra,* and *Access Hollywood.* KTLA Channel 5 did a story on Scott entitled "Where Young Hollywood Goes and Studies" and referred to Scott as "one of the hottest coaches in town."